SKOOB *Pacifica*

No. 2014

WRITING S.E./ ASIA IN ENGLISH
Against the Grain,
focus on Asian English-language Literature

SKOOB *Pacifica*

Joint Series Editors: C.Y. Loh & I.K. Ong

Available Titles

Forthcoming

Shirley Geok-lin Lim

WRITING S.E./ ASIA IN ENGLISH:
Against the Grain,
focus on Asian English-language Literature

SKOOB BOOKS PUBLISHING
LONDON

Published in 1994 by
SKOOB BOOKS PUBLISHING LTD
Skoob PACIFICA Series
11a-17 Sicilian Avenue
Southampton Row
London WC1A 2QH
Fax: 71- 404 4398

ISBN 1 871438 49 7

Agents:
Skoob Books (Malaysia) Sdn Bhd
11 Jalan Telawi Tiga, Bangsar Baru
59100 Kuala Lumpur
Tel/Fax: 603-255 2686

Graham Brash (Pte) Ltd
32 Gul Drive
Singapore 2262
Tel: 65-861 1335, 65-862 0437
Fax: 65-861 4815

Atrium Publishing Group
11270 Clayton Creek Road
Lower Lake
CA 95457
Tel: 1-707-995 3906
Fax: 1-707-995 1814

Printed in Malaysia by POLYGRAPHIC. Fax: 603-905 1553
Colour Separation by Tranlitho. Fax: 603-717 6068

SHILREY GEOK-LIN LIM, Professor of English & Woman's Studies at the University of California in Santa Barbara, was born in Malacca, and her work reflects both her Chinese-Malaysian heritage and the landscape of the United States. She received a Ph.D. in English and American Literature from Brandeis University and her first book of poems, *Crossing the Peninsula* (Heinemann, Writing in Asia Series) won the Commonwealth Poetry Prize for 1980. One of her short stories won second prize in the 1982 Asiaweek Short Story Competition and appears in her collection of stories, *Another Country* (Times, Singapore, 1982). She has published another two volumes of poetry, and has edited/co-edited *The Forbidden Stitch* (recipient of the 1990 American Book Award), *Approaches to Teaching Kingston's The Woman Warrior, Reading the Literatures of Asian America,* and *One World of Literature.* Her book *Nationalism and Literature: English-Language Writing from the Philippines and Singapore* was published in 1993. Her most recent book *Monsoon History,* selected poems from *Modern Secrets* and *No Man's Grove* with the complete *Crossing the Peninsula* has been published in tandem with *Writing South East/ Asia in English: Against the Grain,* a focus on S.E. Asian and Asian English-language literary criticism.

By the same author

Poetry
Crossing the Peninsula (1980, *winner of the Commonwealth Poetry Prize*)
No Man's Grove (1985)
Modern Secrets (1989)
Monsoon History (1994)

Prose
Another Country (1982)

Literary Criticism
Nationalism and Literature: English-language Writing from the Philippines
  and Singapore (1993)

Books edited/co-edited
The Forbidden Stitch (*recipient of the 1990 American Book Award*)
Approaches to Teaching Kingston's The Woman Warrior
Reading the Literatures of Asian America
One World of Literature

Contents

Acknowledgments

My collective debt to mentors, teachers, colleagues, good friends, and good texts extends well beyond a page of gratitude. My gratitude goes first to those mentors who challenged me and wrote letters of references supporting me in my search for both a livelihood and an intellectual institution, and whose own works serve to inspire me. Among them, I thank Lloyd Fernando, Head of the English Department at the University of Malaya when I was a young tutor, and whose book, *Cultures in Conflict* (1986), is a major influence on my readings of South East Asian literature, and Nancy Miller, Distinguished Professor at the Graduate Center, City University of New York, whose élan and complex feminist positions continue to illuminate my thinking. Similarly, my colleagues at the University of California, Santa Barbara, have offered me a model of intellectual rigor to aspire to: Sucheng Chan, Richard Helgerson, and Paul Hernadi.

Specifically, for the genesis, development, and revisions of chapters in this volume, I am indebted to editors and scholars in "Commonwealth Literature," postcolonial literature, and feminist writing — whose decades-long labor in these fields have encouraged me to do likewise: Shirley Chew, Wimal Dissanayake, Diane Freedman, Gayle Greene, Coppélia Kahn, Bruce King, Deidre Lashgari, Anna Rutherford, Sidonie Smith, Julia Watson. From the South East Asian region, I have taken much from critics, librarians, administrators, and staff members that cannot be conveyed through lists of "Works Cited." Among them, I thank Anne Brewster, Koh Tai Ann, Leong Liew Geok, Kernial Sandhu, Kirpal Singh, the staff of the Institute of South East Asian Studies, Mrs Nambier of the National University of Singapore Library, and Professor Thumboo whose encouragement was particularly significant.

As always I owe an immeasurable debt to writers whose works speak intimately to my concerns and who had generously shared their time and materials with me. To name a few: Hedwig Anuar, Frankie Sionil Jose, Stella Kon, Edwin Thumboo, Arthur Yap, and Robert Yeo.

To those friends who encouraged me in my aspirations, Angus Caldor, Jan Kemp, Richard Lim, and Abdul Majid, among others, thank you. I am grateful to Ike Ong and his splendid staff for their dedication to Malaysian literary culture, and to Noelle Williams, Eileen Fung, and Pearly Kok for help with the manuscript. And as always, I am profoundly grateful to my family, Charles Bazerman and Gershom Kean Bazerman, who have affectionately shared their word-processing skills and lives with me.

Much of the actual research and writing was completed during a number of fellowships. I am grateful to the following institutions for invaluable support during those years: in 1982, as a National University of Singapore Fellow; in 1985-86, as an Institute of South East Asian Studies Fellow; in 1987, as a National Endowment for the Humanities Summer Seminar Fellow at Barnard; in 1988, as a Writer-in-Resident at the East-West Center, Hawaii; in 1983 and 1986, as a Mellon Community College Fellow at the Graduate Center, City University of New York; in 1989, as an Asian Foundation Fellow at the Centre for Advanced Studies, Singapore. Finally, I thank the University of California, Santa Barbara Senate for grants awarded between 1990 to 1994 that have supported my work.

Many of the chapters in this volume have previously appeared in earlier form as articles and chapters. I have used some of the same language, or developed upon ideas previously published in these texts: "Gods Who Fail: Ancestral Religions in the New Literatures in English from Malaysia and Singapore," *Commonwealth Novel in English* 3:1 (Spring-Summer 1983): 39-55; "Arthur Yap - "two mothers in a hdb playground," *Critical Engagements*, ed. K. Singh. Singapore: Heinemann Asia, 1986: 25-33; "Poetics of Loss and Nostalgia," *Reviews Journal Center for Regional and National Literatures in English* 1 (1986): 22-25; "Voices from the Hinterland: Plurality and Identity in the National Literatures from Malaysia and Singapore," *World Literature Written in English* 28:1 (Spring 1988): 145-153; "The English Language Writer in Singapore," in *The Management of Success: The Moulding of Modern Singapore*, eds. K. Sandhu and Paul Wheatley. Singapore: Institute of South East Asian Studies Press, 1989: 523-551; "A Poetics of Location: Reading Zulfikar Ghose," *Review of Contemporary Fiction* (Summer 1989): 188-191; "Finding a Native Voice: Writing in English from Singapore (1940-1980's),"*Journal of Commonwealth Literature* XXlX:1 (1989): 30-48; "Semiotics, Experience and the Material Self: An Inquiry into the Subject of the Contemporary Asian Woman Writer," *Women's Studies* 18:1/2 (Summer 1990); also in *World Englishes* 9:3 (1990), ed. Wimal Dissanayake; "Malaysia and Singapore," in *The Commonwealth Novel Since 1960*, ed. Bruce King. New York: Macmillan, 1991: 87-104; "A Problematic of Identity: Margaret Leong in Singapore," in *Perceiving Other Worlds.*, ed. E. Thumboo. Singapore: Times Academic, 1991: 139-150; "Kamala Das: One Woman's Revolt," in *Decolonizing the Subject: Politics and Gender in Women's Autobiography*, eds. Sidonie Smith et al. Minneapolis: U. of Minnesota P., 1992: 346-369; "Social Protest and the Success Motif in Singapore Novels in English," in *From Commonwealth to Postcolonial*, ed. Anna Rutherford. Sydney: Dangaroo Press, 1992: 292-299; "The Scarlet Brewer and the Voice of the Colonized," in *The Intimate Critique,* ed. Diane Freedman et al. Durham: Duke U P, 1992: 191-195; "Reciprocity and Resistance: Asian Women in Anglo-American Feminism," in *Subjects in Process: The Making of Feminist Literary Criticism.*, ed. Gayle Greene and Coppélia Kahn. New York: Routledge, 1992: 240-250; "Language, Race, Nation, and Gender: A Postcolonial Meditation," *Chapman* No. 72 (Spring 1993): 42-48; "Up Against the National Canon: Women's War Memoirs from Malaysia and Singapore," *Journal of Commonwealth Literature,* 1993; also in *Violence, Silence, and Healing Anger in Twentieth Century Writings by Women,* ed. Deidre Lashgari. Charlottesville: U. of Virginia Press, forthcoming; Shirley Geok-lin Lim, *Nationalism and Literature: English-Language Writing from the Philippines and Singapore,* Quezon City: New Day Publishers, 1993; "Race, Nation, and the Subject of the Subject: Timothy Mo's Novels," *Proceedings of "The Fusion of Cultures" Conference*, ed. Peter O. Stummer, University of Munich, forthcoming.

Preface

A collection of essays written for different occasions and published in highly diversified journals and volumes can be a dispiriting production. When the immediate contexts for their original appearance are lost, there is the danger of losing both the sense and significance of their publication. Sharp engagement may now read as dated and topical; textual analysis may be overtaken by newer interpretations; a different theoretical position calls to question the course of past discussions. With these dangers in mind, in selecting specific essays for this volume, I was careful to construct a strict boundary: only those essays that focused on South East Asian and Asian English-language literatures were considered.

Indeed, I had been writing on these literatures since my undergraduate years at the University of Malaya, when Lloyd Fernando approved the first course in Commonwealth literature in 1966. Even now I remember vividly the shock of recognition in reading the novels of George Lamming, R. K. Narayan, V. S. Naipaul, and Chinua Achebe, a shock that tropical geographies and brown people were the subjects of literature, and a recognition that the English language was the possession of whoever would use it, rather than a British possession. Writing in English was against the grain of dialect speech and national language dominance for many of those writers. But the English of Narayan, Naipaul, and Achebe carried the colors of their communities as well as Tennyson's English carried the grey of Victorian evenings.

In the English Seminar Room, then a hallowed space in which copies of the *Times Literary Supplement* and *Listener* were housed, I found Ee Tiang Hong's poems and a copy of Wong Phui Nam's *How the Hills Are Distant*. (Let me confess it now: that copy has followed me through nomadic decades, and rests close at hand in my study.) This undergraduate conversion, the belief in the necessity for a literature of one's own, has remained my unshakable creed, even as the identity of "one" — under the multiple deconstructive interrogations of psychology, anthropology, sociology, global economics, politics, linguistics, revisionist history — has grown progressively more shaky.

Thus, I have organized the chapters around three major and interrelated fields, each taking up a central proposition of identity.

Part One, "Positioning the Subject," examines the relation between the critic's multiple and shifting subject positions — woman, Chinese Malaysian, Asian, postcolonial — and certain cultural texts. The four chapters construct an autobiography vivified by books, as befitting the life of a bookish woman, to put to question propositions of gender, racial, language, and national identities.

Part Two brings together chapters on three very different English-language Asian writers. The first, Zulfikar Ghose, from India, is now a US immigrant teaching in Texas. The second, Kamala Das, continues to live in India. And Timothy Mo, born in Hong Kong, writes his novels in London. Whether we read them as diasporic or Asian writers, their works do not fit easily in the borders of country literatures that confirm other writers in their national canons. Yet they are not international writers, if by international we mean a cosmopolitanism that disavows local identities. Their writings testify to an ever increasing late twentieth-century phenomenon, the appearance of the transnational writer, moving between national cultural boundaries, who makes explicit the very complicated activities of human societies as new technologies (satellite stations, air-travel, faxes) and old catastrophes (war, famine, disease) dislocate cultures.

Part Three returns to what appears to be the original place for my critical interests: Malaysia/Singapore. But what is being written today of and from the region is markedly different from those early works by Ee Tiang Hong and Wong Phui Nam. One chapter focuses on problems within Singapore English-language writing — which has historically valued a Western-based aestheticism — in negotiating a role for itself in its swiftly modernizing society. This "redundancy" anxiety manifests itself differently in the themes of social conflict that pervade the contemporary Singapore novel, as seen in the second chapter in the section. The last chapter, written during an Asia Foundation Fellowship at the Centre for Advanced Studies in Singapore in 1989, brings together theoretical and political concerns that remain central in my work: how the identities of "woman," "nation," and "race" become constituted in texts, and how texts, in turn, get re-constituted in the context of nationalism.

The volume — ten chapters written between 1986 and 1993 — demonstrates an evolving reading of South East/Asian cultures. Above all, they demonstrate that South East/Asian subjects writing in English, against the grain of national languages and national canons, have much to tell us about place and region, about the peoples formed within place and region, and also about the nations that their imaginations press upon from the outside of linguistic borders.

1994

PART ONE

POSITIONING THE SUBJECT

The Scarlet Brewer and the Voice of the Colonized

I was eleven when I had my first poetry reading. Sister Finigan read my poem to my absent mother aloud to the Standard Six class. Rumors went around that my essay on a day in the life of a cock had been read to the senior students, the Form Five class in the new building across the street. When I was twelve and a Form One student in one of the ground floor classrooms in the new building, I had a poem published in the *Malacca Times*. I received ten Malayan dollars for it and immediately spent the entire sum on noodles, ice-cream, sour plums, and dried orange peel which I shared with my second brother who had mailed the poem for me. Do all writers find their beginnings in such minor triumphs, hedged by school-day tyrannies, poverty, and the almost palpable presence of a community?

At twelve, the inchoate desire to write poetry that probably characterizes the unhappy childhoods of many withdrawn insatiable readers focused itself on a book. Somewhere among the Convent School's mildewed books sent by missionary agents in Ireland was a red linen-bound copy of R. F. Brewer's *The Art of Versification and the Technicalities of Poetry*. In fact, in later life I had misremembered the book, confusing it with George Saintsbury's better known *Historical Manual of English Prosody*. Before writing this essay on intellectual memory, I walked along the library stacks in search of the 1910 edition of Saintsbury's *History*. Instead I found the unevenly aged scarlet cloth-cover of Brewer's book and recognized it immediately, despite the almost thirty-five intervening years.

Published in 1931, this University of California copy is almost an exact replica of the one the twelve-year-old child took to bed with her. I remember the heavy yellowing paper with its uneven cut edges, the ornate character of the large print, the skinnier italics, and the plainer appearance of the reduced print used for the verse selections. Especially, I remember the magisterial categorization. Under "Kinds of Poetry," Lyric divides into Ode, Ballad, Hymn and Song, and Elegy; then there are Epic or Heroic, Dramatic, Descriptive, Didactic, the Sonnet and the Epigram. Who would undertake today to lay before us such a simple and grand sweep of poetry, a sweep besides that ignores *vers libre*, the major domain of the idiosyncratic and of the American transAtlantic speaking voice? No wonder as a university woman I had suppressed memory of Brewer and chose instead to reconstruct the more liberal Saintsbury as my saint of poetic form.

Yet Saintsbury was himself influenced by Brewer, whose work he lists in his bibliography. This scarlet book of my childhood had first been issued in 1869 as *Manual of English Poetry* (the only book in Saintsbury's bibliography with the word "Manual" in its title, indicating perhaps its prominent influence on Saintsbury's later historical study, *Historical Manual of English Prosody)*. Brewer's *Manual* was enlarged and reissued as *Orthometry* in 1893, and it was this late nineteenth century version, essentially the same except in a new scarlet suit, that had enthralled me in my precocious pre-adolescence.

Remembering the many books that have found a permanent home in my life, I suddenly see myself as a basket case. Reliquaries held sacred by British imperialists are scattered like altar figures in a shambling cavern, one lit by faith as much as by skepticism. Shakespeare's plays, every single one of them, published in tissue-thin paper in a collected edition that somehow found its way to the school library. I remember best the poems that filled the back of the volume, although to an Asian child in the tropics, "When icicles hang on the wall/ And Dick the shepherd blows his nail" must remain at best exotic words on the page. For me, English words, lines of English poetry, seemed to glow in the brain even in the brightest of languid steamy afternoons.

There were also, in a book-poor community, numerous copies of Everyman's Classics and Oxford University Press World Classics, among them Oliver Goldsmith's *The Deserted Village, The Poetical Works of Gray and Collins,* and Lord Alfred Tennyson's *Selected Poems.* These were required Senior Cambridge Examination texts in the 1940s and 50s, part of that British Literature canon schoolchildren in every British colony would have to master if they hoped to succeed in the colonial administration. Ibo and Yoruba, Ghanaian and Egyptian, Tamil, Punjabi, Bengali, Ceylonese, Burmese, Malay and Chinese studied this canon in order to get on in the British Empire. We studied mysterious volumes in which alien humans wandered through mossy churchyards, stood under strange trees called elms and yewtrees, suffered from dark, cold, gloom, and chills, and hailed "the splendour of the sun" *(Poems of Lord Alfred Tennyson* 242). Pacing the walled garden of the Buddhist temple to which I escaped from the disheveled two bedroom shack in which my five brothers and I barely breathed, in the near ninety degree glare of the equatorial sun from which there was no escape until swift night at 6 p.m., I somehow made out the sturdy figures of the English language under the encrustments of Victorian ethnocentric sentimentality.

That is, thinking hard now through layers of early colonized consciousnesses — the girl-child saw something in the poems beyond the cultural differences that eluded her imagination. This something was what Brewer's *Orthometry* made manifest for me: the mysterious English poetry of the British imperialists was laid bare for me in this revolutionary red book as the bones of craft. Brewer's book of forms demythologized once

4

and for all that literary culture the English taught colonized native children to memorize and fear. Through Brewer, Gray's stanzas written in a country churchyard lost their awesome alienness. Deconstructed as prosody, they re-emerged as iambic pentameters in rhymed quatrains, or as Brewer categorizes them, "Four heroics rhyming alternately. . . [to] constitute the Elegiac stanza" (73).

The simple naming of craft as craft unweighted the imperialism in English poetry and sent it floating deliriously within my grasp. What Brewer's *Art of Versification* proved to me was that the English language was not a natural possession of the English people; like me, like every governed subject of King George V, English was also a language that the English had to learn. English poets learned from other poets; there were versions, variations, imitations, parodies; they borrowed the rondel, the rondeau, and the sestina from the French and the Italians. English poems were not acts of inspired imagination issuing spontaneously from English genius and yielding their meaning only to like spirits. Instead they were mindful things constructed out of reading, observation, care, learning, and play with language and form. According to Brewer's late nineteenth-century primer, English poetry was socially constructed, not innately inherent in race and genius. The respect for craft that breathes in a book of forms, as in Karl Shapiro's *Prosody Handbook*, is also the respect for any reader who will study it.

The clarifying idea that an English poem can be understood because it is written as language using known traditions of expression was revolutionary in a time when literature teachers arriving fresh from Cambridge and Oxford warned students against studying English litera-ture. Was it Mr. Piggott or Mr. Price and does it matter who said with helpful concern, "You haven't grown up in the British Isles — it's impossi-ble for you to get the idioms of the Lake District to appreciate Wordsworth." Or Scottish dialect to understand Burns. Midlands speech for Hardy. British history for Shakespeare. English gentility for Austen. In short, although we were compelled to study this foreign literature, the iron bar Mr. Piggott, Mr. Price, and all the other colonial university teachers raised before us was that English literature was really only for the English people.

The triple bind of force-fed colonial literature, cultural imperialism, and denigration of ability has only begun to loosen in ex-British colonies. But iron and bondage will produce their own kind of revenge. Today, generations of postcolonial peoples are writing in English, warping it into their own instruments, producing other traditions, the way the Miltonic sonnet evolved from the Petrarchan Italian, the way that Marilyn Hacker's sonnets evolve from the English. Wole Soyinka, Chinua Achebe, Bessie Head, Naruddin Farah, R. K. Narayan, Salman Rushdie, Bharati Mukherjee

— these are the illustrious non-English names that appear in English-language literature from Africa, India, Pakistan. But the postcolonial canon is more than those admitted by Anglos into their mainstream. It is the numerous nodes of writing in English produced by local national writers, read perhaps only by their local national audiences, the entire rhizomous planet of minorities, as Deleuze and Guattari would argue, replacing the hegemonic and hierarchical world view of the imperialists.

To my young mind, Brewer's *Orthometry* displayed the human skeleton of poetry; it deflated the Occidental Mystique of English Culture, and offered in its place a material body of social language, although one mediated through measures of syllables, interruptions of caesura, waverings between perfect and imperfect rhymes.

I can no longer read the scarlet Brewer with the intense pleasure of a child discovering the secret of adult power. Brewer's choice of lines and stanzas come too heavily freighted now with my own adult sense of power, the solid materially-inclined intelligence occluding the mere sensory motions of sound and music. Brewer, I see all too clearly, was a Victorian patriarch. While he approached poetry seriously, it was for him a moral and emotional helpmate, a feminine sublime, the way repressed men want their wives to be: full of good feeling, good judgement, beautiful shape. His selected passages expressed narrowly prescribed ideals of elevated emotion and noble thought: "There is a pleasure in the pathless woods" [Byron, cited in Brewer 182]; "Small service is true service, while it lasts:/ Of friends, however humble, scorn not one;/ The daisy by the shadow that it casts,/ Protects the lingering dewdrop from the sun" [Wordsworth, cited in Brewer 142]. Through bitter intelligence, I see how Brewer took strong poems and inevitably extracted their safest pulp. No wonder then that after twelve, I never returned to the book again.

Why have I picked this antiquarian volume as a foundational piece in my biography of mind? Probably to remind myself that a colonized childhood is composed of strange accidents of isolation and community; that, like Robinson Crusoe on a deserted island, a chest can wash to shore and we can find unexpected help — a book published in Edinburgh in 1931, read by the loneliest child in Malacca (or so I imagined myself to be) and leading her to believe that the English language could be as much hers as anybody's. Claiming English as my own was my first step out of the iron cage and into a voice, and who is to say it is not my language and not my voice?

1991

Works Cited

Brewer, R. F. *The Art of Versification and the Technicalities of Poetry.* Edinburgh: John Grant, 1931.

Deleuze, Gilles and Felix Guattari. "What is a Minor Literature?" *Mississippi Review* 11:3, 1983:13-33.

Gray, Thomas. *The Poetical Works of Gray and Collins.* Edited by Austin Lane Poole. London: Oxford University Press, 1950.

Saintsbury, George. *Historical Manual of English Prosody.* 1st pub. 1910. New York: Schocken, 1966.

Shapiro, Karl and Robert Beum. *A Prosody Handbook.* New York: Harper & Row, 1965.

Tennyson, Alfred. *Poems of Lord Alfred Tennyson.* Oxford: London, 1950.

Semiotics, Experience and the Material Self: an Inquiry Into the Subject of the Contemporary Asian Woman Writer

It is a tautology to term the concept of self a problematic especially as conceived in the context of Asian women writers. Why they write is a mystery because their readers are still marvelling at the fact that they write at all, rather like a gaping crowd in wondering confusion at the sight of a spelling or counting dog who never stops to ask why the animal would ever want to spell or count. But women are not dumb beasts, although historically and still in many societies they are seen as such. The marvel that they write at all in fact has as much to do with their reasons for writing; simply to articulate, to create another body than their given circumstanced physical selves, is, for Asian women, as much as for their Asian male audience, a moment of confused wonderment. In Western terms, it is a continuous epiphany, and prepares us for lyrics in ecstactic mode, in which the excitement of expression overrides the poetic genre, whether in Japanese haiku and tanka, Malay pantuns, or Malayalum or Indonesian lyrics, which are some of the few poems by Asian women written and preserved in the native languages.

Having only cursorily studied these poems in very selected translations usually edited by Western or Western-trained men, I do not pretend to be knowledgeable about the traditions of Asian women poets writing in languages other than English. The body of Asian women's literature written in English, a minor cultural phenomenon observable in India, Pakistan, Malaysia, Singapore, Hong Kong, the Philippines, that is, in countries and territories once under the rule of Britain and the United States, the two great Anglophone nations of the modern era, is more accessible to readers like me, proficient in English, trained in the canon of British and American literature, in love with the power of language, and thoughtful and curious about the place of marginalized persons, societies and cultures from which we have our origin and with which we identify. This body of literature is still small; Asian women usually published only after the men had settled the field.[1] (Yet they were educated in missionary schools and universities years before they began to publish. It is not too speculative to believe they must have begun writing poems and stories in English at the same time as they were receiving the education their brothers did, that language was for them, as much as for men, that particular cultural material in which their experiences were shaped; and that there have been numerous poems, diaries, journals, letters, prose pieces dashed off or slowly composed and later thrown away before some anxious mother, some nosey aunt or suspicious husband could discover them and dissolve the writer to that tearful figure of the fallen woman, fallen into the seductions of dangerous Westernized influences.) Early twentieth-century Indian women poets writing in English, for example, adopted strategies of the fugitive, the adaptive chameleon.[2] Like the black slave woman, Phillis Wheatley, Toru Dutt wrote patriotic English poems that could be read with approval by British critics in London; with the move for political home rule and independence from Britain, Sarojini Naidu wrote patriotic national poems, and engineered her acceptance into the new old boys' Parliamentary club by her activism in the cause of male-dominated Party lines.[3]

But this chapter is not a scholarly examination of native-language or English-language Asian women's materials and strategies for survival and acceptance in their colonized and indigenous societies. Nor will it analyse the struggles of a later generation of women poets and writers whose works display like scars the deleterious effects of multiplying marginalizations. Asian women writers in the twentieth century were and continue to be marginalized first by gender, in socio-political structures that have no functions for women except as nurturers (nurses, teachers, lovers, mothers, what is called the helping professions). They are marginalized, also, in nations where national identity has been forcibly equated with a national language policy, by their choice of writing in English. If members of a minority ethnic or regional group they are further marginalized by a majority ethnic power structure. Generally also women who write in English are Western-educated members of a professional middle-class, a narrow segment in basically peasant societies still undergoing development. A woman writing and publishing English-language poems and fiction in India, Pakistan, the Philippines, Hong Kong or Malaysia in the 1980s (and perhaps even more in the year 2000?) is still a freak, like that spelling dog. (Only in Singapore is there a mercantile and manufacturing base, a national language policy in which English has a place, and a substantial middle-class population, factors that make publishing by women more acceptable.) In many of these countries, the publishing women writers can be counted on one hand; two at the most.

It is precisely because there are so few of us (and I use the plural first-person as a problematic, occasioned by the definitions of this essay, and in the context of time past, which is always present in time present and time future) that I defer the analysis of sisterhood in the examination of self and the Asian woman writer, and revert instead to a meditation, a prologue, an open and sundried inquiry into what only I and no one else has as much acquaintance with, that primary subjectivity of my "self." Nor do I offer this yet-to-be-shaped because yet-to-be written "self" as representative, type, or allegorical figure; it is the concrete particular, the specific facticity, the materiality, "earth," through only which any abstraction can take color, size and shape.

And yet what will be offered is as abstract as architecture; for it is only through having read enormous bodies of literature, some offered as poetry, some as fiction, some yet as ideas or theory, and much believed to be knowledge, that I am able to "see" this ground, to "smell" this sensate life, to offer in language, that most abstract of symbolic discourse, the specifity of "self." So I will begin with the abstract, the "theory" that having been pieced together through unrelated readings across gaps in time, space, and societies appears to me now to make a pattern of the whole. I stress the temporality of this signifying pattern; it may be a conjunction of lack of sleep, increased caffeine intake, and the particular although accidental texts I had been reading just this past week that has produced an illusion of clarity, as tired eyes see entertaining designs on worn walls that disappear with rest. Or it may be that the pattern is inscribed within myself, to be obsessively projected on worn walls whenever fatigue, leisure, and over-stimulated nerves combine to break down that efficient corporate eye and leave it prey to the mute projectionist who will madly play and replay the same primal scenes to ever-changing music.

I shall provide the commentary by which you will approach the script and its editing. As the shapes begin to form on those blank worn walls, as director and sole survivor in the plot I shall provide the voice-over. For the "self" can be imaged as a movie in which one is producer, scriptwriter, director, actor being directed by other two-bit directors, projectionist, and audience.

I would argue that "self" cannot be, has never been, that unitary imperial "I" of Kantian thought. Freud, for all his masculinist orientation, pointed the way to areas of self that are outside the knowing "I": the concept of the unconscious self that works so deeply on behavior, feeling, and thought has shattered forever the myth of self as understandable, graspable, integrated, a positive agent defined by its colonization of experience, and negative only in its absence. After Freud, philosophers and psychologists such as Sartre and Laing accept the notion of self as divided, fragmented, in conflict, composed of contradictions, acting in bad faith, encompassing its own double, displaying the energy of a dialectic between presence and absence. Feminists such as Kristeva have seized upon these descriptions of the subject as more accurate of female experience: fractured between Others in their biological/maternal circumstance; the boundaries between mother and self entangled in the pre-Oedipal bond; their consciousness of self en-gendered as female desire or lack (a notion Lacan has popularized among some feminists).[4] Writers such as Tillie Olsen and Doris Lessing have portrayed this suffering experience of female subjectivity in stories such as "Tell Me a Riddle" and "To Room Nineteen." To the

10

unitary conception of the subject, as Domna Stanton tells us, "Kristeva opposes one already in process and in question, 'no longer simply explaining, understanding, and knowing, but an ungraspable subject because it is transforming the real'" (74). Kristeva postulates a female principle — the semiotic — that predates the symbolic, a preverbal locus situated at the moment when the child is bound up with the mother's body; and she conceptualizes this as a stage of silent production in which instinctual drives are organized. "Only the eruption of the semiotic into the symbolic can give reign to heterogenous meaning, to difference, and thus subvert the existing systems of signification" (Stanton 74).

Kristeva's postulation of the semiotic female principle articulates what many writers, male and female, have acknowledged, a principle, spirit, or agent in the self that is preverbal, a-logical, ungraspable, but whose violence to existing symbolic systems is the self's most significant because most transforming act upon 'reality'. This is the principle that acts upon the material subject to produce the "auto" in autobiography, transforming a life to the specificity of a subject.

Of course, that other aspect of self, the "bio"graphy which includes history, society, community, family, gender, race, class, geography, the materiality of a particular situated world, is as important a counter-balance to my view of self. These can be rendered as organized rather than organizing entities, like items listed for a Who's Who, identifying without bestowing identity; as untransformed facticity. It is and is not the material of literature, although the Asian woman writer suffers greater constraints from it. Her ambitions must be narrower, for her freedoms are less. Her energies, which for writers are inscribed in writing, in the "graphic" creations of self, must necessarily be dispersed or dispensed on material "creations" — childbirth and childcare, the planting of gardens, preparations of meals, weaving and sewing of clothing. The Asian man is not free of material constraints either, but there has long been in Asian societies a tradition of male as writer that was denied to women: the Confucian scholar; Brahmin priest; court advisors; government bureaucrats; recorders of social action and journalists; privileged nationalists selected for foreign education and service. These roles had been male prerogatives for centuries, and from these traditions have been drawn the majority of English-language writers from Asia.

For the Asian woman poet, therefore, her "bio" must largely remain on the ground floor of experience. The semiotic presses on life as experience, the daily unfolding of smells, bustle, sensations, endless movement, those pressures of personalities on the self as receiver. According to De Lauretis, experience is "the general sense of a process by which, for all social beings, subjectivity is constructed. Through that process one places oneself or is placed in social reality, and so perceives and comprehends as subjective (referring to, even originating in, oneself) those relations — material,

11

economic, and interpersonal — which are in fact social and in a larger perspective historical."

The Asian woman, however, is seldom an active agent except in the most domestic of situations, so for her the subject is often emptied of political content. For this subject to change its centuries-old separation from the political, a revolution must take place. Ding Ling's portrayal of woman, in "Shanghai in the Spring of 1930," as material self resisting ideological transformation — in the character of Mary (Mother of us all) — acknowledges that a psychological transformation must occur before the political can take place.[5] Mary is a non-conformist student from a wealthy Chinese family: "She had talked a lot, been very lively, conspicuously drunk a great deal...her proud and free ways, her charming insolence, had particularly captivated him" (66). Her lover, Wangwei, adores her, but when she comes to live with him in Shanghai, she discovers that he is absorbed in his work in a socialist organization. Mary rejects the social stereotypes for women, but Ding Ling points to the vacuity in the selfish individualism of her rebellion:

> But she loved nobody other than herself. She knew that she depended entirely on the beauty that youth had given her...From all the novels she had read and films she had seen she knew that once a woman married her life was over. To be a docile housewife, then a good mother, loving her husband and her children, losing all other forms of happiness for the so-called warmth of a family, then in an instant find your hair turned white and your hopes all dashed when your husband was still healthy enough to be going out and fooling around. All you could do then was cultivate benevolence and wait patiently to become a grandmother. What was the point of it?...She was very satisfied with her present freedom (81)

Wangwei attempts to involve her in political activism, but her half-awareness of the moral vitality of these socialist activities only pains her by illuminating the ugliness of her "debauchery, idleness" (98).

For Mary, "love" — the sexual bond between man and woman — was the meaning of her existence. Ding Ling contrasts Wangwei's devotion to the political cause to Mary's a-political self-centered subjectivity. To remain with Wangwei, Mary would have to "obliterate her own self to turn herself into someone with a head like his" (112). Wangwei himself had been transformed by the political process: "He was so ruthless now. She had no idea what could have given him the strength to be like that. It terrified her. She could not make the change with him. Her circumstances and her character were too different" (112). This 'difference' is not simply that of male and female but rather one of class. Ding Ling suggests in the minor characters of Feng and the conductress an idealized proletarian male/female relationship uncorrupted by liberal subjective values. Wangwei, the bourgeois male, makes the successful transformation to a revolutionary consciousness, but Mary, encumbered by her ideals of individual freedom, happiness, and capitalist consumption of goods, cannot change. The story ends with Wangwei in a Black Maria, arrested for demonstrating, seeing Mary with her arms full of shopping by the entrance of a department store (120-121). As Kristeva points out and Ding Ling's short story portrays, "no sociopolitical transformation is possible which does not constitute a transformation of subjects" (Stanton 73).

Self as the semiotic principle that constitutes the subject; self as experience in which both agent and receiver act and are acted upon; and finally self as constituted by the Other, which is the field of the political. Together they form not layers of a self like the flesh of an onion easily peeled apart but rather types of chemicals whose different properties bind to produce for each individual a unique process, reaction, and alchemical substance.

The Asian woman writer, like women everywhere, continues to be constituted by a Male Other. When we look at ourselves in maturity, the gaze we have re-constituted from our culture is male. Our valuation of our selves, our femininity, learned from our mothers, is inexorably the market value of the male world. Our physical size and shape, our choice of coverings, the pitch of our speech, our gestures and walk, the lift of our eyes, our abilities and capacities are always measured against male-constituted desires. We learn to desire for ourselves what men desire in us, an endless regression of desire in which the self cannot separate from the Other except with the most violent repercussions (as portrayed in Doris Lessing's *The Summer Before the Dark*). For Asian women, therefore, not only is the personal political, but sex is often the field in which the political is waged.[6] In the absence of a tradition of political engagement in the world, they articulate political engagement of their most private encounters with the Male Other. The poetry of Indian women poets such as Kamala Das, Gauri Deshpande and Maumta Kalia, read in this light, is not simply the poetry of "sighs and thighs" but an acknowledgment and articulation of the political in their experience.[7]

It is not surprising, therefore, that Kamala Das's novel, *Alphabet of Lust*, for all its many descriptions of marital and illicit sexual encounters, is a political narrative of an Indian woman-poet who becomes Prime Minister of India.[8] Manasi, a forty-year-old poet, unhappily married to an honest therefore poor older man, is lured by ruthless ambitious Vijay into an affair that eventually leads her to a Cabinet position in the corrupt Government. Das paints a cynical picture of depravity and greed among the Indian ruling elite in which women are offered as bribes, treated as sexual objects, and degraded at every turn. For Srinivasachari, "ageing chairman of a leading Public Sector undertaking," "All his life he had loved a life of luxury and had needed beautiful things around him to create for him a state of well-being. The beautiful things included women" (92). At parties, he "fondled secretly their thighs and kept a seemingly innocent hand tucked half beneath their warm seats" (93). Das, like Ding Ling, sees women not as mere victims but as conspiring in their own oppression. "Which women of middle-class," she asks in the novel, "can resist a successful man, even if he is nearly seventy and has discoloured teeth?" (93)

Manasi tacitly conspires with Vijay and becomes the elderly Prime Minister's mistress. Through a lurid progression of sensational events, including a near rape, incest, and a couple of murders, the novel flays the male political animal represented in Vijay. Ironically, Manasi's only corruption is in the area of the sexual. She 'prostitutes' her body to Vijay and to the Prime Minister for political office, and when the Prime Minister is suddenly paralyzed by a stroke finally achieves "the highest office of the land" (147-148). In *Alphabet for Lust,* Das shows the corruption of the sexual by patriarchal power, the woman's subversion of this power through the only weapon given to her, her sexuality, and the final transformation of sexual desire to political desire. The novel concludes with Manasi leaving Vijay and her family for New Delhi: "There was nothing on her mind now except the long-felt desire to be the head of the country" (147). Politically empowered, the woman is finally able to look into the mirror and smile at her own reflection: "she smiled into the mirror while brushing her thick hair vigorously before getting ready for sleep" (148).

In looking for the selves in Asian women's literature, however, one is more usually frustrated to find something one may not wish to recognize because it has been mutilated by an Other which imposes weakness, marginality, inferiority, and absence of being:

> Mid-life stalled, I look for women.
> Where are they, my mothers and sisters?
> Help me. I've fallen asleep,
> Fallen among sleepers.[9]

As many critics have pointed out, colonial and post-colonial women have suffered a double colonization, alienated from the free exercise of their power by a foreign race and also by a native patriarchal society.[10] Whether the society is Confucian, Hindu, Muslim, Christian, animistic, Jain, Parsi, Buddhist, the female is always already a colonized subject.

In order for the woman to write in this doubly colonial world, the self must be in exile; she has to leave the rule of her community and become, if only in her writing, undomesticated, wild. Thus I begin with myself as the feral child.

If my mother had not abandoned us, five sons and a daughter, when I was eight, I may never have become a writer. I remember her then as a feminine mother, that is, she liked fine clothes, gold jewelry, creams and powders, to visit friends and gossip. She had prepared herself for an idle life. Her collection of sarongs was of the most expensive batiks, hand-blocked with vivid Javanese birds and flower motifs, crisp with starch. Her *kebayas* were fine transparent voile, their seams worked painstakingly by hand, and the front openings and sleeves pieced into delicate lace. Such *kebayas* are hardly ever seen in Malaysia now that Malay women conceal their bodies under Arab purdahs and Nonyas like my mother have become Westernized and copy dresses and pants from British Hong Kong. When she dressed carefully to visit her friends in Malacca, she wore three or four gold bangles on each wrist. They were brassy twenty-three carat gold, patterned with vines and petals. A thick gold chain, closely linked, circled her round throat. Like other Nonyas, she wore a modest chemise under the airy kebaya, and fastened the blouse with *kerosong* in the shape of a trailing string of flowers. In the hot afternoons at home she mixed a paste of rice powder and water, and this *bedak* she smoothed on her face to keep her complexion white and unlined. But for night before bed she had large jars of Ponds Cold Cream which smelled like sugar syrup.

Did I love my mother then? I don't know. Her luxuries made her a distant figure, organized for a different world. Between a girl child not yet constituted in this version of the feminine and a mother absorbed in preparations for a presentation in the economic world, little can bind them beyond the biological. And even that was not conscious, for she had three sons after me, a fact that now strikes me as totally significant but which then passed before me as unremarkable. Her continuous pregnancies must have been unwelcome and unpleasant, for I can recall no festivity associated with any of them. The last son was handed over to an aunt at two weeks of age. There was some explanation that a fortune teller had warned the infant would harm his mother's health, and at four I had no curiosity over a displaced brother. That she did give over the last child now falls into a signifying act, for a few years later she gave us over to our father and left the small town for Singapore City.[11] The childbirth weeks impressed me then only as food sensations: chicken feet boiled in soy and sugar; pork kidneys scored like graph paper and tasting of rice wine and ginger; rice porridge rich with minced pork and scallions. These were foods for after-birth. I can taste them still in memory even though no picture of baby brothers or maternal bliss appear.

In this way I must have been a cold child, already separated from the mother and plunged into experience. This very early indifference to my

15

mother can be explained by my strong attraction to the sensate world, the world of play, activity, intervention, the rough coarse world of my brothers who ran wild in the narrow back lanes of Kampong Pantai. The street in front of my father's shoe-shop carried its Malay name, Beach Village (Pantai for beach-front), from ancient days, but it was a thoroughly South Seas Chinese street. On our side, the side I travelled every day, trailing behind the boys as they ran past the shop-fronts, were piles of discarded damaged cans and foodstuffs from the two sundry shops on the right. On the far right the street was anchored by a small Chinese temple behind a walled open-air courtyard which you entered through an ungated entrance. A large red clay urn, closed on the top but with apertures on the sides, stood beside the entrance, and here the worshippers burned silver and gold paper money. The urn was always full of ash and blackened leaves of burned paper not yet consumed to ash.

One day my brothers found some battered, rusted cans of grapes among the rubbish pile in front of the sundry stores. I still recall the pale peeled fruit loggy in thick syrup, an exotic, exciting taste made dangerous because it had been discarded, then discovered, like hidden treasure.

Behind the street a narrow land divided our row of shophouses from the backs of yet another row of houses. The outhouses for every house were at the back, and their back walls each had a small opening at the bottom where the buckets of excrement were taken out in the early mornings and emptied. I never saw the bucketman, although occasionally we would walk down the narrow unpaved lane lined with these outhouse openings. Fat flies with purplish-blue iridescent wings buzzed in and out of the holes, and a heavy fetid odor hung over the air. I did not find the odor then unpleasant. It was strong, like the thick sandalwood smoke that hung like a frieze over the inch-fat joss-sticks sticking out of the urn's many mouths.

I was never a delicate child, and it seems to me now that my father, so abundant with male sperms, having eight sons from two women, must have created a half-boy in me. I wanted to play my brothers' games and would stand in tears, outside a locked door, listening to them whispering inside the magic room of their boys' companionship, wailing for entry. It was not love I wanted from my brothers, only admission to their games. When they made catapults out of whittled crooked branches and rubber bands and shot at each other with hard unripe berries from waste bushes, all scavenged from visits to relatives who lived outside the town, I wanted to learn to shoot also. I wanted to cheer and dodge, to hit a target, to be triumphant. But on the rare occasions that they permitted me to join their game, I was never handed a catapult; I was always the hunted, hurtling from the whooping savages with winded lungs, and crunched behind a box or pillar with painfully thudding heart. When I was allowed to play their games, I was always clumsy, fumbling, falling behind, half in tears, terrified. I would hold a catapult for that brief precious time it was loaned to me when the game was over. The wood had been sanded smooth, the two arms of the weapon strengthened by rubber bands lashed around them. The cradle from which the pellet-berries were slung had been cut out of the inner tubes of bicycle rubbers. The catapult was a crafted artifact, solid, powerful, and I was never taught how to draw back the cradle, how to position the berry, how to throw it with such force that it would fly for yards and sting your enemy on the cheek.

Earnestly following after my brothers, crying at their curt demands that I leave them, terrified when they let me play, whether I was hiding or seeking, my mother was no where in my mind. Or rather she was that female self I did not desire, that repressed consciousness into which was thrown everything that I rejected: the bland and vain behavior; petty, narrow, concerns; boring social meetings; passive pregnancies; repeti-tious, meaningless gestures of motherhood. She was my negative, my brothers my positive model.

But I myself was a vacuum of energy, restless, unsettled, unbelonging, neither girl nor boy. Subjectivity is still to me a kind of drift, an active with-holding of identity, when you don't know who you are because the world is still too new, and you can only know yourself if at all by letting the world be, and letting the shape of your experience of this world shape your knowledge of your self. This active with-holding of identity appears like a kind of passivity but needs a high intensity of observing without prior sight, like an articulate baby with all the tools of a mature language looking at things for the first time.

This must have been my experience of my brothers' half-familiar, half-alien world. My sense of my self was always in abeyance, under their interrogation, and in the experience of my failure as a boy. It is the failure of this kind of identity which has created the consciousness of a gap between myself and others (that is, unlike Freudians, I do not believe that female subjectivity is simply penis envy but when successfully passed the stage of recognition of difference, an active and self creative energy). It is this consciousness of the eternal separation reproduced in myself that has involuntarily organized my instincts to be an observer and a writer.

The feral child and the coldness of an intense isolated subjectivity are elements of my self that only I can know. But there are elements of a life that are there for public record. My father had lost his business because he had invested the little money he had on a get-rich scheme presented to him by one of his best-friends, a pawn-broker whose shop was across the street from my father's shoe-store. When my mother abandoned the family, for a few years we were dreadfully poor. After my grandfather's house was sold and my father's extended family broke into separate households scattered over the town, my father, brothers, and I, six members in all, finally settled into a tiny two-bedroom house in a row of four such houses, all roofed with the same long sheets of zinc that burned in the afternoons as if to bake our brains and rattled in the monsoon storms like an unending army of red ants invading our ear-drums.

Those years were vividly full. I was finally in a situation, a game, just like my brothers. In our wild, abandoned state, we had become equals. We were always hungry, usually having only one meal in the evening each day. One of my brothers would ride his bicycle to a cheap restaurant set up in one of the shacks jumbled together by the river beside the town-market. We waited impatiently for his return with the three-tiered tiffin carrier. The bottom container was filled with rice, although never enough rice for us; the second container held soup, a waterish liquid flavored with dried anchovies, a few pieces of cabbage; if we were lucky some strips of grey pork intestine or tripe. The top container was only half-filled, with bony ribs or fatty pork with thin strips of lean or chunks of ray meat which we chewed cartilege and all. The family dinner was our civilized hour, after which father would start a sing-a-long or some of us completed our homework or studied for exams, then went to bed.

But the hours between the end of school at two and mealtime at six were our wild children's hours. The land around us was still unbuilt. The few houses were attap in style, with palm-leafed thatch, plank walls, and raised from the ground on low concrete pillars. Each had an unattended yard, muddy ground, and scrawny chickens and red-combed, multi-colored, tailed roosters scratching the dirt. Trees bearing all kinds of fruits stood in these unfenced compounds. Right in front of our shabby house was a short leafy tree which bore hundreds of berries. The berries turned pink then bright scarlet when ripe; they were soft, sweetish, with a flesh of tiny specks like miniscule fish roe. The best thing about those berries was that they ripened at different times. It was almost always possible to find a couple of semi-ripe or ripe berries hidden behind limp velvety leaves. Often we could each pick a handful. I learned to climb trees, feeling for toeholds in crannies of bark, testing each branch with my weight before hauling myself up yet another branch to where reddening berries were still hanging. Small aboreal animals, my brothers and I supplemented our diet with stolen fruit.

Often the owners were not home yet from work when we raided their guava or mango trees. Some fruit ripened only every few months. Driven by hunger, we picked them small, hard, and green and devoured them, crunching the young sour mangoes with relish, and gnawing at the *jambu batu,* breaking through the bitter skin to the stony core, and eating every part. Fortunately, many of the trees bore fruit which ripened unevenly. We ate unnamed fruit which broke the insides of our mouths into blisters; we scrubbed needled spines from the skins of the butterfruit and swallowed the creamy insipid flesh in lumps. The world was brightly colored and focused in our quest for garden food. We found sugar cane strands behind the fence separating the common ground from the gardens of the Buddhist Temple, which was also our landlord, and we ran home like victorious hunters, arms full of green-yellow cane still gracefully leafed. We stripped the tough sleek cover from the cane with our teeth and with our teeth broke pieces off the juicy stalk, then chewed and sucked so hard that only dry stringy woody balls remained.

But there was never enough fruit to fill me up. I walked two and a half miles to the missionary school to save the five cent bus-fare and schemed on what it could buy that had the biggest bulk. A wonderful day came when I discovered that five cents would buy a large handful of dried dates, the very sweet, sticky dates that came in sacks, clumped together and matted with straw, rope, pebbles, and who knows what else. Chinese Malaysians never ate these dates for they were the food of fasting Malay Muslims, and the Chinese stores carried them only for the Malays, many of whom were as indigent as we were.

Was I unhappy? Hunger is a drive, and like all drives it gives meaning to the world. I was too hungry to be unhappy, and remember above all the pure joy of discovering food and having food. Moving from gathering area to gathering area, animals do not stop to wonder what it all adds up to. The smell of a ripe banana appearing as it were from one's search in the world gives rise to an emotion of concentrated pleasure that has nothing to do with our usual associations with deprivation and hunger. There is a resilience in the human animal beyond psychological understanding, taking place at the level of instinct, a pleasure in surviving which explains the laughter of refugee children, the ability of raped women to love the children of the rapists.

> At eight I become an animal.
> Hunger sniffs, growls
> at every corner, the dragon
> stomps and dances on my poor head.
>
> Every tree's a meal —
> butterfruit pulped in its
> fuzzy jacket, stone guavas
> with gravelled hearts; even
> tropical cherry-berries
> which squish like birdshit.

I cannot find my mother;
I can find every hiding
place where you can never
find me — dark under

flaming hibiscus,
cool of a back drain.
Crawl into my skin,
keep under cover,

in quiet listen
to the boastful dragon
shaking and shaking. We
were born together,

but I am wild.
I want to eat grass,
frangipani white as sugar
crusts, just like the sun eats me

melting in drops and licking
me, little by little,
like a lolly. I hold
hunger tightly,

gratefully. It is
my gift from the sun.

Of course, unless one is practising a kind of Zen meditation, it is difficult for the mind to be emptied of content. The kind of with-holding of identity while one looks at the world easily spills over into a looking at the self; into self-consciousness. What is commonly described as wool-gathering, staring into space, being lost in thought is that process by which the subject separates the observer/subject from the object/subject, transforming subjectivity itself into mental objects for study. The self-conscious subject, when it uses its capacity for reflection, is in the process of claiming its own subjectivity.

But this claim as autonomous subject is often not legitimized for the Asian woman writer. Where women are situated as objects for others' possession, their attempts to observe, reflect, and articulate their subjectivity in art and literature are seen as dangerous or decadent. Expressions of female subjectivity are most accepted only in the domestic world; hence women's art historically is seen in weaving, pottery, basket-making, home decoration and so on. Written discourse which is in the public domain — history, fiction, poetry (as opposed to letters and diaries) — is traditionally seen as the realm of male expression, and women attempting to use such discourse are perceived as competing with men and unwomanly. In Asia, women writers must face the possibility of social ridicule, censure, and distrust. Ding Ling, for example, was silenced and exiled to the Great Northern Wilderness from 1958 to 1979 for, among other things, the decadence of themes in her early stories (stories which deal explicitly with sexual self-consciousness and self-conflicts in young women). Kamala Das has been excoriated by both male and female critics for the strongly sexual nature of her work, its subjective autobiographical style. Vimala Rao, for example, dismisses Das's poetry on the grounds of its self-preoccupation: "Constant self-exposure in itself does not become lyrical or confessional poetry — it can only descend into a glaring deadening exhibitionism. In life such self-exposure is suicidal; in art it is unpardonably boring" (96).

The pressure of social inhibition (self-exposure presented as suicidal) on the Asian woman writer marks her expressions of her self. The chief marker is the kinds of silences evident in the literary history of her society. Feuerwerker points out, for example, that although "women had been relatively visible in traditional [Chinese] literature...they had been presented less as subjects in their own right than as objects or images catering to the needs, desires, and projections of a preponderantly male authorship" (20).

Beginning with the twentieth-century, Asian women's literature displays the marks of what I had described as a female experience of consciousness including an intense subjectivity which is extremely sensitive to sensual experiences while at the same time cold and isolated. It is a kind of subjectivity which has been criticized as self-indulgent, fragmented, or ideologically rightist because selfishly pre-occupied with subjective needs. When the Asian woman writer becomes conscious of her own subjectivity, she becomes conscious first of the fracture between her desire for the sensual world in which her being is grounded and the isolated signifying self which grasps the social oppression of the female but cannot overcome its internalized meaning. Thus Kamala Das portrays this rupture in her poem, "The Freaks."

> He talks, turning a sun-stained
> Cheek to me, his mouth, a dark
> Cavern, where stalactites of
> Uneven teeth gleam, his right
> Hand on my knee, while our minds
> Are willed to race towards love;
> But, they only wander, tripping
> Idly over puddles of

Desire...Can't this man with
Nimble finger-tips unleash
Nothing more alive than the
Skin's lazy hungers? Who can
Help us who have lived so long
And have failed in love? The heart,
An empty cistern, waiting
Through long hours, fills itself
With coiling snakes of silence...
I am a freak. It's only
To save my face, I flaunt, at
Times, a grand flamboyant lust.[12]

This rupture is between society and the woman (she's a freak), between the man and the woman (he can satisfy only the senses but not her other hungers), and within the woman who acts out an inauthentic desire. The question left unasked is who is the authentic self behind the mask of sexual desire. What is it woman really wants? What is the true object of her desire? The "heart" (the core of self) is signified only by threatening silence. What the poem expresses most successfully of women's subjectivity, therefore, lies under the sound and fury of the sensational and sexual autobiographical, confessional self; it is the silence of the frustrated because not yet created self.

Similarly, Ding Ling in "Miss Sophie's Diary" expresses the turmoil experienced by a woman who is torn between the sensual ground of female sensibility and the signifying subject to whom the male object of her sensuality and therefore her entire experience of desire is contemptible. At an early point of Sophie's attraction to the Singapore Chinese student Ling Jishi, she makes a self-discovery: "Yes, I understand myself, I'm only a completely female woman. Women devote all their thoughts to the men they want to conquer. I want to possess him. I want him to give his heart unconditionally and kneel before me, begging me to kiss him. I've gone completely mad" (27). What the character understands later is not that she can possess him, but she has become possessed by the man. Her "madness" lies in her loss of self-control. As the relationship progresses, Sophie understands the full despair of this split in subjectivity: "How can I explain the psychology of a woman who's crazy about a man's looks? Of course I could never love him, and the reason is easily explained: such a low and ugly soul lurks behind his beauty" (61). The division in the self, the experience of painful and contemptible desire and the inability of self to articulate an alternative desire finally silences Sophie, who tells us "this diary is now coming to an end because Sophie no longer needs to give vent to her resentment and find consolation through tears. This is because I feel that everything is meaningless" (61). The only "victory" possible in this civil war in the female subject is the satisfaction of acknowledging a self-hatred rising from this self-knowledge. In the chaos of absence of identity or self-possession, even a hateful identity is a victory. "Yet all I find in this satisfaction is a sense of victory, a victory in which I find desolation and an even deeper sense of how pathetic and ridiculous I am" (61).

Ding Ling's portrayal of women is dynamic because she does not present them as mere passive victims of a repressive society. Often, as Feuerwerker points out, the "seemingly uncontrollable ambivalence in Ding Ling's stories...stems from Ding Ling's view that women suffer not only as victims of society but also from self-defeating female weaknesses" (33). Ding Ling herself has said, "Actually I strongly dislike the weaknesses in women" (Feuerwerker 33).

Even when Asian women become conscious of strengths, these strengths are often seen as male qualities or as betrayals of a feminine self. With the dawning of liberation for women in Asia, the woman as autonomous subject maker of her own destiny, separate from the traditional roles of mother and sexual possession, will become increasingly the topic of women's writing. Yet Asian women may not be comfortable with these changes; without, as Kristeva says, a radical transformation of the psychological subject, there can be no social revolution. It is understandable therefore that faced with the choice of claiming their subjectivity, many women have retreated instead into the anonymity of purdah (as in Egypt or Malaysia) or the counter-claims of total maternal consciousness (as in Japan where many women stop working to devote themselves to their children's education).

The contemporary Asian woman writer is shadowed by this double, of active self seen in the background of traditional social expectations that continue to complicate and subvert the process of claiming subjectivity. This scene of self and society, like a visual trick, can shift foreground and background, and the Asian woman will alternately place self first then place family and community before self with hardly a sense of the contradictions involved. But the writer who becomes conscious of this doubling of moral vision can be tormented by inconsistency, self-contempt and hatred.

The Double

She too dreamed the grand dream,
wished the million dollar wish,
sighed a Cleopatra heart,
claimed the heroine's part.

She too tightened waist,
unbuttoned her blouse,
halfed self and parted thighs,
laughed loudly above her cries.

She too smelled treachery,
worked the crowds, kissed strangers,
forgot her child, stayed up late
plotting her life. Her I hate.

The modern Asian woman writer is least likely to acknowledge a self as material, which is the field of politics for the empowered male. Because she has had little experience with political power, receiving the vote late and even now very seldom included in governmental roles, her imagination has not absorbed the material reality of consciousness. The Other to her has not moved beyond the first barrier of the Male Other. The Asian woman for centuries has been used by a patriarchal society as an object of economic exchange, de-centered in traditional customs as arranged marriages, child brides, dowries, polygamy, and prostitution. Not possessing economic power, she has been able to value herself only in the biological and domestic reproductive system, as mother and home-maker, values that rest on her ability to attract a mate, on her sexuality. As I've said earlier, for Asian women writers like Ding Ling, Kamala Das, or Gauri Deshpande, the sexual is the political.

Ding Ling was able to move out of her early sexual themes to a consciousness of the material world, expressed in novels such as *The Sun Shines Over the Sanggan River,* a rare development only matched by some Western women writers as Doris Lessing and Adrienne Rich. The future of self for the Asian woman writer must lie in this vision (or re-vision as Rich calls it in her essay, "When We Dead Awaken: Writing as Re-Vision"), in which the material world emerges from its possession by males to the grasp of the woman.

My own poems and fiction have hardly begun to glimpse this material self. Although my work is often situated in Malaysian and Singaporean landscapes, the subject expressed in them, while sovereign, is dimunitive and sometimes phantasmal. Poverty, hunger, desire, confusion are reflected through a single lens spot-lighted on a single scene, a vision which lends itself to the short poem and short story but not the novel. It is also a myopic vision, in which feeling is foregrounded. In so far as literature is a social construct, the self which is expressed in it is also a social construct. Social constructs are organized ideologically; that is, they are created by, express and reinforce the ideology (the visible assumptions and rules that society uses to make meaning of its existence) of their society. Caught in isolated subjectivity, incapable of leaving behind the sensuous and sensual world, poets such as Kamala Das are doomed to obsession, to repeat themselves compulsively. Psychological transformation of the subject occurs when the material self rather than the subjective experience is foregrounded, as in Ding Ling's novels. In their different ways, Ding Ling and Madonna singing "Material Girl" are expressing that transformation of the female subject in the world.

For me, recognizing a material self is to begin to write politically, with a sense of history and larger forces at work outside the subject. It is to begin to understand how remote history and politics have been for women and how totalizing in their lives. So my father's precipitate decline into bankruptcy was a story of greed, betrayal and stupidity, but more than that it was the common story of small private businesses failing in the face of new aggressive corporate companies that began entering Malaysia after the end of World War Two. It was the story of family businesses destroyed by familial rivalries, and of the harsh laws of bankruptcy imposed by a British colonial government still meting out a Dickensian punishment of the impoverished and unlucky. So too my mother's sudden flight to Singapore, abandoning six children heedlessly, is a tale of selfishness, egotism, an unforgiving resentment of the woman for the man who has abused her. But it is also a tale of an Asian woman influenced by Western mores of individualism, the sociological story of women from the provinces departing for the metropolitan centers and for new economic opportunities.

My story as a writer is also that of a colonized education in which the essential processes of identity formation are ironically the very processes stripping the individual of Asian tradition and communal affiliation. All writers begin as readers, and what I read for British external exams administered in Cambridge and Oxford and for pleasure in the cool thick-walled Malacca library were William Shakespeare, Jane Austen, Lord Alfred Tennyson, T.S. Eliot, Mills and Boones books, Barbara Cartland and Agatha Christie.[13] At that voracious age before puberty, I did not reflect that Hamlet was hardly a character a Chinese Malaysian girl could understand; after all, he was presented as a universal. So we chanted, "To be or not to be, that is the question," and watched Lawrence Olivier in black and white, impressed most by the daring of his exposed stockinged legs. Years later, I read the graffitti on the bathroom walls of a second-hand book store in New York, "Shakespeare: To be or not to be; Sartre: To do is to be; Sinatra: Doobeedoobeedoo" and realized that some native wag had Americanized an Anglo wit. But in Malacca in the 1950s English literature was a very solemn affair, reflecting the seriousness with which the British undertook to inculcate their civilization in us. "The White Man's Burden" was still taken by white men as their responsibility in the Far East, and while we were gifted with the splendid weight of the English language and its poetry, we were also burdened with their images, assumptions, values, history, and ideology, not to mention their prosodic forms, rhymes, silly poses, cheap sentimentality, Cliff Richards songs, tinned crackers, boiled sweets, Cadbury chocolates, all the colonial trivia of Malaysian daily life which adds up to a crackpot culture.

Of course it was a yellow culture we received, whether it was Thomas Peacock's unutterably dull satires canonized by the Cambridge Exams or Denis Robin's ladylike because suggestive pornography for teenage girls and frustrated wives. But then no open society is safe from yellow culture; to put it more positively, from the undesirable influences of other cultures. We were, however, not an open society. We were caged in British colonial culture and like the mynah learned to repeat the master's phrases, a song that we hear in the poems of the early Indian women writers such as Toru Dutt and Sarojini Naidu. The Asian woman writer, once the colonial screen has been lifted, is not yet a free individual, for colonial education has shaped both the spirit of independence and the language of independence that is to free her, and, as Audre Lorde asks, how is the master's house to be dismantled by the master's tools?

When the Asian woman looks to the West for social and economic liberation, she is exchanging a traditional social oppression for a new cultural oppressiveness. Filipino women who advertise for and marry ageing European males are acting out of the ancient role of women as economic possessions to be bought and sold to the highest bidder. When Chinese girls in Beijing deliberately seek Western men to marry, they are moving from one level of colonized mentality to another.

Lost Name Woman

Mississippi China Woman,
why do you wear blue jeans in the city?
Are you looking for the rich ghost
who will buy you a ticket to the west?

San Francisco China Woman,
you will drink only Coca-cola.
You stir with a long straw,
sip ss-ss like it's a rare elixir.

Massachusetts China Woman,
you've cut your hair and frizzed it.
Bangs hide your stubborn brow, eyes
shine, hurricane lamps in a storm.

Arizona China Woman,
now you are in Gold Mountain Country
you speak English like the radio,
but will it let you forget your father?

Woman with the lost name,
who will feed you when you die?

The experience expressed in this poem is an analogue for the precarious situation of the English-speaking Asian woman writer. In "marrying" the English language, the engendering of self occurs as the consciousness of alienation from a native culture. Subjectivity is articulated in a foreign or second tongue. The valuation of self is distorted in a doubly sexist mirror: the mirror of the Asian male that tells her that although she is not as beautiful as the white goddess, she is fated to be the mother of his children; and the mirror of the white male that tells her she is an exotic Susie Wong fated to be his mistress. No wonder then that terms such as deracination, alienation, and anomie ring in her ear like identity markers, a strange condition where no-identity, loss of self, estrangement from traditional society, the single atomized individual is the assumed material identity. Like the fizz in Coca-cola, the rapt reading of Billy Bunter public-school adventures, the crazy gyrations with the hula-hoop to Bobby Checkers' Twist music, this vision of the self is a phantasm created by English-language culture.

There are other selves not yet created in English literature and culture. The story of the Asian woman writer is the yet-to-be-told story of these selves which are dense with facticity, intersected by history and politics. The material self is the most Asian; rejects universality as the lesson of the master's tools; and insists on political realism as the space for self-creation. For me as a Chinese-Malaysian woman writer whose ethnicity marks me as subject to a new colonialism in the name of nationalism, this realism must be deeply insisted upon. To continue to write in English about a Chinese-Malaysian self and world, to insist on the validity of my material history, is the most revolutionary act possible in a society which seeks to deny autonomy or value to people like me.

In naming her experiences, the modern Asian woman writer is an existentialist. To write is to inscribe original identity; "Asian" is a term that is still filling with meaning. The material world is the political world; and the self, which is always already in exile, is also always already in birth.

1988

Notes

I thank Nancy Miller for insights shared during the 1987 NEH Summer Seminar at Barnard; and Wimal Dissanayake for his support during my 1988 summer residency at the East-West Center, Honolulu, which resulted in this chapter.

1. In the Filipino short story in English, women began publishing as early as men. Among the best and earliest short story writers published was Paz Marquez Benitiz, whose short stories began appearing in the 1910s. She edited the *Woman's Home Journal* in the Philippines from 1919 to 1934, and the first anthology of Filipino short stories in English, *Filipino Love Stories*, in 1928. Filipino women writers also generally continue to publish as widely as men do, but with considerably less notice. This phenomenon may be partly explained by the American missionary and colonial system of education which encouraged girls as well as boys to receive English language education. See, for example, the work of such contemporary Filipino women writers as Edith Tiempo, *A Blade of Fern* (Hong Kong: Heinemann, 1978); and *His Native Coast* (Quezon City: New Day Publishers, 1979); and Linda Ty-Casper, *The Hazards of Distance* (Quezon City: New Day Publishers, 1981); *Awaiting Trespass: A Pas'ion* (New York: Readers International, 1985); *Wings of Stone* (Columbia, LA: Readers' International, 1986); *Ten Thousand Seeds* (Manila: Ateneo de Manila University Press, 1987); and *Fortress in the Plaza* (Quezon City, Philippines: New Day Publishers, 1985).

2. See Meena Alexander for a defence of the Asian woman writer's subterfuges in finding a place for herself in a colonized and sexist society.

3. See Sarojini Naidu, *The Golden Threshold* and *The Sceptred Flute Songs of India*. Also Toru Dutt, *A Sheaf Gleaned in French Fields* and *Ancient Ballads and Legends of Hindustan*. Critics are divided between a rejection of Phillis Wheatley's poetry as a fawning imitator of Pope ("one thing she was not permitted to develop (was) the sense of her own distinct identity as a black poet...The barter of her soul, as it were, was no conscious contract" [Richmond 65]) and a re-interpretation of her work as expressive of Afro-American consciousness (She "did indeed manage, in various ways, to have much more Black consciousness, much more concern for her fellow Blacks, than many readers will admit," [Robinson 30]). Perhaps, the sharpest expression of Wheatley's problematic position in the Black American canon is expressed by M.A. Richmond: "To those in the present black generations, who are involved in the assertion and definition of black identity, in the rekindling of black pride, she can represent, with rare purity, the initial deprivation of that which they seek to regain" (Robinson 127).

4. See feminists critics' discussion of Lacan's ideas on the language of desire or female self inscribed as lack; for example, Toril Moi's succinct summary of Lacan's theories on the Imaginary and Symbolic Orders, the Mirror Stage, and the usages of the Other as "the locus of the constitution of the subject"; she points out that "If, for Lacan, it is the entry into the Symbolic Order that opens up the unconscious, this means that it is the primary repression of the desire for symbolic unity with the mother that creates the unconscious."

5. Ding Ling, "Shanghai in the Spring of 1930," *Miss Sophie's Diary*, 1985. All references to the story are taken from this edition.

6. After writing the bulk of this essay, I came across Teresa De Lauretis's summary of Catharine MacKinnon's essay which expresses a similar although larger argument: "To feminism, the personal is epistemologically the political, and its epistemology is its politics" (535).
7. Monika Varma's condemnation of Deshpande's womanist poetry as limited and sensationalist is a model of the kinds of resistances Asian women critics have set up against Asian feminist writing that transgresses traditional psycho-sexual modesty.
8. Kamala Das, *Alphabet of Lust,* 1976. All references to the text are taken from this edition.
9. Shirley Lim, "I Look for Women," *No Man's Grove.*
10. See, for example, the anthology *A Double Colonialism: Colonial and Post-Colonial Women's Writing,* ed. Anna Rutherford.
11. I have written on my mother's abandonment of the family in an earlier essay, "When East Meets West: Second Mothers and Abandoned Daughters."
12. *Ten Twentieth-Century India Poets,* p. 23.
13. I have written of the colonial reading experience in previous essays, especially in "Interview with Norman Simms" and "The Dispossessing Eye: Reading Wordsworth on the Equatorial Line."

Works Cited

Alexander, Meena. "Romanticism and Resistance in Sarojini Naidu." *Ariel,* 17:4 (Oct 1986): 49-61.

Das, Kamala. *Alphabet of Lust.* New Delhi: Orient paperbacks, 1976.

———. *The Old Playhouse and Other Poems.* New Delhi: Orient Longman, 1973.

Dutt, Toru. *A Sheaf Gleaned in French Fields.* 3rd edition. London: Kegan Paul and Co., 1880.

———. *Ancient Ballads and Legends of Hindustan.* London: Kegan Paul, 1882.

De Lauretis, Teresa. *Alice Doesn't: Feminism, Semiotics, Cinema.* Bloomington: Indiana University Press, 1984.

Feuerwerker, Yi-tsi Mei. *Ding Ling's Fiction.* Cambridge, Massachusetts: Harvard University Press, 1983.

Gilbert, Sandra M. and Susan Gubar. *The Norton Anthology of Literature by Women.* New York: Norton, 1985.

Kristeva, Julia. "La Femme, ce n'est jamais ca," *Polylogue.* Paris: Editions de Seuil, 1977.

Lessing, Doris. *The Summer Before the Dark.* New York: Knopf, 1973.

———. *To Room Nineteen.* London: Jonathan Cape, 1978.

Lim, Shirley Geok-lin. "When East Meets West: Second Mothers and Abandoned Daughters," *Women and Stepfamilies Voices of Anger and Love.* Ed. Nan Bauer Maglin and Nancy Schiedewird. Philadelphia: Temple University Press, 1989, 162-169.

———. "Interview with Norman Simms," *NZASIA,* Hamilton: New Zealand Asian Studies Society, 1983: 28-46.

———. "The Dispossessing Eye: Reading Wordsworth on the Equatorial Line," *Discharging the Canon: Cross-cultural Readings in Literature,* ed. Peter Hyland. Singapore: Singapore University Press, 1985: 126-132.

————. *No Man's Grove*. Singapore: National University of Singapore English Department Press, 1985.

Ding Ling. *The Sun Shines Over the Sanggan River*. Translated by Yang Xianyi and Gladys Yang. Beijing: Foreign Languages Press, 1984.

————. "Miss Sophie's Diary" and "Shanghai in the Spring of 1930." *Miss Sophie's Diary and Other Stories*. Translated by W.J.F. Jenner. Beijing: Panda Books, 1985.

Lorde, Audre. "The Master's Tools Will Never Dismantle the Master's House." *Sister Outsider*. Trumansburg, New York: Crossing Press, 1984, 110-13.

Moi, Toril. *Sexual/Textual Politics*. London and New York: Methuen, 1985.

Naidu, Sarojini. *The Golden Threshold*. With an introduction by Arthur Symonds. New York: The John Lane Company, 1905.

————. *The Sceptred Flute Songs of India*. New York: Dodd and Mead, 1928.

Olsen, Tillie. *Tell Me A Riddle*. New York: Dell, 1981.

Parthasarathy, R. ed. *Ten Twentieth-Century Indian Poets*. Delhi: Oxford University Press, 1976.

Rao, Vimala. "Kamala Das — The Limits of Over-Exposure." *Studies in Contemporary Indo-English Verse: A Collection of Critical Essays on Female Poets*, ed. A.N. Dwivedi. Bareilly, India: Prakash Book Depot, 1984.

Rich, Adrienne. "When We Dead Awaken: Writing as Re-Vision," *College English,* 34 (October 1973): 18-30.

Richmond, M.A. *Bid the Vassal Soar*. Washington, D.C.: Howard University Press, 1974.

————. "On 'The Barter of Her Soul'." *Critical Essays on Phillis Wheatley*, ed. William H. Robinson. Boston: G.K. Hall, 1982, 123-127.

Robinson, William H. *Phillis Wheatley In the Black American Beginnings*. Detroit: Broadside Press, 1975.

Rutherford, Anna, ed. *A Double Colonialism: Colonial and Post-Colonial Women's Writing*. Aarhus, Denmark: Kunapipi, 1985.

Stanton, Domna. "Language and Revolution," *The Future of Difference,* ed. Hester Eisenstein and Alice Jardine. New Brunswick, N.J.: Rutgers University Press, 1987.

Varma, Monika. "Gauri Deshpande," *Commonwealth Quarterly*, 3:9 (December 1978): 15-27.

Asians in Anglo-American Feminism:
Reciprocity and Resistance

This essay I write as an "Asian" woman owes its presence to an invitation from Anglo-American feminists. The agency which permits my presence has an authority that legitimizes me and that my presence in turn validates. Its authority presides because certain epistemic bodies have privileged it to *speak for* women. So I have permission to speak, but permission to speak as and for a minority; not as an *individual* which is an ideologically majority construct in the United States, but as a *re-presentation* of a minoritism of specified color and race.[1] One can read this already given inequality between Asian women and Anglo-American feminists as that of the moon to the sun, a smaller, unfueled planet illuminated by the atomic radiance of a self-propulsive star. Or perhaps as that of an even smaller orbiting fragment, illuminated by the pale glow of the moon, a light borrowed of a light borrowed from a patriarchal sun.

For an Asian like me, the personal and social significance of "owing," social indebtedness, the unequal relation of being a taker with the implied promise of making a return, is very strong. The bonds of reciprocity are an idealized social construct in both Confucianist and traditional Malay societies. The Filipinos call the construct *utang na loob*, a functional relation in a feudal and patronage-based society whereby the patron, the land-lord, the rich man, the mistress, assists the serf, the tenant farmer, the poor woman. In return, the taker is obligated to return that "social capital" in any number of ways: giving his labor when needed, offering a share of his crops and his livestock, showing due respect and proper distance at all times.[2] Reciprocity as a pre-capitalist function that is as materialist and economically penetrative as colonially introduced capitalism is not simply good or bad; it is a way of constructing social relations when capital is not available to many of the constituents in that society.

As a child growing up in the British colony of the Federated States of Malaya, I was constantly reminded of how much gratitude I owed to all kinds of people. To my father for keeping us children with him when our mother abandoned us. To my step-mother who cooked and cleaned for us. To the nuns of the Convent of the Holy Infant Jesus who taught us the Catechism and how to pass exams. To my many aunts and uncles who gave us an occasional dollar or meal. To the British administrators who gave us the railroad, the macadam roads, piped water, electricity, law and order, and "civilization."

I was always aware of how much I "owed" family, adults, and white people, in that order of importance. And I was expected to moderate my behavior in accordance with these debts. Not merely in saying "thank you" often and sincerely, or holding my posture in a deferential manner, but in what I said, judged, evaluated, and believed. If I were properly grateful, I would not say what I thought, that so and so was a foolish and selfish person. In fact, I would not think negatively — for example, that the British were a racist lot who believed themselves superior to others. Nor would I question the unequal relation of creditor and debtor — does a charitable meal offered to a hungry child make the giver a morally superior being or the child wolfing down the meal a morally inferior creature?

Now that I'm a mother, an adult, and an "Asian American," I am still confused by this miasma, this entangled, entangling net of bonds of gratitude that arises almost involuntarily when white feminists recognize me. Mentoring, that positive spin given to a corrupting old-boys' network, is inevitably, for me, shaded in with the ideal of *utang na loob*.

In order to write an essay on feminism, a term made popular and authoritative by Anglo-American women, I have first to understand wherein and why my relationship to feminism is tangled with those early cultural ideals of gratitude and obligation, and how those ideals, embedded in a Confucianist/Malayan/Catholic background, a colonized/British imperialist mentality, and an Asian patriarchal society, still command the relations between Western feminists and, in my case, an Asian woman.

Filial duty. Gratitude. *Utang na loob.* Obligation. Indebtedness. These terms are not synonymous although they circle around a common set of paradigms: the child to the parent, the wife to the husband, the peasant to the landowner, the colonized non-citizen to the colonizing administrator, the debtor to the capitalist. These paradigms are predicated on unequal relations, between one who is lesser with someone who is greater. The child is dependent on the parent's wisdom, the wife on her husband's protection, the serf on the landlord's plenty, the colonized subject on the administrator's rule, the debtor on the capitalist's loan.

What is missing from the paradigm of reciprocity ironically embedded in unequal relations is the notion of injustice. The analogous relations are constructed around apparently "natural" phenomenon, specifically that of dependent child and protective parent. The "naturalization" of these social and political structures, their ideological propagation, serves to mask their economic purposes. With social reciprocity, dependents do not perceive their powerlessness as caused by the others' agency. The peasant does not understand the landlord's exploitation of his labor; the colonized subject the colonizer's abuse of his land and people to enrich the "mother country;" the wife the husband's possession of her body and services. Instead, dependents perceive chiefly their weakness and the others' power to assist them; and align themselves with the stronger as the means to empowerment. In systems of social reciprocity, oppression is seldom an overt and single act of domination; rather it is comprised of systematic, multiple, repeated, pervasive acts of injustices in which the complicity of the oppressed, their silence, passivity, and yes, cooperation, support and contribute to the power of the oppressor. The "natural" gratitude owed by child to parent becomes enlarged, reified, and ideologized as those Confucianist social hierarchies of family position and state power, just as the British colonialists exploited the Christian ideal of gratitude owed to a good Samaritan to explain the loyalty subjugated natives owed them for their civil government.

At a political and social level, I was raised a colonized child, abandoned by my mother and left to my father's heavy-handed care. According to family legend, my father, who kept all the children with him after our mother ran away, favored me, the only daughter, above his five sons. But he did not hesitate to take a rattan cane to me when, as they said it then, he "lost his temper." Corporal punishment in the 1950s and early 1960s was perhaps more prevalent than in these enlightened times. But :o a child of 8 or 10 or even 15, slaps, blows, and caning on the arms and legs that raise bloody welts can never be rationalized. My first experience of patriarchy, at its most immediate domestic manifestation, made me sharply ambivalent about any future relations with men. I learned that love and brutality existed simultaneously in the "protection" that men offered; but I also learned that there was nothing outside of this social structure that a weak child could appeal to. My mother having blithely abandoned us for the bright lights and freedom of a big city, I also learned that ny father's protection, his attachment to the patriarchal family, was absolutely necessary for my simple existence.

What I understood, even as a child, was that my father's brutality should have been mediated for me by a mother's presence. Even where constraints make it difficult for women to act against men's power, there are strategies available to lessen that abuse of power. These strategies have usually developed over centuries of social formation.[3] My mother, however, like Ibsen's Nora, chose to live for herself. Displacing the Chinese tradition of the good woman as the dutiful mother, she grasped the prickly principle of duty to self.

At the age of 8, I had not read Ibsen. The central experiences of my childhood shaped me to understand not one set of injustices — that of a patriarchal world where men have power to do good and evil to women — but another set seldom discussed by feminists: that of a women-for-women world where women, deciding on their duties to their children, also have power to do good and evil. My early lesson, learned as it were at my absent mother's knee, is that feminism, like patriarchy, is open to critique.

Feminism, as defined in the United States, as ideology, movement and personal practice, is predicated on the belief that women suffer injustices simply by fact of their gender. Feminists concur in an activist vision of correcting these injustices wherever they occur: in the home or workplace, in bed or out on the streets. The social and political agenda has assumed, perhaps inevitably so, a universalist program, that feminism speaks for all women and works for the good of all women.[4]

Women of color increasingly have queried this assumption.[5] Hooks critiques contemporary United States feminism, initiated by Friedan's *The Feminine Mystique,* as dealing with "the plight of a select group of college-educated, middle and upper class, married white women" and ignoring "the existence of all non-white women and poor white women" (1984: 1-2). To hooks, "White women who dominate feminist discourse, who for the most part make and articulate feminist theory, have little or no understanding of white supremacy as a racial politic, of the psychological impact of class, of their political status within a racist, sexist, capitalist state" (Ibid.: 4). An instance of where U.S. feminism fails black women is its intensification of male sexism.[6] Black women do not join the feminist movement, hooks says, not because they cannot face the reality of sexist oppression, but because "they do not see in feminist theory and practice . . . potential solutions" (Ibid.: 75).

For hooks, as well as the Anglo-American feminists who are the objects of her critique, a key concept for feminist struggle resides in the term, "deprived."[7] "Deprived," with the prefix "de-" functioning as a signifier, connotes an act of theft, oppression, upon a set of rights. It suggests not merely a negative state but also a causal agent behind that condition. When you are "deprived," the assumption is that you have had certain items that rightfully belong to you taken away from you by someone or some force. A deprived child in contemporary America is one who should rightfully have more — care, food, shelter, education. Some one or some force has robbed the child of her rights, and, if we are so minded, we can act in concert to return these rights to the child.

It is easy for many women in the U.S., politicized by anti-colonial, anti-establishment movements, to recognize the Confucianist, feudal, patriarchal paradigms as misleading, distorted, incorrect, and incomplete. In place of the benevolent protection that these false consciousnesses of reciprocity had asserted in an earlier colonialist era, Anglo-American feminists posit instead a malevolent inequality of power constructed on economic, military, and political oppression. In place of social reciprocity or bondage, they insist on democracy, individual freedom, and equal rights for women.

The first set of paradigms was pervasive when I was a child. The British colonial system, particularly as conveyed to me through the teaching of missionary women from Ireland, constructed an ideology that in its paternalism supported and replicated the patriarchal, sexist, feudal, and capitalist aspects of pre-Independence Malayan society. In contrast to colonialist propaganda, Aimé Césaire's unrelenting critique of colonialism provides no space for compromise: "Between colonizer and colonized there is room only for forced labor, intimidation, pressure, taxation, theft, rape, compulsory crops, contempt, mistrust, arrogance, self-complacency, swinishness, brainless elites, degraded masses" (21). To Césaire, colonized societies are "drained of their essence, cultures trampled underfoot, institutions undermined, lands confiscated, religions smashed, magnificent artistic creations destroyed, extraordinary possibilities wiped out" (21). All this was true of colonized Malaysia, despite the construction of macadam roads, railways, hospitals, and schools.The British-style institutions that replaced native customs quickened the pace of alienation, which was made irreversible for populations that lost their original languages and became largely monolingual English-speaking. The alienated elite were assimilated into Western culture and were chiefly disaffiliated from any sense of Asian solidarity. The poets quoted T. S. Eliot's *The Waste Land* and wrote from a colorless, that is, Western imagination (Ibid.: 75). I was vaguely aware of this alienation and the need to return to Asian sources of culture before I left Malaysia, immediately after the riots of May 1969, when hundreds of Malaysian Chinese were killed by Malays who resented the Chinese push for electoral representation. My analysis of my homeland's political future then was that of inevitable race-based state power empowering the majority Malay and the increasing economic and social marginalization and dislocation of the minority Chinese.

In my life, therefore, it was not feminism that radicalized me. Instead, it was experiences within Confucianism, colonialism, feudalism, patriarchy, and neocolonialism that led me to feminism. In the United States in the 1990s, the second paradigm that I had been "civilized" in, the paradigm of unequal power, with one pole of the race, class, and gender category oppressed by the dominant pole, has become *au courant*. The shift from the first to the second paradigm is usually what is meant by the term "radicalized." When one becomes radicalized, the first naturalized ideological universe tilts, as it were, left. Usually, the radicalized person comes to view the conserving powers of capitalism, imperialism, and patriarchy as an undifferentiated epistemic oppression of dispossessed groups.

But as an already multiply colonized subject, I do not see these oppressions as coming from a hegemonic center. Instead, I see a colonial subject as the cultural site for the contradictions inherent in the intersections of multiple conserving circles of authority. These authoritarian domains overlap each other but not sufficiently so as to preserve the illusion of totalization. Ironically, therefore, I experienced those liberatory movements precisely *where* Confucianism, Catholicism, feudalism, and colonialism intersected.

To give an example. An internally consistent system such as Catholicism possesses oppressive weight for the individual enmeshed in its social networks. But its consistency becomes a point of departure or becomes itself a disruptive force when it intersects and destablizes another ideological system, such as Confucianism. Within the stable relations constituted by Confucianism, the female is always subordinate to the male, the younger to the older, the outsider to the insider family member. In the social hierarchy constructed in a Confucianist family, all members of the family know where they stand in relation to everyone else, in an order of social importance that is reiterated in naming (Eldest Brother, Second Uncle, Third Sister, for example) and replicated in official and institutional constructions outside the family. To a young female in this family, the dogmatic constructions of Catholicism can very well take on the lineations of a liberationist theology. The ideals of an order made in Heaven, rather than embedded in familial hierarchies, of loving your neighbor as yourself (and as your parents and siblings!), are frankly subversive, almost anarchic in its effects on retrograde Chinese chauvinists.

That was how I read the role models of those tight-faced hooded virginal nuns in the Convent of the Holy Infant Jesus. At the age of 7 or 8, I saw them as dangerous women, living outside the protection of the Confucianist family, Asians and whites together, thriving in open defiance of what centuries of Chinese civilization have shaped as natural for humans. They lived without men, outside of marriage, without children of their own, doing the kind of work that men do. They were women who were like men. That I was given to their care every day from 7.30 a.m. to 2 p.m., that Chinese parents were deferential to them, were intimidated and made smaller by their presence: these facts did not pass by me unremarked. In Catholicism as lived by these nuns I saw a larger power than Confucianism, and so very early, even before my mother's flight, the Confucianist construct of the good wife and mother lost any significant hold on my imagination.

However, the ideal of ascetic single lives of cloistered women, women who had unerringly destroyed the possibility of Confucianist upbringing for those good little girls entrusted to them by foolish parents, never exerted its ideological power over me. Instead, what fueled my imagination was the multiple lapidary colors of cross-cultural worlds created by a history of colonialism. The Federation of Malaya, a minor protrusion off the southeast corner of the Asian landmass, was all of the world I knew. Malacca, the town in which I spent the first nineteen years of my life, like a frog in a well who measures the night sky and stars from the roundness and depth of her well, was a microcosm of cultures.

Beginning as a Malay fishing village, it attracted Portuguese, Spanish, Dutch, and English colonizers, drew Arab, Indian, and Chinese traders, and was visited by Irish and French missionaries. Australian tourists drank beer in its few bars, American soldiers on R&R drove politely through the narrow streets.

Growing up, I knew a town of small untidy houses and large families, and shops in which cloths, foodstuffs, cosmetics, hair ornaments and other gimcracks were displayed in single rows or heaps. I knew nothing of boredom. The scale of experience in Malacca for a child was near perfect. The few cars sped at twenty to thirty miles per hour on the open roads outside town. In the town itself, crowded with cyclists, trishaws and occasional bullock-drawn carts, the cars moved at ten to fifteen miles per hour. Walking in the short winding lanes, you could see the faces and postures of passengers as the cars passed slowly beside you. It was a town that a child could map on her imagination, could hold in the palm of her mind. Here one's family knew a banker, a rubber estate owner, a Malay government official, a schoolteacher, a trishaw man, a noodle peddler, a temple trance devotee, a gangster, a mad man, a doctor, a gambler, several unfaithful husbands, a hen-pecked man, people much richer than oneself, indigents to be pitied, snobbish Eurasians who thought too highly of themselves, alcoholic Ceylonese, chauvinist Chinese who talked of returning to China: an entire society englobed in one's immediate experience. There was more of color, activity, and bustle in the little town, more that could be grasped by a child sent spinning among its circles of gossips, its sphericities of class and race, than could be contained within the walls of the convent. And it is that contingent aspect of colonialism, its anarchic, entrepreneurial free-for-all of cultures encountering, breaking down, breaking through to others, that re-positioned Catholicism and its universalist apparently gender-free spirituality, so appealing against a Confucianist patriarchal kinship system, as small, provincial, and unattractive to a 13-year-old.

The irony of my present feminist state is that it owes as much to Confucianist patriarchy (a father determined to keep his family together), Roman Catholicism (nuns who offered another model of woman as unmarried and professional), and colonialism (a political system that produced a commingling of radically different races and cultures) as it does to Anglo-American feminist theory. However, it is not these systems but their intersections that offered me points of escape. Situated as I was in Confucianist, Malay feudal, Roman Catholic, British colonial crossways, I was exposed not to systematic political oppression but to continual upheavals. As Fanon points out in his phenomenological critique of colonialism, "There is a zone of nonbeing, an extraordinarily sterile and arid region, an utterly naked declivity where an authentic upheaval can be born" (10).

My cultural world was not monological but multilogical. Given the multiplicity of cultures, the extraordinary subjective feature remained that none of them offered the girl-child a stable, established, supporting society. Each system, oppressive alone, became interrogative and subversive in the matrix of multiculturalism. Their values and beliefs did not co-exist in parallel structures but reacted on each other, calling into question their differences. None was dominant, there was no mainstream, each system was marginal to the other. As subject, agent, and object, I resisted the identity given to me by each of them. I remained between and outside the statements of these systems: non-male, non-Malay, non-Catholic, non-British-colonial. Involuntarily, I moved from my Chinese extended family where uncles, aunts, cousins, and even strangers were endowed with familial and honorific status — third paternal uncle, first maternal aunt, eldest brother — to a missionary school where a Mother Superior ruled over Irish sisters — Sister Finigan, Sister Patrick, Sister Alexis. From the South Seas community known as Nanyang Chinese and the Irish Convent (locally known as the French Convent), I moved on to a high school whose Principal was a Sandhurst Military Academy Englishman. Colonel Wade presided over prefects in the imago of characters from *Tom Brown's Schooldays,* characters already phantasmically related to Roman senators traced through a classical Latin imaginary. Trained intellectually on the British model of Parliamentary debate, we moved suddenly to the phenomenon of *Merdeka* (Independence) with a Malay Royal Prince, Tengku Abdul Rahman, as the first Prime Minister and Malay Sultanates standing in line every five years to rule as kings over our now Malaysian nation.

Significantly, I experienced none of these systems as closed. They were present as contradictions opening multiple counter-possibilities, offering questions rather than answers, divergences rather than oppressions, ferments rather than ideologies. Cultures (not Culture), differences (not Centrism), form the base of inquiry for me. Before coming to the US, before coming to feminism, I understood pluralism as the ground of experience. Thus, although the ethos of American democracy is relatively recent to me, a by-product of an interracial, international marriage and of immigration, and although feminism in its Western form is even newer, a still evolving force that has reached me via academia, the media, and theory, they bear the traces of something familiar and ancient, the lineations of civilizations rising from the crossroads where natives and travellers are indistinguishable, trading, babbling in a multitude of languages, and engaging in activities both seductively mysterious and dangerously alien to each other.

The attack on patriarchy as an entrenched political system preserving the privileges of one gender on the back of another is for me also an anti-colonialist position. Men have colonized women, exploiting their labor for their own purposes, creating a society of unequals, and reifying these injustices through a series of legislative acts. Women, passive, long-suffering, complicit, have been colonized subjects for centuries. The critique of patriarchy not merely parallels but reinforces and broadens the critique of colonialism, moving it from a historical specific moment to a profoundly ahistorical theoretical acknowledgement of the relations of power and powerlessness. Having had my being always already on the margins of circles of power, I recognized this construction of (male, colonialist) power over (female, colonized) subject as authenticated in and authenticating my life. Theory and experience match in this moment of feminist consciousness.

But what keeps me going as a feminist in the United States is the promise of community that Anglo-American feminists hold out to women of color like myself. Unlike Malacca of my childhood, the United States is a continually hegemonizing society. By that I mean that political, institutional, and social forces are continually contesting for a foreground, and that American culture generally is defined and defines itself as a conflict of centrisms. Not to name oneself as centric is already to accept marginalization. And the material, professional, and social rewards accrue generally to centric positions. Even young children in the United States are trained in observations of centric positioning, especially as manifested in material behavior. Possessing specific brand-name items, sharing in specific activities and behavior, can create a sense of being in the mainstream. But other determinable aspects also dictate the individual's position in American society, among them race, color, national origin, class, gender and language-possession. As if to counter the pluralistic immigrant influx, American society has constituted hegemonic cultural processes, through education, employment, media, the military, governmental and social agencies, so that millions of Americans while they recognize their marginality are continually pressed to give it up to assimilate into a cultural center that is Standard-American-English-speaking, European-civilization-based, and middle-class in consumption and aspiration. American feminism appears to offer a counter-community. Commanded by its rhetoric of the privileging of difference, it promises a community that paradoxically is constructed not on commonality but on difference.[8]

Already a feminist in my post-colonial progressive marginalizations, two significant events mark my entry into an overt commitment. The first was my coming to motherhood at 35; the second my summer at Barnard working with the prominent feminist scholar of French Literature, Nancy

Miller. No feminist, I believe, can understand woman's special position of social enslavement/social empowerment without understanding the psychosocial dynamics of maternality. The maternal role entails the kind of physical labor, daily drudgery, and social bondage that equalizes most women with the working poor. But it also enables an ideal of noble sacrifice, a social bonding that functions as referent for human behavior, that has almost universally made a mystique of motherhood. Becoming a mother late in life, and determined to maintain my professional position, I soon discovered the needs for woman-bonding, for woman-centered community, that an academic career can ignore. Mothers who can babysit, mothers who share information on child-care, mothers who understand the stresses, guilts, and joys of raising children — I hungered for these contacts as much as I had hungered for books in my impoverished childhood.

This need for woman-centered community received a theoretical shape in 1987 when Nancy Miller gathered twelve women in Barnard to discuss feminist issues in literary criticism.[9] Among the twelve were three women of color; and it was the white women whose community dominated. Perhaps the most meagre place to look for community is among competitive and research-oriented academic women; but Miller offered an intensely brilliant summer when the decade-old conversations among feminists were replayed for us. If a colonized, Confucianist, feudal apprenticeship prepared me for the zone of upheaval, difference, and question, Miller's readings provided me with the language that shaded me as a feminist ideologue.

But it is this very shading, this feminist vocabulary, that I now interrogate, for I see in my relation to Anglo-American feminism the same troubling imbalance of power that characterized my earlier experiences. Fanon, from his own situated colonized experience, noted that

> Every colonized people — in other words, every people in whose soul an inferiority complex has been created by the death and burial of its local cultural originality — finds itself face to face with the language of the civilizing nation; that is, with the culture of the mother country. The colonized is elevated above his jungle status in proportion to his adoption of the mother country's cultural standards. He becomes whiter as he renounces his blackness, his jungle. In the French colonial army, and particularly in the Senegalese regiments, the black officers serve first of all as interpreters. They are used to convey the master's orders to their fellows, and they too enjoy a certain position of honor. (19)

I hold similar ironic observations of myself. Adopting the rhetoric of feminism that allows me to be heard by white feminists, I am also at the same time elevating the culture of that "mother country." Speaking of Asian experience to white feminists or of feminist agendas to Asian Americans, I am also serving as mediator and interpreter, conveying the "mother-culture's" position to my fellow Asians. In that mother-culture of feminism, have I not buried my own original "jungle status," that local piecemeal of plural civilizations manifested in the South Seas Chinese-Malay-British cultures-in-process and in-contact?

Feminism that predicates its viability on a recognition of gender difference has yet to make space for the plural cultural utterances of gender differences. Feminism as ideology leaves no space for gaps of being in which psycho-social upheavals can occur. It has yet to listen to the voices of colonized women from deep within their oppressions, to recognize the divergent race, national, class, religious, and linguistic selves among women. Too often, as hooks argues, in its Anglo-American form it serves careerist, middle-class white women and, as complicit servitors, those women of color admitted into this professional feminism.

Yet, in its liberatory mission, US feminism has served me well. In the ideal of sisterhood, it has given me a sense, an affect, of community larger than nation, race, religion, or class. In the "conversations" of women from Nancy Miller to bell hooks and Catharine Stimpson, it has provided me with the analytical tools that permit me finally to segue through the intersecting systems of twentieth-century oppression that have directly borne upon me. More importantly, it has made a space for women of color like myself to be heard. How easy then to be grateful to one's sisters, to commit oneself to the community of women.

None the less, the Asian woman who comes to feminism via Anglo-American theory would do well to resist the Asian cultural pressures of reciprocity and the historical colonial construction of inferiority that paradoxically support each other in her induction into the ideology. The relation between Asian woman and Anglo-American feminist theory must be continually interrogative and provisional as long as it remains a relation of unbalanced power, with Anglo-Americans formulating the theory and Asians consuming it. Fanon argued that colorless literature produced by black people was a manifestation of their colonized imaginations; similarly, we should read "colorless" feminism, feminist theory that ignores the place of cultural and racial difference in women, as an expression of Anglo-American-centric colonialist theory. A feminist canon of foremothers that centralizes Anglo-American writers such as Virginia Woolf and Gertrude Stein and constructs a theory out of their privileged white upper-middle-class oriented lives and works can only speak marginally to my concerns. When such a theory is presented as essentially speaking for women, I perceive the same kinds of imperializing patterns that characterize white male culture.

It is especially distressing to observe how white feminists, arguing the model of sisterhood and shared narratives of oppression and victimization, have moved into postcolonialist discourses. My distress does not arise from perceptions of appropriation but of misappropriation. If white feminists are open to instruction about women of color, about women as diverse and different, their speaking for these differences would be welcomed. Instead, some white feminists, claiming to speak for postcolonial women, offer a discourse that takes only more white and privileged women — Olive Shreiner, Jean Rhys, Isaak Dinesen, and Nadine Gordimer — as women's voices from the Third World. The Eurocentric view prevails over and above the feminist critique. In light of such narrow, intolerant, culture-bound canons, it behooves the Asian feminist to read U.S. feminism as yet another manifestation of Anglo-American imperialism. Until white feminists become embarrassed at the gaps in their critiques of society, and until feminism becomes a cluster of culture-specific practices, I will have to remain uneasily a resisting sister.

1991

Notes

1. I discuss the unease of speaking as representative of a color and gender in my lecture, "The Ambivalent American: Asian American Identity on the Cusp" delivered at Brown University, 1988; in *Reading the Literatures of Asian America*:

   I was conscious that the invitation to speak was addressed not only to myself, as an individual, but also to the group which I represent. I am a representative, I suppose, by fact of my origin and appearance, my yellow-brown skin and black hair, my birth in an Asian country. . . . It is difficult to be a representative. One must always be more than one is, and in like manner one is always less than one is (13).

   Gayatri Spivak addresses it also in "Questions of Multi-culturalism," an interview with Sneja Gunew, in *The Post-colonial Critic:* "When *they* want to hear an Indian speaking as an Indian, a Third World woman speaking as a Third World woman, they cover over the fact of the ignorance that they are allowed to possess, into a kind of homogenization" (60).

2. See Fred Eggan:

   In one form or another reciprocity is basic to all social life everywhere. . . . The most important feature of this reciprocity system in the Philippines is that much of life goes on among relatives, and others, too, on a basis of just give and take, of agreements and compensations for agreements. If one goes beyond this and *voluntarily* performs a service or helps someone out of a difficulty, then he puts the individual he helps under a special obligation. It is an obligation which cannot be repaid in money, but which has to be repaid in services and should be repaid upon request. (10)

3. Margery Wolf discussed women's strategies for influence and survival in traditionally structured peasant families in *Women in Chinese Society.* As Kay Ann Johnson points out, "in fairly regularized ways the influence of women often went beyond their legitimate limits in informal and sometimes surreptitious ways" (20).

4. See the kind of universalism appealed to in the introduction to *New French Feminisms:* "Feminism owes its existence to the universality of misogyny, gynophobia, androcentrism, and heterosexism. Feminism exists because women are, and have been, everywhere oppressed at every level of exchange from the simplest social intercourse to the most elaborate discourse" (Marks and de Courtivron 4).

5. For example, see critiques of white feminist theory in Mitsuye Yamada (71-5) and Trinh T. Minh-ha. Yamada asks uneasily for support from white feminists:

this path (feminism) is fraught with problems which we are unable to solve among us . . . in order to do so, we need the help and cooperation of white feminist leaders, the women who coordinate programs, direct women's buildings, and edit women's publications throughout the country. (71)

Trinh addresses ironically the restricted role of difference that a Third World woman must play to her sponsors:

Eager not to disappoint, I try my best to offer my benefactors and benefactresses what they most anxiously yearn for: the possibility of a difference, yet a difference or an otherness that will not go so far as to question the foundation of their beings and makings (88).

6. Hooks points out that

the poor or working class man who has been socialized via sexist ideology to believe that there are privileges and powers he should possess solely because he is male often finds that few if any of these benefits are automatically bestowed him in life. (73)

The reluctance of black women "to publicly discuss sexist oppression," (74) she explains, comes from a fear that "it could simply lead to greater victimization" (76).

7. For example, hooks uses the concept of comparative deprivation to critique the white feminists' privileging of work as liberatory, because it ignores the exploitative and dehumanizing aspects of many jobs held by people of color. Many Anglo-American feminists interpret work narrowly as professional careers, leading to an influx of bourgeois women into the marketplace. The success of these professional women have taken attention away from the fact that many more women, especially women of color, are still exploited and devalued in low-paying service jobs (95-105).

8. Feminist scholars, in attempting to rearticulate woman against traditional and patriarchal norms, privilege complexity, conflict, and difference. See, for example, Gayle Greene and Coppélia Kahn, "Feminist scholarship and the social construction of woman," for a cogent review of feminist revisions in

anthropology, history and literature that insist on "restor(ing) conflict, ambiguity and tragedy to the centre of historical process" (Fox-Genovese 28, cited in Green and Kahn 21).

9. Nancy Miller's most recent book, one that she was completing during that summer, *Subject to Change: Reading Feminist Writing*, demonstrates her witty feminist re-reading of "the text's heroine" and the refusal of the patriarchal plot in women's writing.

Works Cited

Césaire, Aimé. *Discourse on Colonialism*. Trans. Joan Pinkham. New York: Monthly Review Press, 1972.

Eggan, Fred. "Philippine Social Structure," *Six Perspectives on the Philippines*, ed. George M. Guthrie. Manila: Book Mark, 1971.

Fanon, Frantz. *Black Skin White Masks*. Trans. Charles Lam Markmann. New York: Grove Press, 1967.

Fox-Genovese, Elizabeth. "Placing Women's History in History." *New Left Review* (May-June, 1982): 5-29.

Greene, Gayle and Coppélia Kahn. "Feminist Scholarship and the social construction of woman." *Making a Difference: Feminist Literary Criticism*.London:Methuen, 1985. 1-36.

hooks, bell. *Feminist Theory: From Margin to Center*. Boston: South End Press, 1984.

Johnson, Kay Ann. *Women, The Family and Peasant Revolution in China*. Chicago: University of Chicago Press, 1983.

Lim, Shirley Geok-lin. "The Ambivalent American: Asian American Identity on the Cusp." In *Reading the Literatures of Asian America*, edited by Shirley Geok-lin Lim and Amy Ling. Philadelphia: Temple University Press, 1992. 13-32.

Marks, Elaine and Isabelle de Courtivron,eds. *New French Feminisms*. New York: Schocken Books, 1981.

Memmi, Albert. *Dominated Man: Notes Towards a Portrait*. New York: Orion Press, 1968.

Miller, Nancy K. *Subject to Change: Reading Feminist Writing*. New York: Columbia University Press, 1988.

Spivak, Gayatri Chakravorty. *The Postcolonial Critic: Interviews, Strategies, Dialogues*. Edited by Sarah Harasym. New York: Routledge, 1990.

Stimpson, Catharine. *Where the Meanings Are*. New York: Methuen, 1988.

Trinh T. Minh-ha. *Woman, Native, Other: Writing Postcoloniality and Woman*. Bloomington: Indiana University Press, 1989.

Wolf, Margery and Roxanne Witke, eds. *Women in Chinese Society*. Stanford: Stanford University Press, 1975.

Yamada, Mitsuye. "Asian Pacific American Women and Feminism." *This Bridge Called My Back*. Edited by Cherrie Moraga and Gloria Anzaldua. New York: Kitchen Table Press, 1981. 71-75.

Language, Gender, Race, and Nation:
A Postcolonial Meditation

In the US academy, the axiom that knowledge is power, which has conventionally been read as a race- and gender-free proposition, is almost always applied differently to non-EuroAmericans and to women scholars. Werner Sollors has argued through an examination of selected American literary texts that the construction of American identity proceeds by way of consent, with the individual abandoning a pre-immigrant culture and voluntarily accepting modes of behavior and systems of belief associated with American culture (6-17). Consent as the predominant paradigm of Americanization counters the descent paradigm, in which identity remains embedded in genealogical blood-lines, and the individual is constrained in construction of identity to some essentialist notion of birth-affect and tribal influence. Sollors' reading of the consent-descent dichotomy of ethnic identity formation is appealing precisely because it appears to support the ideological matrix of democratic individualism that is usually presented as the American way. His consent theory to explain the relatively smooth process of assimilation by European immigrants into the American social mainstream, however, overlooks how the descent paradigm operates differently for people of color (that is, all distinctively non-European-looking Americans).

Let us take the problem of language requirement in one area of the knowledge industry. In the field of American literature, scholars are still expected to have a reading knowledge of at least two other languages than English. In the sub-field of Asian American literature, more and more the expectation is that the scholar should have at least one major Asian language in hand. As Asian American literature is to a large extent written in English by writers who are themselves unable to write in the language of their Asian ancestors, this expectation points to an unacknowledged emphasis on descent. The racial origin of the producer, validated by the possession of a "descent" language, is presented as having a significant bearing on the reproduction of knowledge in that particular sub-set. Thus, in treating American ethnic literature, the racial identity of the interlocutor is valorized as a significant signature, assigning authority, authenticity, and validity to his or her reading. The same kind of descent association is not made of mainstream American critics: for example, Lionel Trilling's Jewish identity did not prevent him from discussing Anglo-American writing, nor does one ask that a critic be versed in Armenian or Yiddish to write on William Saroyan's or Bernard Malamud's works.

Colonial and Postcolonial Non-Consent

This ascription of authority to descent does not take into account the diachronic and provisional dimension of language/knowledge acquirement (as in the question of language acquirement in a recent past, for example, the colonized world of Malaysia), but reads discourse in the synchronicity of the contemporary. The critique of colonized cultures is well rehearsed by writers such as Franz Fanon, Memmi, and Chinweizu. Post-independence, the sociopolitical model of an anomic, alienated, English-speaking native intelligentsia-elite produced by a British imperial administration is accepted in these critiques as replicable whether in Trinidad, Singapore, Ghana, Kenya, or India. However, in both colonial and postcolonial constructions of the intelligentsia-elite and the relation of language choice to its construction, the crucial factor of consent is overlooked. The colonial government, in setting up English-language schools and a system of civil-service rewards based on English-language acquirement, did not require the consent of the populace.

Similarly, beginning in 1970, in dismantling that English-language educational and civil-service structure, and in establishing a native language-base power structure, the Malay dominant government in Malaysia did not ask for the consent of its non-Malay citizens. In colonial and postcolonial societies, language policies took effect, whether to the empowerment or displacement of the English language, *de facto*, outside the area of democratic discussion and decision. In place of consent, the paradigm of descent remains ascendent in matters of language choice. That is, the bias remains that individuals do not so much choose a language of affiliation or have that choice politically foisted on them as that the choice has always already been made through the essential bond of race and blood-line.

The Chinese Malaysian and language choice

What seems to be a straightforward proposition of identifying language with the people, "the folk," can be seen as problematic in post-colonial societies. In a nation like Malaysia nothing can be taken for granted in examining the relationship between the individual's localized speech world and national language culture. Chinese Malaysians, for example, would be expected to feel an affiliation for Bahasa Malaysia, the national language. Embracing place as origin, the Chinese Malaysian may adopt the national language in an assimilative act similar to the Nonyas and Babas of the Straits Settlements. However, if Bahasa is seen as an instrument for empowering one racial group and consequently for disempowering the Chinese Malaysians, the language itself may rouse strong feelings of disaffiliation, to be used only when necessary. The same Chinese Malaysians may turn to the language of descent to express their resistance to a national formation that appears to erase their identity. The language of race may be Mandarin, the elite Chinese of writing and communication. Or, having lost any sense of affiliation with the Chinese of origin, some Chinese Malaysians may simply continue to use their dialect, asserting a local ethnic, as opposed to national Chinese, identity. Or Chinese Malaysians, rejecting both Malay and Chinese cultural nationalisms based on paradigms of racial descent, assent to an international language that opens the future for themselves and their children, English. These Malaysians, in choosing the future over the past, consent over descent, are choosing a potential international identity formation over national identity politics that reinscribe ancient tribal feuds and territorial imperatives. They are choosing the potential open border of immigration over the already closed boundary of the nation-state.

Exiles, Refugees, and Immigrants

In a postcolonial world, where exiles, refugees, and immigrants form a sizable part of its citizenry, language choice must increasingly be dissociated from racial origin and possession, a matter of descent, and become associated with matters of economic, political, and material circumstances. Language choice and possession are less an unproblematic voice of a people, a marker of tribalized identity, a mythologized origin, an idealized notion of racial purity and authenticity, reified in time, changeless, than problematized products of economic forces that include the movements of peoples globally in response to capitalist labor demands, the resistance of indigenous ideologies forming around similar notions of unalienated labor and capital supply, and so forth.

The Little Tree Controversy

Let us return to the expectation that a scholar of Asian American literature should possess one major Asian language. This Asian language requirement is provocative for more reasons than those of disagreements concerning professional certification. At the heart of the provocation is the unspoken issue, who speaks for whom? And behind that the more problematic question, what qualifies the speaker? There may be little disagreement when one operates in the clearly defined areas of political representation. An elected spokesperson is validated by the votes of the majority to speak for his/her electorate. But in the issue of minority or ethnic literary production, complicated issues are raised as to who is qualified to write, for example, of the Native American experience.

The question of author's identity is no easy matter of essentialist false-reasoning or red-herring "authenticity" debates in the example of *The Education of Little Tree,* an uplifting, politically correct tale narrating the experiences of a young Native American, which sold as a best-seller until it was discovered that the author was in fact a white American racist who had written speeches for the Ku Klux Klan.[1] This "discovery" of white racism in the author who wrote *The Education of Little Tree* immediately casts doubt on the "sincerity" if not authenticity of the text, reminding us that literary texts as social productions are therefore open to such social questions as sincerity and authenticity. Literature can no longer be hidden behind, protected by an argument of its sacral textuality: it is exposed as vulnerable, as we human cultural producers and reproducers are, to social, political, and economic contingencies and critiques.

Does the author's racism change the nature of the text of *The Education of Little Tree?* This question cannot be put aside easily. The signature (source of authority) must necessarily taint the text, for a white racist, one may reasonably suspect, may not fully believe in what the text purports to demonstrate. The relation between a fiction and the imagination that produces it is not unsubstantial. A reader forearmed with the knowledge of Little Tree's non-Native American white supremacist past, begins to read the text in a different context, one of hidden racist or racialist signs, of duplicity, manipulativeness, and artifice, significantly, politically removed from the artifice of fiction. Who is doing the speaking is as significant in affecting the ways we decode that language as what language he chooses to speak in.

Feminist Criticism: The Signature of the Woman

In such an ethnic-marked situation, racial identity is a factor in influencing and guiding interpretation. The emphasis on identity is also marked in much of US feminist criticism. In an odd conjunction of theoretical concerns, the most positivist and materialist of feminists critics in the US, women usually concerned with political and economic analysis for specific corrective social agendas, agree with a number of French feminist theoreticians that the identity of the speaker is crucially related to the nature of the language deployed. Nancy Miller, a US-based French literature critic, argues that authorship is a complex "contextual activity" that involves agency and shows the "marks of a producing Subject" (16). It is important that we maintain the signature of the woman writer for political reasons, as this woman's signature leads to "resistance to dominant ideologies [and] is the site of a possible political disruption" (17).[2] In looking at language, we must continue to emphasize the gender identity of the producer, the "feminine" tradition that the text contributes to and that forms the context by which the text is to be politically understood. For Miller, in reading a woman's text, we undertake "a double (intertextual) reading — of the auto-biography with the fiction" as a way of "deciphering a female self" (108).

Many French feminists work against the usual critique of language as a phallocentric — because logocentric — institution: Hélène Cixous and Luce Irigaray argue that this phallocentricity can be transformed by woman's language: "Because the economy of [woman's] drives is prodigious, she cannot fail, in seizing the occasion to speak, to transform directly and indirectly *all* systems of exchange based on masculine thrift. Her libido will produce far more radical effects of political and social change than one might like to think" (Cixous 252).

Marguerite Duras argues that men and women live in different linguistic territories and write from radically different perspectives. Women must resist plagiarism of the masculine tradition, must resist taking off from a theoretical platform already in place, but must instead be translated from the unknown (Duras, quoted in Yeager 955).

US critics, more grounded in praxis, argue for a modification of this radical otherness of woman's language: Showalter, for example, calls for "a feminist criticism that is genuinely women-centered, independent, and intellectually coherent," but concludes that "women writing are not, then, *inside* and *outside* of the male tradition; they are inside two traditions simultaneously" (247, 264). From such a pragmatic position, one can argue that the novel, the form that most offers possibilities for the multivocal, the polyphonic, the dialogical, the non-unitary and heteroglossic operations of language (Bakhtin 1981), would appear to be a woman's form that subverts the monological, logocentric language of the male tradition.

Many feminists have appropriated the theme of difference, once used to oppress and subordinate women, and re-deployed it to serve feminist purposes. There is something deeply seductive about a theory of language that dichotomizes its properties through means of gender identification, and reverses the usual patriarchal social constructions that place male as superior and female as inferior. Woman's language, to follow through with this line of argument, is in its form closer to woman's lived experience, at the center of which is the body. Ideas of otherness and the body are linked because the only visible differences between men and women is that of the body. This emphasis, however, may be dangerously essentialist, for "In today's context, with oppression not having ceased, to insist on Difference (without analyzing its social character) is to give back to the enemy a proven weapon" ("Variations on some common themes" 10). The illusory claim to woman's language, the counter-theoreticians argue, is based on a current literary style that is just as academic and therefore as masculine as other literary languages. To claim that this language is closer to the body also implies an expression of the body that is not mediated by the social structure, thus denying the power of social mediations which give to feminist criticism its political edge. Radical feminists see it as their mission to attack the social roots of difference, including *écriture féminine,* and define women as a class, sociologically defined in (from, within, by) a material and historical relation of oppression, but whose oppression is itself ideologically related by the dominant group to a so-called biological determination of the oppressed class ("Variations on some common themes" 17).

Intersections

This radical definition of woman, resisting old or new mythologies of difference and insisting on a material analysis, is just as valid if we replace gender with race, specifically those people of color who are minorities in white majority societies, as African Americans in the US; or who are ethnic minorities in majority rule by other people of color, as in Malaysia; or even a majority colonized by a minority group, as in South Africa. Minority or colonized race is a class, sociologically defined in a material and historical relation of oppression, whose oppression is itself ideologically related by a dominant group to a so-called biological determination of the oppressed class, and of that class alone.

As a Chinese Malaysian ethnic minority woman now resident in the United States, I cannot theorize the relation of language to gender without simultaneously incorporating the categories of class, race, and nation. Reading Cixous, Irigaray, Showalter, Judith Newton, and, yes, even Alice Walker, bell hooks, and Barbara Smith, any number of European and American feminists writers on gender and language, I note how post-colonial, exilic, and Third-World women of color and their specific positions are continuously omitted.[3] Despite their theoretical interests in rethinking the category of woman outside the institutions of patriarchy, many feminist critics operate within these patriarchal structures without interrogation and with ease and privilege. National identities and borders, formed by a history of male wars, agents, and interests, confer on these women safe within their borders securities, powers, and material advantages seldom disavowed.

Similarly, in their focus on language as the field of the female subject and as directly related to the speaking body of the woman, continental feminists frequently forget that the female body in other places is still the possession of patriarchal economic powers, is still a slave without voice and without subject identity. Rather than a site of pleasure, of autonomous defiance and disruption of patriarchal institutions, the female body in most societies is still the locus of alienation, of male rape and pleasure and female pain, disease, and unwanted child-bearing. Many European and American feminists do not ask how the pleasures of their language, their utopian feminist projects, are perhaps related to the material dystopias, the awful and increasing silence from the majority of women, but chiefly women of color, in the world.

While it is important to ask whose language is it that is associated with colonial depredation or neo-colonial rapacity, while it is also important to ask who is doing the speaking, I believe we should also ask what is being said. If "patriarchal power rests on the social meanings given to biological sexual difference" (Weedon 2), then does Western feminist power rests on the social meanings given to racial, national, and class difference? Feminist theory seeks to explain how and why people oppress each other; it is "a theory of subjectivity, of conscious and unconscious thoughts and emotions, which can account for the relation between the individual and the social" (Weedon 3). Feminist theory, therefore, must enlarge to include categories of race, nation, and class, to account for the construction or destruction of subjectivity. If this "burden of women's content" merely replicates the pleasures of Western bourgeois literature, without expanding and breaking down those global boundaries that keep poor, disaffiliated, women of color in disintegrating national economies in their places, then this women's language is both complicit with and corrupted by those very patriarchal institutions from which it seeks to separate itself.

To return to the beginning of the meditation, the position of the exilic woman of color attempting to maintain her grip on the circulation of knowledge that girds any strategy of power in the academy today while defending the language choice by which she has made her entry into this academy and while skeptical of the relation between her gender and that language as theorized by some of the major producers of that knowledge that she is consuming — that position demonstrating such a narrow specificity as to raise intrusive issues of representation — who is speaking, what language is she speaking in, what is she speaking of — that is a position that may be taken to deconstruct or reconstruct other women's positions. If we believe that such a position would be more representative were it located in a native and national discourse, then we must acknowledge our privileging of political and patriarchal systems of nationalism and mythologizing of essentialist origins. If we hold that the subject position would have more force of representation were it situated in a class node, for example, a Third-World service or working class, then we acknowledge that class supersedes, indeed forms the material base for subjectivity, and the gendered position is disqualified. Speaking as a woman in an interstice of class (in but not of an academic elite), race (a minority in a majority culture), and nation (of Chinese ancestry in a Malay dominant nation-state; and an exile-immigrant in a dominant native-born Caucasian society), I note that certain versions of the native and of the relations between language, the native, and woman, hold more social and institutional sway than others. If I am painfully a ware of the non-representational conclusion to be drawn from the specificity of my location, this awareness is also an articulate consciousness of how specificity resists the pressure of institutional explanations, and so resists the replacement of the individual woman with her universalized and canonized figure as Third-World victim, which is the way that the woman of color is usually put into Western discourse. Speaking as I do from the precarious position of discourse contradictions and resistances, I am subordinate both within and outside dominant cultures and ideologies. My position as exilic/immigrant Third World woman is inherently marginal, marginalized ironically by my use of an international language, and marginalized in the discourse of feminism in the United States, where I make my second home, by my other identities in the categories of race, class, and nation.

1992

Notes

1. Henry Louise Gates. Jr. sees the *Little Tree* hoax as a crucial instance to analyse how "race" gets constructed socially in the US. Susan Hegeman notes that "the study of these traditional native American materials is thus poised not only between two disciplines [literary and ethnographic], but between two different conceptions of the object of study, and two different systems of evaluation of their objects" (266).
2. See Frances L. Restuccia, "Of Ungrammaticality," for a reading of Miller's position.
3. Gayatri Chakravorty Spivak's two collections (1987, 1990) and *Third World Women and the Politics of Feminism,* among more recent books, do address the position of the postcolonial, "Third-World" woman.

Works Cited

Bakhtin, M. M. *The Dialogic Imagination.* Trans. Caryl Emerson and Michael Holquist. Ed. Michael Holquist. Austin: University of Texas Press, 1981.

Carter, Forrest. *The Education of Little Tree.* Albuquerque: University of New Mexico Press, 1990.

Chinweizu, et al. *Decolonising the African Mind.* Lagos, Nigeria: Pero, London: Sundoor, 1987.

Cixous, Hélène. "The Laugh of the Medusa." Trans. Keith Cohen and Paula Cohen. *New French Feminisms.* Edited by Elaine Marks and Isabellede Courtivron. New York: Schocken Books, 1981. 245-267.

Duras, Marguerite. "An Interview with Marguerite Duras." By Susan Husserl-Kapit. *Signs* 1(1975): 423-34.

Fanon, Franz. *Black Skins, White Masks.* Trans. Charles Lam Markmann. New York: Grove, 1967.

Gates. Jr., Henry Louis Gates. "'Authenticity,' or the Lesson of Little Tree." *New York Times Book Review* (Sun, Nov 24, 1991): 1+.

Hegeman, Susan. "Native American 'Texts' and the Problem of Authenticity." *American Quarterly* 4: 2 (June, 1989): 265-283.

Memmi, Albert. *The Colonizer and the Colonized.* Trans. Howard Greenfeld. New York: Orion, 1965.

Miller, Nancy K. *Subject to Change: Reading Feminist Writing.* New York: Columbia University Press, 1988.

Mohanty, Chandra Talpade, et al., eds. *Third World Women and the Politics of Feminism.* Bloomington: Indiana University Press, 1991.

Restuccia, Frances L. "Of Ungrammaticality," *Novel* 24:1 (Fall 1990): 108-110.

Showalter, Elaine. "Feminist Criticism in the Wilderness." *The New Feminist Criticism.* Edited by Elaine Showalter. New York: Pantheon, 1985.

Sollors, Werner. *Beyond Ethnicity: Consent and Descent in American Culture.* New York: Oxford University Press, 1986.

Spivak, Gayatri Chakravorty. *In Other Worlds: Essays in Cultural Politics.* London and New York: Methuen, 1987.

—————. *The Post-Colonial Critic.* Edited by Sarah Harasym. New York: Routledge, 1990.

"Variations on some common themes." Editors of *Questions Feministes. Feminist Issues,* Summer 1980.

Weedon, Chris. *Feminist Practice and Poststructuralist Theory.* Oxford, U.K.: Basil Blackwell, 1987.

Yaeger, Patricia S. "'Because a Fire Was in My head': Eudora Welty and the Dialogic Imagination." *PMLA* 99:5 (Oct 1984): 955-73.

PART TWO

SOUTH EAST / ASIAN POSTCOLONIAL LITERATURE

A Poetics of Location: Reading Zulfikar Ghose

Any attempt to read Zulfikar Ghose as a serious poet is beset by problems. These difficulties are caused not by the poetry, which is sensitive, substantially wrought and worthy of critical attention, but by the larger issues attending the act of reading itself. In interpreting and evaluating a body of poems, certain issues can and do take precedence over those posed by the language of poetry. For one, there is the problem of context. A poet's use of language and poetic forms can only be fully understood in the context of the local history in which it is embedded, to which it appeals. Reed Way Dasenbrock defines this "contextualist" or "localist" position in his interesting paper on "Intelligibility and Meaningfulness in Multicultural Literature" as an "explanatory kind, filling in gaps between the author and the reader and offering information that makes the text intelligible" (12).[1] That is, before one can "read" Ghose's poems intelligibly, many gaps have to be filled in first, and certain kinds of "local" information, specific to Ghose's set of nationalistic and historic circumstances, elucidated.

One of the major tasks of critical reading is an evaluation of a poet's accomplishment arrived at only by reading him within a larger context and history of other poets' works. Together with the local information that allows the reader to make sense of a text is the larger literary tradition to which the critic refers in order to evaluate the text's significance. Sense or intelligibility, as Dasenbrock pointed out, is not synonymous with significance (12), although the latter can hardly be arrived at without an attempt at the former. What critics are getting at in their corporate endeavors in maintaining or revising the canon is significance rather than sense; that is, the value of the poems' meaning and the meaning of the poems' value rather than the poems' meaning itself.

Eliot said all that and more in his analysis of the relation between tradition and the individual talent.[2] Eliot, however, had a Western tradition in mind, a specifically Graeco-Roman-Christian tradition composed of poets such as Homer, Virgil, Dante, Shakespeare, and Milton. English poetry, for Eliot, was inseparable from the mainstream of Western literary tradition. Eliot wrote his famous essay in 1919, at least three decades before the British Empire broke up into numerous national autonomies, and at least a generation before it became clear that the English language would no longer be the sole possession of Western people.

Eliot's career represented an appropriation of Anglo-European traditions by a national group outside that history he valued (his "conversion" to monarchist Anglicanism made visible the convergence of American and British traditions). So a future generation of writers can be seen to further problematize the relation between their individual talents and English literary tradition. Ghose's talent, like the individual talents of V. S. Naipaul, Salman Rushdie, and Derek Walcott, calls into question the ways in which we read and evaluate literature written in English, indeed, perhaps the way in which we categorize literatures as products of a national history.

The major problem is of location. When we pick up a book of poems, our first assumption is that it can be placed somewhere. It is a book by a woman, or by a Nigerian, or by a confessional poet. That is, we locate the work in a number of ways, by gender, by sub-genre, and chiefly by nationality (sometimes offered as geographical and regional). The work's identity is generally conveniently located in the author's identity. This initial categorizing activity permits a crude location of the individual writer in a tradition. That a book of poems in English is written by a Nigerian tells the reader that his reading and evaluation should occur in the light of a Nigerian history of literary development, that the traditions appealed to may be non-Anglo and ethno-specific to Ibos, that the shifts in literary tradition that the work demands occur within a body of Nigerian poetry first before it can be read in that enormous and amorphous body of world literature written in English. This is how Achebe is read, as a Nigerian writer writing out of his tribal and national bailiwick, whose appeal lies in his African-ess, and whose talent in the English-language novel affords him an international audience.

But there are permutations and shadings to this basic nationalist/ethnographic frame. Derek Walcott, for example, while seen as a West Indian writer writing of St. Lucia, is also read as a poet whose enormous talent has not been restricted to a provincial stage; his wide-ranging geographical themes, institutional affiliation to Boston University, and travels have made him increasingly North American in appeal. As the writer aims at and is able to moult out of his national or provincial origin, he usually becomes identified with one metropolitan culture. Camus, an Algerian, became French; Claude MacKay, a West Indian, an American; Naipaul, as he limns it in *The Enigma of Arrival,* chose to become British. Thus, many writers, usually situated in conditions of exile, also display elements of choice in their careers.

Born in a place, seemingly a mere biographical item, the writer must do something about location in his work in order to affect the conditions under which he is to be received. Ghose's poetry suffers from these problems of reception, for, biographically, the problems of location are more extreme in his case. Born in Sialkot, then part of British India (and now part of Pakistan) in 1935, Ghose moved to Bombay at age nine, then to England at seventeen, and finally to the United States at thirty-five. His life forms a series of nationalities, and his poetry reflects and expresses these hyphenated and multiple states. However, because critical reception is ruled by assumptions of location, critical attention has not kept pace with his work.

A cursory examination of the ordinary tools of bibliographical reference will demonstrate that the critical/academic complex has not yet arrived at a conceptualization and formulation of the problems of location that Ghose's body of writing poses in an exemplary manner. *The Modern Language Association International Bibliography,* for example, categorizes all items by national literatures. The principle of arrangement, the explanation goes, "is based on the concept of national literatures, using the combined considerations of geography and language. The macro arrangement is by geographical region, with individual literatures within those regions arranged alphabetically. When the national designation and the language of the literature are not logically linked or when there are two or more languages prominently used within a given country, access to the language is given in the index" (1983 vols. 1 7 ll v). This principle of arrangement, as the qualifier indicates, raises perhaps more exceptions than rules. Geography and language frequently do not give rise to permanent, clearly demarcated, national boundaries. In the Philippines, for example, writers writing in English will slip in and out of Tagalog or Pilipino, the national language, in the same text. A writer will write in both English, the dominant language of international trade, and in her provincial language of origin, like Visayan or any of the other 76 languages of the Philippine islands. In Sarawak, a native-born writer may write in Mandarin, a language considered not participating in a national literature by state agencies in Malaysia.

Aside from the kinds of language controversies that haunt definitions of national literatures, there is the other major feature of the individual writer's shifting nationality. Take, for example, Michael Ondaatje or Timothy Mo or Yasmine Gooneratne who have relocated geographically, often following the trajectories of powers of access in their language of choice.[3] *The MLA International Bibliography* tells us, "In general, subject authors have been placed within the national literatures in which they are most closely associated. If a user is unable to locate a particular author, the subject index should be consulted, because it includes every author listed in the classified sequence" (v). Where national boundaries or language possession cannot identify the author, the author should be traced as "subject": a sovereign individual. This "other" category, a "subject" index supplementing the "national" category, however, does not work as a full supplement, because it will only list authors already listed in the classified sequence. In short, in order to appear as a "subject" you must already have a "national" affiliation.

Taking Ghose as the exemplar of an author who has not been placed nationally (the question why can only be answered by a sociopolitical sophistication concerning the murderous Indo-Pakistan history and by psycho-social speculations concerning the author's attitudes toward self and being-in-the-world), it becomes clear that Ghose's achievements as a writer in English cannot be recorded in an instrument such as the *International Bibliography.* (When he is listed, he appears as an Indian writer.) He is never listed as Pakistani; this despite the "accident" of birth in Sialkot, an event and location radiant with meaning for the younger poet. Pakistan appears as a mirage of political construction on his consciousness in his autobiographical pieces.[4] But Ghose has explicitly constructed his identity as Indian, albeit a Mosle Indian. The India of sensations, an India of unity of family prior to the Separation, forms the bedrock of his early poems, and persists in rising like igneous heights in his later work. Then, for seventeen years, he was an alien Englishman, like Naipaul, approaching the mystery of English landscape, the substantiality of English history, with a melancholic reverence reserved perhaps only for those who can never be admitted into them. In that period, Ghose appeared in print with heavyweight English poets such as Gavin Ewart.[5] Had Ghose remained in England he may have been admitted, like Naipaul, into the *International Bibliography* with British Authors, if not into British history.

But in mid-life, at thirty-four, Ghose crossed over the Atlantic and began teaching at the University of Texas in Austin. His later poems as selected in his collection of poems, *A Memory of Asia,* have the breadth, grit, and feel of this latest adopted homeland. They are American poems, in so much as America is also an immigrant's vision of America. But they are not American enough to admit Ghose into the *International Bibliography* with American authors. There, bibliographical information on Isaac Singer takes up almost a full page, although Singer's fiction is often written not in English but in Yiddish and although the world his fiction portrays is often non-American, perhaps eve non-European.

What made Singer an American writer and Ghose not yet American? The question is useful in examining aspects of reception. Although Singer has lived in the United States longer than Ghose, the crucial point is not length of tenure. The central issue, it seems to me, is that Singer has a defined, loyal audience in the United States, an audience first of relocated Eastern European Jews like himself, who share a minority language and culture. Despite its small size, this audience is a growing influential group in the United States. Once Singer was "taken up" as an American Jewish writer, he was assured of a prominent place in American literature: he could be both himself, a minority writer, and American, a mainstream author.

Ghose has no such loyal minority audience. Coming from the Indo-Pakistani sub-continent, the politics of Separation have made him unacceptable to both Pakistanis (Ghose is a secular Moslem who had claimed himself to be an Indian) and Indians (Ghose is a Moslem who has renounced his Indian nationality). He was perhaps most clearly defined as an orphan of the British Commonwealth, formed by an imperial world culture, and by the disintegrative violence that broke the empire into numerous unstable nation states. His seventeen years in Britain were years of orphanage, and his poems of that period have that poignancy of the outsider adrift between worlds, disowning and ownerless. It is in this period that he approaches closest to Naipaul's biting perspective on postnationalist societies: an "objectivity" arrived at after great disillusionment; an intellectual stance constructed on derision of subjective states of mind and subject nations; a mind that questions romantic gestures and colors.

But unlike Naipaul and Conrad, their equal forebear, Ghose chose yet another society, the United States. His faithfulness to story-telling, an art Naipaul rejects in his turn to the reportorial and inquisitional, is seen in his continued fictions of the marvellous, the mysterious, and the romantic. Also, unlike Naipaul and Conrad, Ghose has continued to write poetry. The history of his poetry (evolution is perhaps too legalistic a word for poetry which slips past national boundaries and developments like an illegal immigrant across cultures) most economically tells the range of his split complexities.

Critical response to Ghose's poetry has been extremely narrow. Reviewers and critics repeat what they find to be his major themes: alienation, rootlessness, disorder, deracination, fading in his later poems to nostalgia. In 1964, Furbank finds the poet of *The Loss of India* "float(ing) comfortably in a permanent state of mild displacement" (949). In 1972, the reviewer in the *Times Literary Supplement* remarks on "the solemn sense of deracination" in Ghose's third book of poems, *The Violent West.* Reviewing the recent collection of poems, *A Memory of Asia,* K. S. N. Rao again discusses "the theme of the alien" in Ghose's work (317). Of course, these materials are present to be pressed into the services of a generation of theme-hunters. Critics have had much to say about Ghose's themes of the wanderer, the exile, and the displaced person.[6]

But as universal as they are in their application, these themes do not explain Ghose's poetry. Ghose writes not so much of homelessness as of different homes: the Pakistani home of origin, the Indian home of childhood and of political awakening, the deluded English literary home of empire, the Texan home of real-estate value. These biographical homes are always grounded in the recognized larger ironies of the myths of home: Ulysses sailing for Ithaca, the personal mythopoetics of memory, and Asia as figure of home for the Asian immigrant.

Moreover, grounded even more deeply and resonant with unrecognized ironies is the poet's unshaken claim to a home in the English tradition. Some of Ghose's critics begin with the legitimacy or illegitimacy of his claim to an English literary homeland, together with the likes of Shakespeare, Auden, Beckett, Larkin and Gavin Ewart. Indeed, Goldberg's light dismissal of Ghose as "an adaptable tumbleweed" which can "thrive anywhere" (214), a response to his Brazilian fiction, misses the point. As a writer, Ghose could not thrive in Pakistan, the home of origin, or in India, the home of political awakening. He took root as a writer on English soil, and in the case of his poetry, he carries like Aenias rather than Ulysses the penates of his ancestors, English writers such as Shakespeare and Beckett, on his back.

Poetry, unlike fiction, cannot mimic other men without losing its voice. Ghose, for all the various ventriloquisms he pulls off in his prose narratives, possesses a core poetic identity that forms a major motif in the collection, *A Memory of Asia*. Here, the poems operate like the layers of an archaeological dig. The poet's various "homes"— countries and nationalisms — are present in the poems' subjects and themes, not as a comfortable cosmopolitanism but as sharply experienced localities in the moment of their biographical realities. An early poem such as "Across India: Feb. 1952," written in his early twenties, vividly narrates a motor journey the seventeen-year-old Ghose undertook from Bombay to Delhi with his father just before the family emigrated to England. The poem is specifically "Indian"; its meaning can only be approached through the nationalistic context of post-Independence India. In contrast, "Mutability," set in London, has the nervous rhythms of metropolitan movements of an English poem. "A Private Lot," however, speaks out of a Texan context. All three poems, read together, suggest the migrant's shift across borders and cultures. Together they form a panorama of incipient multinationalism and multicultures, although thematically sounding certain plangent notes easily categorized as alienation, deracination, and exile.

The central theme of the collection is not exilic loss, although that too is sounded, for example, in the poems "The Attack on Sialkot" (52-53) and "The Lost Culture" (55-56). The newer poems pick up Ghose's career narrative, his personal myth. Set against the more easily discerned because familiar story of the wanderer, the Odysseus figure, arguing against "an ancient fraud" of home (in "The Pursuit of Frost" 68-79), also enacts the modern story of the writer who is staging the drama of his personal myth. In the title poem, "A Memory of Asia," two vivid localities are recalled: the

Asia of Hindu temples, still gaudy, forms one layer of the archaeology. Then there is the immigrant's vision, composed of "white P & O ships sailing away to England" (3). But both stages are subsumed under the central scene of the writer in the act of writing:

> But this is a version: I've put some
> of these phrases together before. (3)

The superstructure, the self-conscious act of writing, rises above the local gaudy concretions of nationalities:

> I keep altering an image, it's like waxing
> an old car until I begin to believe
> I see the original polished surface. (3)

"The original polished surface," the "reality" of local experience, may be recuperable upon "waxing" the old car, a figure suggesting the body of the poet's writing. But the old car, the vehicle, also suggests the body of all literature on which images are reflected, suggesting that Ghose is working also on the body of the English language with all its manifold traditions and artifacts. The significance of his poems lies in their place in the story of language itself, in the tradition of writing, which must be seen today in a multinational, cross-cultural context.

Ghose consciously intersects his personal story with the story of language, presenting this thought as a "complication":

> There's this other complication, when what's
> remembered occurs to the mind as a line from
> someone's poem or a phrase from a fiction
> (and that very language of remembering is someone else's
> style which one's own voice is convinced is its own (5)

The passage reiterates Ghose's original position, that the signifying event is the writing act. It alone participates directly, without boundaries, in the universe of literary and language creation. The "fact" that memory refers to is therefore actually a phenomenology of experience that demands a critical poetics:

> the recognition of the individual, compelling one
> to reject the notion of an abstract form in
> a more comprehensive observation of details (11)

The subject of the memory is insignificant (although it may be necessary to make it intelligible in order for the poem to be "understood"). The irrelevance of "local" history (memory's accuracy) or "fact" leads to the recognition of a more compelling form of individual truth, in the confluence of "comprehensive observation of detail" (a phenomenological sensitivity) and "grammar."[7]

Pushed to another conclusion, if poetry as image is not related to "truth," then a poetry that denies any absolute claim to truth is the only significant kind possible. Here Ghose comes close in spirit to the Absurd writers (in his critical essays, he claims Beckett as his model).[8] The mockingbird is Ghose's symbol for the art of poetry, a language that mocks the pretensions of local and universal images to serve as conveyers of truth, and that is meaningful for its own sake. In "The Mockingbird," the bird is also the figure of the poet whose language mocks because it imitates, and so calls to question "the pretension of / a supposedly true language" (16). Ghose celebrates the ultimate freedom of the poet without national boundaries, who can sing "with no insistence on meaning: his is / a beautifully arrogant irresponsibility" (16).

The image of the meaning-denying bird to celebrate poetry's unboundedness is deeply contradictory. Overleaping the significations that boundaries and nationalities can and do confer on an individual talent, Ghose insists on the status of poetry whose meaning derives from its participation in the broadest universal, language. His career therefore challenges the institutional ways in which readers locate writers. Situated in national interstices, he could possibly have been multiply read: Indian/Pakistani/British/American poet/critic/novelist/scholar. But the reception has not been optimistic. Ignored by the various centers, he has centered his poetry directly in the tradition of the language. Only a more mature institution of criticism that can read literature in the context of multiple nationalities, cultures and world languages will find a place for poets such as Ghose.

1987

Notes

1. Much of my thinking in this chapter was influenced by Dasenbrock's essays, "Multicultural Literature in English" and "English Department Geography." Dasenbrock argues for a radical comparative literature approach to arrive at the significance of works in English outside the traditional canons of British and American Literatures: "Literature in English can no longer be represented as a sum of national literatures. . . . [There] would be genuinely comparative distinctions, and it is towards a comparative literature in English that I would have our discipline move, recognizing national differences where appropriate

but also seeing common elements beyond and above national differences. English then would denote the language alone and not the country, and we would see a concern with that language as the abiding focus and continuous thread of all the various discourses that constitute our field today" ("English Department Geography" 22-23). My chapter suggests that although Ghose does not belong to any one single national literature, he would benefit from such a comparative approach because his work contains the range for a comparative literature approach within its own multinational integrity.

2. To Eliot, writing at about the time of Nazi propaganda and in response to similar reifying forces of nationalist sentiment, "tradition involves all those habitual actions, habits, and customs, from the most significant religious rite to our conventional way of greeting a stranger, which represent the blood kinship of 'the same people living in the same place'" (20). His privileging of "blood kinship" explains his critical stance that "not only the best, but the most individual parts of (a poet's) work may be those in which the dead poets, his ancestors, assert their immortality most vigorously" (22). Literary tradition involves "the historical sense," and to Eliot, a Western man, it specifically signifies writing "not merely with his own generation in his bones, but with a feeling that the whole of the literature of Europe from Homer and within it the whole of the literature of his own country has a simultaneous existence and composes a simultaneous order" (23). Ironically, Eliot was himself an immigrant attempting to write with the whole of his *adopted country* as his tradition. When Eliot moved from location politics to observations of his own creative process, his ideas on the individual talent, written fifteen years before his notion of tradition overlapped with the definition of "blood kinship," parallel closely Ghose's theory and practice of poetry. Ghose's ideas expressed in "A Memory of Asia" coincide with Eliot's notions that "the poet has, not a 'personality' to express, but a particular medium;" that "[t]he business of the poet is not to find new emotions, but to use the ordinary ones and, in working them up into poetry, to express feelings which are not in actual emotions at all. And emotions which he has never experienced will serve his turn as well as those familiar to him" (28-29).

3. Ondaatje was born in Sri Lanka when it was known as Ceylon, and was educated in England and Canada. He is now a Canadian citizen and writer. Timothy Mo considers himself a British citizen and writer, but he writes of Chinese immigrant experiences and has based much of his fiction in Hong Kong, his family's place of origin. Yasmine Gooneratne, from a prestigious Sri Lankan family, was educated partly in Britain, but is now considered an Australian writer.

4. The opening chapter on Sialkot, in *Confessions of a Native-Alien,* describes Ghose's memories of a birthplace: "some images of that time persist as obsessions" (1). Ghose sums up poignantly his enigma of departures in this opening chapter: "The British were ruling over their sunny Empire then and Sialkot was my India. It was the India of the future Pakistanis. When we left Sialkot in 1942 for Bombay, the latter was the India of the future free Indians. When we left Bombay in 1952 for England, we were leaving two countries, for in some way we were alien to both and our emigration to a country to which we were not native only emphasized our alienation from the country in which we had been born. This distinction between the two countries of my early life has

been the schizophrenic theme of much of my thinking: it created a psychological conflict and a pressing need to know that I do belong somewhere" (1-2).

5. In the Penguin collection, Ghose appears with Gavin Ewart, who was a candidate for the Poet Laureateship of Britain, and B. S. Johnson. The collection appeared in 1975, only four years after Ghose's poetry was included in an Oxford University Press collection of eight Pakistani poets, *Pieces of Eight*. The flexibility of boundaries that permitted his work to be read then as Pakistani and as British no longer applies now. Ghose is categorized as a Pakistani writer in a few major bibliographies; more frequently the difficulty in locating his national category has resulted in an absence of bibliographical information.

6. These themes, revolving around words from geography and travel, are, as Joseph Warren Beach pointed out, popular with many writers from the 1930's and 1940's. As political and economic instability continues to produce refugees, and as writers leave the provinces for the metropolitan cultures, they have persisted as the obsessive themes of the modern age.

7. The notion of art making the transitory moment of delight permanent has parallels with the Romantic privileging of poetry and the Imagination. Ghose's symbol of the hummingbird's flight captured in words echoes the Keatsian image of the Grecian Urn. The evolution of the hummingbird-turned-into-words image into the image of the mockingbird as a figure for poetry points to Ghose's re-cycling of the Keatsian nightingale figure. But where Keats insisted on the equation of Beauty (or art) with Truth, Ghose ironically equates poetry with non-truth. Poetry does not reflect the world in a truthful manner: its truth resides not in the matter of the art but rather in the art of the matter. Or, as he explained it elsewhere, "Truth is to be perceived not by looking at the world but by looking at the way in which images have been structured to complete the internal, imaginative order of the work" *(The Fiction of Reality 10)*.

8. See, for example, his critical essays in *The Fiction of Reality* where he is concerned, not with fiction as representation of the world, i.e. as mimesis, but with its ontological nature: "Of the many uses of words the most obsessive one concerns the invention of reality which must daily be shaped somehow not only in our normal dealings with our families and colleagues at work to whom we must make the effort not to appear to be lunatics but also in the abstract world of our own inner silence which has to be filled with those words which soothe, clarify, bring meaning. But we've been made fools by the language we've invented by imposing upon it the burden of meaning and by charging that it contain a capacity for truth" (4).

Works Cited

Anonymous. "Bedtime Initiations." *Times Literary Supplement* (1972): 873.

Beach, Joseph Warren. *Obsessive Images: Symbolism in Poetry of the 1930's and 1940's*. Minneapolis: University of Minnesota Press, 1960.

Dasenbrock, Reed Way. "Multicultural Literature in English." *PMLA* 10:1 (1987): 10-19.

————. "English Department Geography." *ADE Bulletin* 86 (1987): 18-23.

Eliot, T. S. *Selected Prose.* Hammondsworth, England: Penguin, 1953, rep. 1955.

Ewart, Gavin; Ghose, Zulfikar; Johnson, B. S. *Gavin Ewart, Zulfikar Ghose, B. S. Johnson Penguin Modern Poets 25.* Hammondsworth, England, 1975.

Furbank, P. N. Review of "The Loss of India." *The Listener* LXll:1863 (1974): 949.

Ghose, Zulfikar. *The Loss of India.* London: Routledge and Kegan Paul, 1964.

————. *Confessions of a Native-Alien.* London: Routledge and Kegan Paul, 1965.

————. *Jets From Orange.* London: Macmillan, 1967.

————. *Pieces of Eight Eight Poets from Pakistan.* Karachi: Oxford University Press, 1971.

————. *The Violent West.* London: Macmillan, 1972.

————. *Hamlet, Prufrock and Language.* New York: St. Martin's Press, 1987.

————. *The Fiction of Reality.* London: Macmillan Press, 1983.

————. *A Memory of Asia.* Austin, Texas: Curbstone Publishing Co., 1984.

Goldberg, Gerald Jay. "Tumbleweed Fiction." *The Nation* 236:7 (1983): 214 215.

Rao, Narayana K. S. Review of "A Memory of Asia." *World Literature Today* 59:2 (1985): 317.

The Modern Language Association International Bibliography. 1 & 2 New York: MLA Press, 1983.

Terms of Empowerment
in Kamala Das's *My Story*

A popular approach to Western women's writings is to categorize the best of them as the achievements of exceptional women, women who were able to move beyond the socio-cultural confines which kept other women "domesticated" and invisible. Such exceptional women forced a re-ordering and re-visioning of seemingly stable social relations and roles for women; their works, therefore, have been privileged in the canon of Euro-American women's literature.[1] In Sappho, Aphra Behn, Jane Austen, the Bronte sisters, Emily Dickinson, and Sylvia Plath Western women persistently find models of exceptional women to study and emulate.

Recently, the privileging of exceptional Anglo-American women has become open to interrogation in critical exchanges about the intersections of race, class, and gender and the sociopolitical implications of "sisterhood." Bonnie Thornton Dill, succinctly outlining the racist and classist biases that have historically accompanied white American middle-class women's liberation movements, tells us that "contemporary scholarship on women of color suggests that the barriers to an all-inclusive sisterhood are deeply rooted in the histories of oppression and exploitation that Blacks and other groups encountered upon incorporation into the American political economy"(131-50). Dill calls, therefore, "for the abandonment of the concept of sisterhood as a global construct based on unexamined assumptions about our similarities" and urges us to "substitute a more pluralistic approach that recognizes and accepts the objective differences between women" (146).

American readers, however, are generally ignorant of non-Western women writers whose literary production has set them apart in their traditional societies. In the Asian world, the works of such women writers as Ding Ling and Kamala Das possess a power to enable their readers to re-read social relations and to participate in a revolution of consciousness.[3] Such a revolution, Julia Kristeva rightly insists in *Revolution in Poetic Language,* must precede changes in the materialist/political horizon (17). The transforming power in Ding Ling's and Das's work and its impact upon readers precede and/or parallel the effects of works by Anglo-American and ethnic women writers and critics such as Adrienne Rich, Alice Walker and Barbara Smith. Ding Ling's and Das's writings contain the themes of women's revolt and the interrogations of the processes of women's subjectivity as it is situated in frankly portrayed male/female power relations that many Western readers associate chiefly with Anglo-American feminist literature.

Kamala Das is a prolific bilingual Indian woman poet, fiction writer, and essayist. She is the author of numerous novels in Malayalam, collections of English-language fiction and poetry, and an autobiography, *My Story,* published in 1976.[4] She is not entirely unknown to American readers; Sandra Gilbert and Susan Gubar have included her as the only representative from Asia in their *Norton Anthology of Literature By Women.*[5] As none of her Malayalam novels has been translated into English, I will address only her English-language writing.

For the purposes of this essay, I am interested in Das's autobiography as a document expressing the writer's own ambiguity — what Bakhtin characterized as "the internal dialogism of double-voiced prose" — as a woman asserting subjective power in a traditional patriarchal society.[6] Her materialist critiques propose precisely those themes that give her writing its vividness and compelling power to arouse and disturb. Her female subjects destabilise our notions of what is female or feminine and dislocate given Indian cultural and social relations; in short, they give her writing a transformatory dimension that accounts for both the repulsion and the fascination it has provoked.[7]

Das's autobiography is a strongly public work, exhibiting a deliberate consciousness of audience. The audience is both the reader of the autobiography and the readers of her poetry prior to the writing of the autobiography; that is, the poet's audience appears in her life story as an active catalyst and agent. Before turning to the autobiography, however, I would like to summarize her critical reception to date, as that reception helps explain the "double-voicedness" of her narrative (Bakhtin 324).

Das has had two audiences. Her own native Indian audience is mostly English-educated and middle-class. Its class mobility and its choice of the English language for expression are generally associated with a modern, Westernized mentality (that is, with an unstable indigenous cultural identity related to an assimilation of socio-political values influenced by Anglo-American norms and cultures).[8] Her other, more vocal and welcoming, audience is an international group of readers, chiefly from Australia. These non-Indian critics are interested in non-Western writing in English. They represent the old Commonwealth Literature school of thought reincarnated as postcolonial, post-Orientalist sensitivities to new or national or world literatures in English.[9] While the emphases are different, both audiences share common assumptions and make similar conclusions in approaching Das's writing.

Das is acknowledged by both Indian and Anglo critics as working within a "strong tradition of female writing. . . with a venerable ancestry"(*KD* 2). The consensus from both interpretive communities is that her achievement is limited to themes of female sexual and physical experience. Hostile readers, both Indian and international, debunk her subjects, describing them variously as "a poetry of thighs and sighs," "salacious" fantasies, and "flamboyant," "weak," "selfindulgent" obsessiveness.[10] Friendly critics valorize her as "a poet of feminine longings"(Dwivedi 20). She is praised (chiefly by male critics) for that "feminine sensibility [that is] manifested in her attitude to love, in the ecstasy she experiences in receiving love and the agony she feels when jilted in it"(Rahmin 7). According to her most fervent defenders, both Indian and Western, her feminine sensibility is expressed in her total involvement with the sexual male Other.

The publication of a selected collection of her work by the Centre for Regional and National Literatures in English in Adelaide, Australia, accompanied by critical essays, all by white Australian critics, would seem to confirm a hardening of these interpretive lines.[11] Many of the essays in the volume argue that Das's heterosexuality has its highest apotheosis, its Indian rationale, in Das's identity as a devotee of Krishna. As Dorothy Jones informs us, Krishna, eighth avatar of Vishnu, is traditionally represented in Indian culture as "an important focus in Hinduism of Bhakti, the experience of intense religious adoration in which the soul [the female representation] abandons itself in ecstasy to the divine [the male representation]" (Jones 203). Jones is only repeating a paradigm, first articulated by Das herself, whereby the "vulgar" (and arguably Westernized "confessional") topos of brutal or illicit sexuality becomes transformed into the "high" topos of licit Brahman mysticism.

In approaching Das's evident concentration on sexual themes, however, the non-Indian reader would do well to keep in mind that erotic sexuality is strongly inscribed in Indian, specifically Hindu, culture. In using these materials, Das is able to appeal to both the Western tradition that emphasizes confessional writing and the Hindu tradition which places a high and visible valuation on male-female eroticism. By a shift in authorial (and critical) perception, the sensual complexities of a "sensational" — because exceptional — life are reduced to an abstract allegory of religious quest and devotion. (No American reader, however, would find Das's so-called confessions of extra-marital affairs memorable if set among the Hollywood memoirs appearing today!)

Many critics have participated in this sanitization of the female subject Das constitutes in her autobiography and her poetry, and have acquiesced, even contributed, to obfuscating the notable "revolt" against male-dominant terms of sexuality in her themes. They have interpreted the persona in her poems and autobiography to be a "smoothly" acceptable, because traditional, worshipper of that most adulterous, most privileged male Indian god, Krishna. Mohan Lal Sharma, for example, argues that Das's career exhibits a "pilgrim's progress" towards Krishna-worship; thus, he congratulates her for her faults in poetic style, since, for him, they demonstrate her religious achievement (97-111). "'He shining everything else shines' is the ultimate Upanishadic dictum" (100), Mr. Sharma advises us, unself-consciously reflecting his patriarchal reconstruction of Das's work in his choice of dictums. Sharma's male-centered critical orientation, moreover, is itself a reflection of the patriarchal structure of communities dominated by Krishna-worship. Adopting a similar critical approach, non-Indian critics such as Syd Harrex, Vincent O'Sullivan and Dorothy Jones similarly turn Das's very specifically located materialist critiques of class and gender into a phantasm of Krishna-worship.[12]

I argue that Das's writing and life display the anger, rage, and rebellion of a woman struggling in a society of male perogatives. Her best work cannot be read either as a celebration of love or as an allegorical abstraction of Radha, the Gopi cowmaid, worshipping Krishna in his many manifestations. I find that the informing energy in the autobiography springs, like the pulsating rhythm of a popular sixties rock 'n' roll song, from its central poetics, "I Can't Get No Satisfaction." Teresa De Lauretis, among other feminist commentators, has pointed out that "to feminism, the personal is epistemologically the political, and its epistemology is its politics" (235). "Satisfaction," therefore, while it encompasses the notion of sexual desire, emerges in the autobiography, as it does in Das's novel, *Alphabet for Lust,* as epistemologically the domain of female struggle in a patriarchal society.[13] The inequalities and social oppressions suffered by Indian women are many and profound. As Marilyn French reports for a 1985 United Nations-sponsored publication, "Most Indian women are married young by their families to men they have not met before . . . . They then move to their husbands' parents' home, where they are, essentially, servants" (174-201). French documents a series of social horrors: the dowry system, bride-burning, male abuse, the ban against divorce, women's isolation, job discrimination, female infanticide, poorly paid or unpaid female labor, high female illiteracy. Das's autobiography vivifies the connections between personal/sexual and social/political struggles for a female protagonist in this traditional male-dominated society.

In her preface, Das locates the origin of her autobiography in the confessional impulse attending the deathbed. She indicates that the autobiography was written during her "first serious bout with heart disease," and that she "wanted to empty myself of all the secrets so that I could depart when the time came with a scrubbed-out conscience" (Preface). This intention indicates a particular understanding of the autobiographical genre, one attuned to the confessional tradition of Christianity exemplified in Augustine's *Confessions*. The expressed wish for a "scrubbed-out conscience" itself prepares the reader for representations of "sinful" or immoral subjects, secrets which defile a conscience, and for some kind of remorse undertaken within a religious or spiritual frame of reference. Yet Das candidly reveals that she wrote her autobiography as a commercial publication, a series of articles for a popular magazine, because she needed money to pay off her medical bills (Preface). The spiritual impulse and the commercial intention are both evident in the dialogic, ambiguous, and contradictory features of the text.

The autobiography, republished in book form in 1976, possesses the characteristics that mark it as a book written hurriedly and structured to the formulaic requirements of serial publication. It has fifty chapters, each from two and a half to about four and a half pages in length. The organization of materials into so many short chapters is clearly governed by the necessity of chopping the life into as many marketable pieces as possible, thus revealing more about the magazine format and the attention span of its popular audience than the writer's craft. Moreover, the serial form dictates the anecdotal, essayistic structure, allowing little room for analysis of difficult issues or exploration of psychological experience.

The contradictions between the commercially dictated features of the text and the narrator's stated "spiritual" intention have led many critics to view the autobiographer as unreliable. "After reading such a confession," Vimla Rao says astringently, "it is difficult to determine where the poseur ends and the artist begins" (Rao 88). Dwevedi describes the work as "more baffling and dazing (sic) than her poetry" (42), and Jones admits that "it is hard to know how to respond to this book which, while adopting an openly confessional tone, conceals quite as much or more than it reveals" (192). Because they cannot read her autobiography as a faithful account of her life, critics have generally preferred to treat it as an appendix to her poetry. Sharma claims that Das's autobiography "is the single best 'Reader's Guide' to the design and meaning of her work" (108). Jones more cannily allows that "if considered as a literary rather than a factual recreation of the writer's life, it often serves as an illuminating comment on her poetry and fiction, exploring many of the same dilemmas and situations" (197).

In fact, the obvious unreliability of the author's intention foregrounds the postmodernist qualities of Das's "autobiography." Thus, instead of approaching it as a text containing an authentic account of a life unmediated by literary conventions, I argue that our understanding of the constituted "autobiographical" female subject should be negotiated through features of the text. These features include ones that conform to a mass market strategy (the simple anecdotal structure, unrelenting focus on sensational and popular themes, attention to domestic and marital relations as appealing to a women's readership), and ones that derive from the self-reflexive nature of the prose. In "deconstructing" Das's autobiography, then, I want to elaborate how it achieves its impact less from its separate parts than from their sum. While each chapter offers a distinct picture or theme, together the chapters resonate in their emphasis on the domestic details of food, familial relations, marriage, child-birth, sexual liaisons, and the internal and external struggles of one woman in a sociopolitically repressive world.

The opening chapters, for example, depict a colonized childhood, resonant with the later theme of oppressed womanhood. The father, a Rolls Royce and Bentley salesman, stood as a middleman between the British corporation and the Indian upper class. Das similarly showed the characteristic alienation of being suspended between indigenous and colonized cultures. Unhappy as one of the few brown children in a white school, the young girl "wondered why I was born to Indian parents instead of to a white couple, who may have been proud of my verses" (8). Significantly, the child's very mastery of the colonial language, English, provoked the psychic break between herself and her (native) parents. This separation between English-language child-poet and Indian parents, a consequence of colonialism, prefigures the later rupture between the English-language woman writer, engaged in the project of claiming her own subjective autonomy, and traditional patriarchal Indian society. Das's autobiography, therefore, in its very "doubleness" of commercial and spiritual intentions and of suspension between colonized or Westernized and indigenous cultures, provides a valuable recording of the hybridized, "impure" cultural conditions in which postcolonial English-language writers from non-Western societies often find themselves writing.[14]

Setting the opening scene on the internal division in the colonized subject, Das prepares the reader for the move to the theme of an older division, the division between genders. By implication, the colonized child brings to her womanhood those perceptions of division arrived at when she learns to value her talent and simultaneously learns to reject her Indian parents, who do not value it. The longing for "white parents" is a powerful psychic aberration, expressing and demonstrating the embedded racism in the colonizing (and colonized) experience which the child has internalized. As the opening psychological drama, it contains those contradictions and ambivalences, between the privileging of "verse" and "self", at times recognized as a specifically "white" or Western-based value, and the respect to be accorded to one's "parent" society. In her representations of gender divisions, Das similarly oscillates between two contradictory positions: one the exceptional woman in conflict with her traditional society, struggling for a subject status specifically endowed through her writing, and the other, that most unexceptional of Indian women, the Krishna devotee. Das's subsequent examinations of her woman's experiences are informed by these postcolonial ambivalences — the contradictions between Westernized and indigenous sociopolitical values — as well as by gender and feminist concerns.

In the autobiography's dialogic representations, therefore, the interest does not lie in the frank revelations of illicit sexual encounters. In fact, the autobiography has so little of the pornographic in it as to make credible a critic's description of Das as "Matthew Arnold in a sari" (Harrex 155). Instead, it compels our reading because it offers, among other things, a critique of the victimization of women in a patriarchal society. The autobiography is itself a gesture enunciating the empowerment of the female when she speaks in protest, in rejection, in an infinitely recessive "desire" within a powerfully restrictive psychosocial matrix.

The dominant figure in her autobiography, also present in her fiction and poems, is the female as "desiring" subject. Female "desire" is figured in the psychological longing of a neglected daughter for a remote father, the physical drive of a virgin for sexual experience, the marital yearning of a young wife for emotional union with her husband, the ecstatic enjoyment of a mature woman with her lover, the depraved lust of a disillusioned older woman with a host of unloving and unlovely paramours, and finally as the ecstasy of the older devotee in the ancient worship of Krishna, a female soul seeking her divine bliss. "Desire," as embodied in the autobiography, is multiply manifest, attending a range of female roles. The narrator presents herself in turn as a girl-child with a crush on a teacher, the naive object of lesbian exploration, an innocent child bride, the victimized wife, loyal and loving wife, adoring mother, sexual tease, easy lay, and spiritual goddess seeking union with the divine. The narrator lives out these stereotypical roles.

The central attribute of this "desiring" female is that, in order to maintain her subject condition and the economy of energy which constitutes her being, she cannot be satisfied. As "self" is constituted in desire, and desire is given shape by the energy of an absence of satisfaction (whether in innocent longing, brutalized sex, cynical promiscuity, the range of female sexual experiences), the story of "self" is constructed on a continual series of arousals and deferments of satisfaction. The life in the autobiography is continuously plotted as a drama of desire, and the female protagonist becomes the representation of female desire.

Significantly, the narrative first provides the reader with a series of empowered female subjects. Chapter four is a rewriting of Das's matriarchal past. The narrative is yet another version of the legends surrounding her grandmother's home, Nalapat House, which had been mythologized in earlier poems.[15] The poem, "My Grandmother's House," for example, identifies the place with an idealized time in the poet's life, "where once/ I received love" (*KD,* 14). In Das's auto-mythology, the maternal home is also the trope for the condition of proud and loving freedom, a condition that the poem raises as absent in the degraded adult woman's life:

> . . . you cannot believe, darling,
> Can you, that I lived in such a house and
> Was proud, and loved. . . I who have lost
> My way and beg now at strangers' doors to
> Receive love, at least in small change?

In the autobiography, Nalapat House becomes a symbol of the way in which the contradictions in traditional Indian women's roles can be resolved. Das traces her lineage to her ancestress, Kunji, a wealthy aristocrat who, at age fifteen, fleeing from the war between the English and Dutch, "was made to change her route by an amorous chieftain who brought her over to his village and married her" (11). The delicate phrasing masks the more sensational possibilities of abduction, rape and forced marriage; it suggests instead a romantically blurred portrayal of a male figure motivated by "amour", a male figure moreover who "was well-versed in Astrology and Architecture" and who set his bride up in the magnificent Nalapat House. The maternal home was dominated by "the old ladies" — "my grandmother, my aunt Ammini, my great grand-mother, her two sisters" (12). Only two males intrude in this woman-universe, the remote and idealized political saint, Mahatmaji Gandhi, whom the uncomprehending girl saw as a brigand whose "diabolic aim was to strip the ladies of all their finery so that they became plain and dull;" and her grand uncle, the famous poet-philosopher, who is seen as lonely and indigent. The girl-child falls under the influence of these women, especially her aunt Ammini, "an attractive woman who kept turning down all the marriage proposals that came her way." Ironically, it was from this virginal literary woman that Das "sensed for the first time that love was a beautiful anguish and a *thapasya*" (12). Deepening the theme, the following chapter is devoted to an even earlier ancestress, "my great grandmother's younger sister," Ammalu, "a poetess." Like Ammini, Ammalu "was a spinster who chose to remain unmarried although pretty and eligible" (14-15). What kind of female models do these relatives offer the girl-child? Both women were ascetics. Ammini "chose to lead the life of an ascetic" (12), while Ammalu "was deeply devout and spent the grey hours of dusk in prayer" (15). Both loved poetry. The former recited it and the latter "read profusely and scribbled in the afternoon while the others had their siesta" (15). Das locates the existence of an ancient female ambition for writing, expressed, and perhaps only capable of being expressed in the strict and narrow social structures of the time and place, as religious longing. This writing ambition, while associated with female spinsterhood or chastity, is made more complex by its juxtaposition with intimate symbols of female sensuality. As a middle-aged woman, Das returns to her maternal home and discovers books containing Ammalu's poems. Together with "the leaves of her books, yellowed like autumn-leaves," Das finds "in the secret drawer of [Ammalu's] writing box, a brown bottle shaped like a pumpkin that smells faintly of Ambergis" (16). The archetypal resonances in the symbols of "bottle" (container, receptacle, vagina, womb, female desire), pumpkin (round, swelling, female, fecundity), and ambergis (perfume, sensuality, arousal, sexuality) are meaningful cross-culturally, and the significance of their placement in "the secret drawer of her writing box" is deliberate and emphatic. If these ancestresses are literary spinsters, they also are familiar with female desire, with the knowledge "that love was a beautiful anguish." For Das, their biographies offered a knowledge of the complex intersections of asceticism and sexuality that form major thematics in her autobiography.

What separates this knowledge, the surface thematics of Das's autobiography and much of her poetry, from the usual sentimental drift of popular women's romances is that it is inseparably, intricately woven and innately situated in the thematics of woman as writer, that is, woman as speaking subject. The identity of her ancestresses, while associated with love or yearning, remains woman- or subject-centered; and this subject condition is integral to and invested in the literary enterprise. In these maternal figures, therefore, the protagonist is able to find an indigenous tradition that her English-educated childhood had denied her. Only in Nalapat House, in a matriarchal society, do the identities of Indian, woman, and writer coalesce. Only here, as the poem suggests, are love and pride coeval, in contrast to the patriarchal society where love becomes coeval with degradation.

Nalapat House and the women in it, while representing ideologically one pole of female empowerment, are also perceived as limited in what they can offer the active child. In the poem, "Blood," for example, Das shows in painful detail the decline and fall of this matriarchal tradition. Its "chastity" and isolation from "the always poor" and "the new-rich men," its venerable ancestry ("Now three hundred years old,/ It's falling to bits/ Before our very eyes" (*OP* 17) result in its destruction. The adult Das, while finding her source of identity in it, cannot resurrect this matriarchy:

> O mother's mother's mother
> I have plucked your soul

Like a pip from a fruit
And have flung it into your pyre. (*OP* 19)

Yet, even as the autobiography narrates the sordid "reality" of a bad marriage and unsuccessful affairs, the matriarch as native spinster and writer remains a powerful representation that resonates in the background.

Similarly, foregrounding the native sources of the narrator's feminism, the early chapters narrate an active engagement with those Indian cultural elements which valorize unchallenged female power. The strongest symbol of female empowerment in the protagonist's early ancestral memories is Kali. Kali is the most feared deity in the Indian pantheon, the goddess to whom is attributed the power of death and destruction. Significantly, the narrator devotes her longest description to her worship. Describing the annual ceremonies, she writes, "When Kali danced, we felt in the region of the heart an unease and a leap of recognition. Deep inside, we held the knowledge that Kali was older than the world and that having killed for others, she was now lonelier than all. All our primal instinct rose to sing in our blood the magical incantations" (26).

What is constituted in this "recognition"? The shift from "I" to the communal "we" emphasizes Das's explicit recognition here of a collective female "primal instinct" associated with the repressed aspects of womanhood, the un-nurturing, destructive forces of female passion. Paradoxically, Kali represents a collective identity of powerful isolation. Thus, she is called the "lonely goddess." Her affection, we are told, is specially reserved for the aboriginal pariahs, people who are normally "regarded as outcasts and held at a distance" (25). Only in the month of Makaram, between January and February, a time set aside for the worship of Kali, do the Pariahs become important members of Indian society. Kali worship, as a form of carnival, permits the reversal of social hierarchy and encourages the transgression of social rule. Kali's power in Indian society is such that it also permits a crossing of gender identity; in the Kali rituals, the oracle who takes on the role of Kali is a male: "He ran up and down through the crowd of people brandishing his scimitar before a trance thickened. . . . His voice changed into the guttural voice of the angry goddess" (26). During the month of Makaram, young women perform a processional ritual in which they enter into a trance-like condition: "The drums throbbed against their ears, mesmerizing them so that their walk began to resemble the glide of a somnambulist and their eyes began to glow, nesting in their pupils the red flame of their lamps" (26). The passage describes an ecstatic state at the level of sensuous experience that Kali-worship permits these young women, and stands in contrast to the later devotional passages on Krishna worship, in which the god is described in abstract terms of non-physicality, as "the bodyless one."

The Kali figure returns in a later chapter, to represent again those forces of fearful female isolation that can protect the outsider, the pariah, against "feudal" "enemies" (178). In response to the villagers' persecution, Das decided she "too should try some magic to scare my foes away. I hung a picture of Kali on the wall of my balcony and adorned it daily with long strings of red flowers, resembling the intestines of a disemboweled human being" (178). The Kali figure represents the usually repressed energies of the female psyche whose release transgresses and crosses social hierarchy and gender. This mythic female power is capable of both destruction and protection, and it therefore has to be pacified through intercession.

In the early chapters Das sets up female figures, each of which, like the iconic representation of Kali, provided her as a girl-child with a "leap of recognition." In Ammina and Ammalu we recognize the woman writer influenced equally by sensual and ascetic passions, a woman recognizable in Amherst's Emily as well as in Nalapat House's Ammalu. In her grand-uncle's wife, we recognize yet another face of the empowered female. The wife is woman as voluptuary and seducer. She is "never seen even at night without her heavy jewelry, all gem-encrusted and radiant, and the traditional cosmetics of the Nair woman" (19). And the object of her life is to "*enslave*" the man "with her voluptuous body" (20; emphasis mine).

These early portrayals of female types make apparent, contrary to general critical consensus, that Das's focus is less on the male (or male-female relations), than it is on the female. The female types that fascinate the young girl range from those in the women-centered community in Nalapat House to the self-authored woman as subject (Ammalu), and the fearfully empowered Kali figure. Together they form an original patterning of proud and powerful womanhood against which the narrative of patriarchal marriage and abuse develops.

Despite the rhetoric of scandal Das employs to describe them, the male-female relations depicted in the autobiography are significant more for their sociopolitical themes than for any scandal in them. For instance, in the narrative of her arranged marriage we see a critique of that institution beneath the apparently confessional surface. The fifteen-year-old Das, having experienced only school-girl crushes, the attentions of lesbians, and clumsy seduction attempts, is married to an older man because "I was a burden and a responsibility neither my parents nor my grandmother could put up with for long" (73). Her marriage begins in sexual brutality. She calls the wedding-night encounter an unsuccessful rape. She suffers through her husband's selfishness and neglect of her emotional and physical needs. The cook prepares only breakfast and dinner, and the young pregnant bride falls ill. After an early separation, they attempt a reconciliation when they move to Bombay, but she has a nervous breakdown at twenty after the birth of her second son. Das's critique of Indian marriage as patriarchal oppression is more damning when the reader keeps in mind that middle-class and professional Indian women, a very small minority of Indian society, generally receive greater legal and social protection than the vast numbers of poor and peasant Indian women.

Exactly in the middle of the autobiography, in chapter 25, the narrator locates an instance of insight, an epiphany that permits the protagonist to move beyond the passivity of her female bondage to a more integrated existence. Faced with the failure of her marriage and the impossibility of leaving it, with her son's illness, and her husband's rejection of her in favor of a homosexual attachment, the protagonist finds herself poised on a balcony in a moment of suicidal temptation: "I felt a revulsion for my womanliness. The weight of my breasts seemed to be crushing me. My private parts was only a wound, the soul's wound showing through" (94). In this moment of recognition, the young wife acknowledges the powerlessness of the female body, that understanding that woman's fate as suffering victim is tied to her physical body. The narrator expresses for us the knowledge that, for the victimized woman in a patriarchal society, sexuality does not only make her vulnerable physically, a prey to rapacious men; it is inherently bound up with her emotional and spiritual vulnerability. This moment of insight gives fresh meanings to the Freudian maxim that anatomy is destiny. It is a powerful because profoundly ironic reconceptualizing of woman's fate as victim; her experiences as victim, we cannot be reminded too often, goes beyond the plane of material pain to encompass mental and spiritual conditions when her very identity as woman and her own body become the instruments of her torment.

But the woman does not throw herself off the balcony. Instead she "lit the reading lamp . . . and began to write about a new life, an unstained future" (94). Again, as in the early chapters, the autobiography shows a female subject coming to her own ministry, becoming herself a mistress/ancestress of "an unstained future." Centrally located in the text, the passage repeats the central theme, of woman writing her self, not only as one act of identity among other acts, but as the primary act. She saves her life by telling her life. It is perhaps an example of cross-cultural concerns that this passage foreshadows a later passage by the French feminist, Hélène Cixous, who asserts that a woman must write her self to mark "her shattering entry into history which has always been based on her suppression . . . . To become at will the taker and initiator, for her own right, in every symbolic system, in every political system" (880). The protagonist chooses writing against suicide, self-inscription against self-destruction, and so takes the first steps of revolt against a symbolic/political system that has oppressed her.

The passage therefore also marks the convergence of the thematics of female psychic emergence with a continued critique of female sexuality in a patriarchal society. It is in the light of this thematic of emergence that we should read the rest of the book, which is heavily interlaced with accounts of extramarital affairs, sexual flings, cynical portrayals of deceit and betrayals, and yearnings for spiritual consolation. After her breakdown and grandmother's death, the protagonist who emerges is a different sexual person. No longer a naif or passive "object" of her husband's actions and victim of the rapes of various strangers, she is now able to take her pleasure, to re-appropriate her sexual self, "with my pride intact and blazing" (100). Her sexual adventures, however, have less to do with actual male others than with her own internal identity needs. As Das aptly makes the point, "Like alms looking for a begging bowl was my love which sought for it a receptacle" (105). Here the conventional association of woman with receptacle, of woman as passive receiver of male desire and sperms, is inverted. In this passage, woman's desire is dominant, aggressively seeking, "a (male) begging bowl." In the bold reversal, the male is passive, the female active and full, signifying plenitude and wealth.

But *My Story* does not conclude on this seeming female victory. Although it continues with the narrative of extramarital affairs (Das apparently had an open marriage; according to her poems and the autobiography, her husband accepted her love affairs rather than encourage the prospect of a divorce), it becomes clear that sexual empowerment in no way satisfies the protagonist's internal identity needs. Thus, even as the narrative dwells on lovers and husband, it incorporates a poem that resists an equation of 'liberated' sexuality with satisfaction of female desire:

> We lay
> On bed, glassy-eyes, fatigued, just
> The toys dead children leave behind,
> And we asked each other, what is
> The use, what is the bloody use?
> That was the only kind of love,
> This hacking at each other's parts
> Like convicts hacking, breaking clods
> At noon. (115)

The poet rejects the sexual act as brutal and futile action committed by "toys dead children leave behind," or by "convicts." Rather than representing or enacting desire, male-female sexual interactions are anomic, penitential, dead.

Curiously, then, what we can read in Das's autobiography is a re-visioning of female desire. Contrary to the Lacanian thesis of female desire as "lack," a wanting, which is itself an extension of the Freudian argument of female as that which is deficient in or missing the potency of the penis, the protagonist of the autobiography emerges from passive victim to active agent possessing fullness and plenitude, needing only a proper recipient. But this female desire, assertive, aggressive, and confident, must still await satisfaction in a sociopolitical context that denies it any expression except in the area of sexuality. The area of sexuality that the adult Das explores, however, is defined in a patriarchal society to the advantage of men, and the narrative's tales of extramarital affairs are also tales of male abuse. In the narrative of her most intense affair, she interrogates the sadomasochistic nature of her relationship: "Years after all of it had ended, I asked myself why I took him on as my lover, fully aware of his incapacity to love. . . . I needed security. . . . Perhaps it was necessary for my body to defile itself in many ways, so that the soul turned humble for a change" (163). Here is yet another recognition of the mental and spiritual damage women suffer on account of their sex; the masochistic rationalization of drives, while more conventionally expressed as religious growth, is itself a chilling example of psychic damage in the female protagonist.

The struggle for sexual and other forms of autonomy in the female protagonist is "exceptional" in the tradition of Indian writing in English, whether by men or women. In the Indian context, female desire, because it breaks social conventions of marital and sexual property and propriety, is inherently illegitimate and therefore doubly exceptional. As French reports it:

> [Indian women's] primary duty, a duty so emphatic as to override their children's well-being and certainly their own, is to 'make the marriage work'. This means that a woman must adjust to her husband. Whatever he is or does — if he is cold or cruel, if he is never home, or does not give her money, if he drinks or gambles or has other women, if he beats her — is her lot. She is expected to submit, serve, and produce a son. (179)

The myth of her origin in the woman-centered matriarchy of Nalapat House enables the protagonist to stand outside and to interrogate the abusive patriarchal world in which she (or her sexuality) functions only as an economic object with market value. When her husband complains that she has not read "the prestigious report of the Rural Credit Survey Committee" — that is, not given him due respect — she answers, "But I let you make love to me every night . . . isn't that good enough?" (114). The protagonist has learned to balance what is "due" to her husband in terms of her sexual availability, and understands that the exchange of her sexual self in the economy of the marriage is a kind of market exchange, "a good" enough for the shelter and material security he provides. The passage makes explicit what is more often concealed or silenced in both Indian and Western literature, that the relationship between male and female is often baldly an economic exchange. This relocation of male-female relationship in an economic world makes it evident that the protagonist's claim to female subject autonomy in matters of sexual relations outside of marriage is even more illegal, for it breaks both the cultural and economic codes.

The narrator goes beyond the economic/sexual bond to examine the place of class in her society. Observing the lives of the working-class and poor who surround the protagonist and commenting specifically on the protagonist's fascination with the poor, the narrator offers these lives in moral contrast to the protagonist's own middle-class ennui. In one striking passage, the poet is in her "drawing room" while "cultured voices discussed poetry" (190). She hears the song that the poor who live in the builders' colony behind the "large new structures" are singing. "Finally," she writes, "unable to control myself any longer, I dragged my husband to the colony one evening" (190). In the squatters' welcome for her, she is able to revise her subjective perspective:

I was pining for yet another settee for the drawing-room while these grand men and women were working from morning till dusk carrying cement and climbing the scaffoldings. And yet they had more vitality than I had of optimism. . . My gloom lay in its littlest corner like a black dog. I had had the idiocy to think of myself as Kamala, a being separate from all the rest and with a destiny entirely different from those of others. (191)

This incident, isolated as it is from any larger examination of the issues of class and caste in Indian society, may be read as a shallow idealization of the working class. To my mind, however, its inclusion in a subjectivist genre like autobiography indicates the writer's unease with her subjective project, of constituting "Kamala, a being separate from all the rest and with a destiny" all her own. The passage contains less a materialist critique of class inequalities than an interrogation of the Westernized, middle-class privileging of the individual, which forms the autobiography's sub-text. In its valuation and equation of vitality and "singing," a communal activity, with the working class (in contrast to 'poetry,' a private affair, equated with middle-class ennui), the passage offers another example of narrative "double-voicedness." The incident represents another instance of the protagonist attempting to break the psychic isolation of a middle-class marriage; but the attempt on this occasion, dragging "my husband with me," is licit and legal and serves to underline her identification with, rather than separation from, the larger Indian society.

In the autobiography, Das comes to a point in her life when she questions her own sense of being exceptional. The same kind of necessity to open consciousness to the dialogic presence of others, whether of a different race (as in the case of the young girl yearning for white parents), class or gender, also admits into the autobiography the other aspect of self, of tradition. Yet it is this aspect of woman as patriarchal mate, that most non-exceptional of women in Indian society, which the autobiographical discourse has been most energetically displacing.

As befitting the story of a woman mediating among and mediated by multiple and contradictory cultures, My Story in its Krishna-consciousness shows the ideological interpenetrations of the Hindu world-view with a feminist, — although not wholly — Westernized, text. For example, in locating the woman as autonomous sexual subject in her familiar world, the narrator moves from the image of plenty looking for a begging bowl to that of devotee: "I was perhaps seeking a familiar face that blossomed like a blue lotus in the water of my dreams. It was to get closer to that bodyless [sic] one that I approached other forms and lost my way. I may have gone astray, but not once did I forget my destination" (105). The immediate contradictions between this passage and the bulk of the book are so large as to suggest the complicated indeterminacy of identity that forms the site of conflict for Westernized Asian women in strongly regulated, traditionally patriarchal societies. Marginalized by their gender, their colonial English education and language, their rejection of patriarchy and its given social and familial norms, and their bourgeois interests in a chiefly peasant society, women writers such as Das negotiate their identity needs among contradictory dominant discourses, each of which offers more grounds for tension than for resolution. As a work by a major English-language Indian woman writer, Das's "story" is less a seamless product of hybridity than it first appears, although the cultural differences, between Indian and Western values and ideas, are obviously present and affect her work. Her autobiography, in fact, shuttles between the gaps, articulating the space between cultures, displaying rather than resolving these differences in the narrative. The conclusion moves out of the discourse of feminism that occupies the foreground of the first two-thirds of the text, to the more conventional discourse of the confessional autobiography.

Arguably, therefore, it is possible to read the major locus of meaning in the slippage between the two tropes, that of alms looking for a begging bowl (female subject desiring/enacting its terms of empowerment/ identity), and devotee worshipping the blue Krishna (female desire as passively situated in the hierarchical construction of patriarchal stasis or tradition). For in the shift in tropes, Das places a Hindu screen before her feminist project, which is up to this point to treat the domain of the sexual as also the field of political struggle. In shifting from the psychosexual and sociopolitical to the Hindu view of woman as Krishna-worshipper, Das attempts to move from the position of the exceptional (and illegitimate) woman to that of the legal, central and iconic Indian female figure.

The presence of Krishna-consciousness (that is, of acceptance of female submission to male godhood) in Das's autobiography, I would argue, is evidence of the process of creative play that Bakhtin describes in *The Dialogic Imagination*, the "struggle and dialogic interrelationship of [the categories of authoritative discourse and an internally persuasive discourse that] usually determine the history of an individual ideological consciousness" (342). Krishna-consciousness in Das's work makes evident the presence of the "authoritative word" of patriarchal Indian culture. The "authoritative word," as Bakhtin defines it, is the word of the fat hers, a prior discourse, located in a distanced zone, with a hieratic language akin to taboo (342). Das's slippages between straightforward feminist discourse, the subjective writing of the body — her internally persuasive discourse — and this "authoritative word" of Krishna-consciousness, testify to the gaps that result from the simultaneous existence of plural, dominant yet contradictory discourses in the same consciousness. The "intense struggle within . . . for hegemony among various available verbal and ideological points of view, approaches, directions and values" (346) defines her inscribed ideological development.

In this regard, Das's inscriptions of the struggles for autonomy of the female are themselves placed in jeopardy, under interrogation. Aspects of female identity are polarized. The autonomous subject actively creating her destiny in an unstained new world stands in contrast to the iconic figure of the female as passive, culturally fixed in an object relationship in which she is always the inferior in search of the Divine Krishna. The weight of these polarities indicates the enormous contradictions that beset a woman living in a strongly male-dominant society. As an Indian woman, she participates in and endures simultaneously those constructed systems of Hindu rationalization that have existed in India for centuries.

To privilege one polarity over the other, however, is to falsely reduce the dialogic complexities of Das's themes and the totality of her achievement.

It is to silence that libido that speaks in and through relations with others. Her autobiography reshapes both our consciousness and our unconscious, by means of its raw, experimental edges. The internally persuasive dialogue of her autobiography shares characteristics with the kind of writing described as "écriture féminine" in Western literature. The enabling myth of matriarchal origin; the genealogical constructions of chaste spinster-writers; the sociopolitical critiques of arranged marriages, child brides, and loveless middle-class marriages; the portrayals of male abuse of women as sexual objects and prey; the narrative of emergence of woman as subject and writer — all these form a counterdiscourse to the later confessional closure. This counterdiscourse, contradicting and attacking patriarchal constructions of male superiority and female passivity, appears forcefully in the early reconstructions of empowered female figures. The Kali figure, for example, sets up a clear female anti-thesis to Krishna-consciousness that forms part of the authoritative word of the father in the second half of the autobiography; this "savage" goddess reminds us especially of "the forceful return of a libido, which is not so easily controlled, and by the singular, by the noncultural, by a language which is savage and which can certainly be heard" (Cixous 880).

Despite the later development of the Krishna theme, Das's autobiography springs from the same impulses of revolt as the rest of her oeuvre. Indigenous cultural elements such as the Kali figure and the matriarchal structure of Nalapat House, provide sources for her critiques of patriarchally constructed heterosexuality. These critiques form major themes in her autobiography and poetry, contributing to a self-reflexivity that provides an intertextual web in which whole plots, incidents, acts, characters, concerns, even sentences and phrases from her other works appear. For example, about halfway through the autobiography, at the point where the protagonist arrives at full although emotionally unsatisfying sexuality (in a chapter titled "For the First Time in my life I learned to surrender totally"), the chapters are prefaced by her poems (e.g. 99, 107, 115, 124, 127). Many of these poems had been previously published and were already notorious.[16] Their appearance in the autobiography suggests that the coming to adult sexuality of the protagonist is also a coming to speaking subjectivity for the poet.

Das's critique of patriarchally constructed heterosexuality and her struggle to construct her own terms of sexual empowerment, while sharing similar concerns with Western feminists such as de Beauvoir, Kate Millet, and Hélène Cixous, remain one exceptional Indian woman's life story. The concluding chapters suggest not so much a retreat as a reconfiguration of her feminist project. A bad heart condition and her aging body lead the protagonist to turn away from male-female sexual relations as the site of conflict: "I had shed carnal desire as a snake sheds its skin" (170). Her sexual desires are imaged, ironically in the stereotypical figure of the spiritual lotus, as "now totally dead, rotted and dissolved, and for them there was no more to be a re-sprouting" (186). She returns to Nalapat House "like a lost woman" (175), in a gesture of retreat into female chastity: "I should never have taken to wearing the coloured clothes of the city. I should have dressed only in white. . . . I belonged to the serenity of Nalapat House" (176). But the retreat is not a defeat; instead the protagonist's libido becomes invested in the writing project, which is described in suggestively erotic terms: "I learnt for the first time to be miserly with my energy, spending it only on my writing which I enjoyed more than anything else in the world. I typed sitting propped against pillows on my wide bed" (183). Yet this emergence of the woman as empowered writer, recalling the return of the ancestral figures of Ammini and Ammalu, is still patriarchally restricted. The narrator represents her readers as lovers: "I had realized by then that the writer had none to love her but the readers" (183). The desire to write, therefore, signifies the desire for a collective libidinous intercourse, a female exposure fantasy: "I have often wished to take myself apart and stick all the bits, the heart, the intestine, the liver, the reproductive organs, the skin, the hair and all the rest on a large canvas to form a collage which could then be donated to my readers" (183). Although a different subject from the woman as sexual being, the woman as writer is again presented as consciousness constructed under the gaze of a patriarchal other, in this case a voyeuristic male deity: "Each time I walked into my lover's houses dressed like a bride, my readers have walked with me. . . . Like the eyes of an all-seeing God they follow me through the years" (183). It is in her intercourse with her readers that the narrative finally arrives at anything like a recognition of satisfaction: "But how happily I meddled to satisfy that particular brand of readers who liked me. . . . And it certainly brought me happiness" (184). This satisfaction, however, while it operates as a sign of empowerment (privileging) of the woman writer, continues to be expressed in the terms of patriarchal (inter)discourse, demonstrating the continued submission of Das's feminist project to patriarchy.

The social restrictions on women writers against expressing that kind of sexual and professional autonomy that we find in *My Story* are as strongly embedded in many Asian cultures today as they were in 1976 when Das's book appeared and will probably prevent any imitators soon. The negative responses of Indian women critics such as Monika Varna, Vimala Rao, and Eunice de Souza to Das's work and to the work of other candid Indian women writers such as Gauri Deshpande and Mamta Kalia demonstrate that perceived transgressions of social decorum and traditional behavior still affect literary evaluation.[17] Moreover, Asian women generally might not find Das's exploration of female subjectivity, as chiefly desire-centered or her portrayal of sexual relations as politically engaged, congenial or helpful. After all, Das's writing can be said to have little material transformatory effect in Indian society. Some 80 percent of India's 700 million people live in the countryside. The status of Indian women, moreover, is woefully precarious, reflecting a profound gender inequality and urgent material deprivations. The age for sacramental marriage, for example, is fourteen years for girls; the 1987 birthrate was 32 percent per one thousand population. More than 75 percent of Indian women are illiterate.[18] Moreover, Das's English-language Indian audience is extremely limited; India has fifteen languages included in its Constitution, and it has been reported that only about 3 percent of the Indian population, a Westernized and class-differentiated elite, uses English with any regularity. Her engaged and disruptive work, however, serves to remind Western readers to avoid any stereotyping of women from postcolonial developing nations. Even in the oppressive sociocultural conditions that the autobiography delineates — conditions too often elided and stereotyped as Third World backwardness — Das's *Story*, proving the exception in her revolt against patriarchal oppression, helps to write the terms of empowerment for Indian women.

1989

Notes

I wish to thank Nancy Miller, Graduate Center of the City University of New York, and Lawrence Lipking, Northwestern University, for their support; Wimal Dissanayake and the East-West Center, Hawaii, for the time and resources that led to this paper; Julia Watson, who gave me the occasion for the paper; Sidonie Smith, whose critical eye sharpened my argument; and the many critics, both East and West, who have provided me with their readings.

1. Adrienne Rich notes that for centuries Western women have been "mothered" by the "unchilded" — that is, exceptional — woman: "Throughout recorded history the 'childless' woman has been regarded . . . as a failed woman . . . . seen as embodiments of the great threat to male hegemony; the woman who is not tied to the family, who is disloyal to the law of heterosexual pairing and bearing. . . . Without the unacclaimed research and scholarship of 'childless' women, without Charlotte Bronte (who died in her first pregnancy), Margaret Fuller (whose major work was done before her child was born), without George Eliot, Emily Bronte, Emily Dickinson, Christina Rossetti, Virginia Woolf, Simone de Beauvoir —we would all today be suffering from spiritual malnutrition as women" (251-52).

2. That we can and should find parallels between Asian and Western women's texts does not imply that we must accept "the concept of sisterhood as a global construct." See Bonnie Thornton Dill, "Race, Class, and Gender: Prospects for an All-Inclusive Sisterhood."

3. See Ding Ling, *Miss Sophie's Diary* and *I Myself Am a Woman: Selected Writings of Ding Ling*, edited by Tani E. Barlow with Gary J. Bjorge.

4. All page references to major texts will be given in the body of the essay. See Kamala Das's *The Old Playhouse and Other Poems (OP); Kamala Das A Selection with Essays on her Work (KD).* Works not discussed in the paper included *The Descendents; Tonight, This Savage Rite: The Love Poems of Kamala Das and Pritish Nandy;* and *Collected Poems.*

5. In Sandra M. Gilbert and Susan Gubar's *The Norton Anthology of Writing by Women,* Das, the only Asian woman writer in the anthology, is represented by one poem, "An Introduction," which encapsulates much of the same material worked in her autobiography.

6. M. M. Bakhtin, *The Dialogic Imagination (DI).* Further page references to *DI* will appear in the essay. Bakhtin's notion of "the internal dialogism of double-voiced prose" that "draws its energy, its dialogized ambiguity, not from individual dissonances, misunderstandings or contradictions . . . but sinks its roots deep into a fundamental, socio-linguistic speech diversity and multi-languagedness [heteroglossia]" (325-62) applies to Das's multi-language background and specifically to what Harrex has termed "cultural dissonances" in the postcolonial Indian world.

7. Das has attracted an enormous critical response, resisting and laudatory, in her relatively brief writing career. There are more bibliographical items on her work than on any other Indian writer in English, living or dead. It is curious that the majority of Indian women critics persists in reading Das's subjects as strongly physical, a "profanity" of love, in contrast to the male and Anglo tendency to sacralize her subjects, to read them counter to the body as manifesting transcendent and Hindu mentality.

8. The phenomenon of erosion or changes within native cultures in response to aggressive colonial education and colonial language imposition has been the focus of numerous studies. See, for example, Chinweizu, Onwuchekwa Jemie, and Ihechukwu Madubuike's classical polemical study of this phenomenon in African states.

9. See Bruce King's introduction in *Literatures of the World in English* for a discussion of the evolution of these literatures from their colonial sources to their complex contemporary national identities.

10. See Vimala Rao, "Kamala Das: The Limits of Over-exposure," for one of the sharpest attacks on the sexual themes and craft of Das's work. See also Eunice de Souza, "Kamala Das, Gauri Deshpande, Mamta Kalia."

11. Harrex and O'Sullivan, *KD.* The essays in the volume are by S.C. Harrex, Vincent O'Sullivan, Dorothy Jones, and Curtis Wallace-Crabbe.

12. See Syd Harrex and Vincent O'Sullivan, "Introduction," 1-3, and Vincent O'Sullivan, "Whose Voice is Where? On Listening to Kamala Das." O'Sullivan asserts that with Das, "We are reading religious poems of a kind that it would be impossible to find in any other woman now writing in English" (190).

13. For a discussion of Das's novel, *Alphabet of Lust,* see Shirley Geok-lin Lim, "Semiotics, Experience, and the Material Self: An Inquiry into the Subject of the Contemporary Women Writer."
14. See Homi Bhabha, "Signs Taken for Wonders: Questions of Ambivalence and Authority Under a Tree Outside Delhi, May 1817," for an insightful discussion of the dynamics of hybridity in colonialist and postcolonialist cultures. In Das's case, her texts are further complicated by the intersections of gender conflict with postcolonial cultural ambiguity, multiplicity and indeterminacy.
15. See, for example, "My Grandmother's House," *KD* 14; and "Blood," in *OP* 16-9.
16. For example, untitled poems beginning chapters 37 (137) and 41 (154) are "The Freaks" and "The Sunshine Cat," both published in her 1965 collection, *Summer in Calcutta.*
17. See Monika Varna, "Gauri Deshpande;" Eunice de Souza, "Kamala Das, Gauri Deshpande, Mamta Kalia;" Gauri Deshpande, *Between Births,* and *Lost Love*; Mamta Kalia, *Tribute to Papa and Other Poems.*
18. Statistics taken from *Women: A World Report* (1985).

Works Cited

Bakhtin, M. M. *The Dialogic Imagination.* Ed. Michael Holquist. Trans. Caryl Emerson and Michael Holquist. Austin: University of Texas Press, 1981.

Barlow, Tani E. and Gary J. Bjorge, eds. *I Myself Am a Woman: Selected Writings of Ding Ling.* Boston: Beacon Press, 1989.

Bhabha, Homi. "Signs Taken for Wonders: Questions of Ambivalence and Authority Under a Tree Outside Delhi, May 1817." *Europe and its Others.* Eds. F. Barker, et al. Colchester: University of Essex, 1985. 89-105.

Cixous, Hélène. "The Laugh of the Medusa." Trans. Keith Cohen and Paula Cohen. *Signs: Journal of Women in Culture and Society.* (Summer 1976).

Chinweizu, et al. *Toward the Decolonization of African Literature.* Washington, D.C.: Howard University Press, 1983.

Das, Kamala. *Alphabet of Lust.* New Delhi: Orient Paperbacks, 1972.

———. *A Doll For the Child Prostitute.* New Delhi: India Paperbacks, 1977.

———. *The Descendents.* Calcutta: Writers Workshop, 1967.

———. *My Story.* New Delhi: Sterling Paperbacks, 1976.

———. *Summer In Calcutta.* Calcutta: Rajinder Paul and Everest Press, 1965.

———. *The Old Playhouse and Other Poems.* New Delhi: Orient Longman, 1973.

———. *Tonight, This Savage Rite: The Love Poems of Kamala Das and Pritish Nandy.* New Delhi: Arnold-Heinemann, 1979.

———. *Collected Poems* vol. 1. Trivandrum, Kerala State. 1984.

De Lauretis, Teresa. *Alice Doesn't: Feminist, Semiotics, Cinema.* Bloomington: Indiana University Press, 1984.

Deshpande, Gauri. *Between Births.* Calcutta: Writers Workshop, 1968.

———. *Lost Love.* Calcutta: Writers Workshop, 1970.

de Souza, Eunice. "Kamala Das, Gauri Deshpande, Mamta Kalia." *Contemporary Indian Poetry.* Ed. Saleem Peerandina. Bombay: Macmillan India, 1972. 84-87.

Dill, Bonnie Thornton. "Race, Class, and Gender: Prospects for an All-Inclusive Sisterhood." *Feminist Studies 9*, no. 1 (Spring 1983): 131-50.

Dwivedi, A. N. *Kamala Das and Her Poetry*. Delhi: Doaba House, 1983.

———. ed. *Studies in Contemporary Indo-English Verse. Vol. 1 (A Collection of Critical Essay on Female Poets)*. Bareilly: Prakash Book Depot, 1984.

French, Marilyn. "Women and Work-India." *Women: A World Report*. New York: Oxford University Press, 1985. 174-201.

Gilbert, Sandra M, and Susan Gubar. *The Norton Anthology of Writing by Women*. New York: W. W. Norton, 1985. 2247-49.

Harrex, Syd. "The Strange Case of Matthew Arnold in a Sari: An Introduction to Kamala Das." Syd Harrex and Vincent O'Sullivan: 155-75.

Harrex, Syd, and Vincent O'Sullivan, eds. *Kamala Das: A Selection with Essays on her Work*. Adelaide: Centre for Research in the New Literatures in English, 1986.

Jones, Dorothy. "'Freedom Became my Dancing Shoe': Liberty and the Pursuit of Happiness in the Work of Kamala Das." *Kamala Das: A Selection with Essays on her Work*. Syd Harrex and Vincent O'Sullivan.

Kalia, Mamta. *Tribute to Papa and Other Poems*. Calcutta: Writers Workshop, 1970.

King, Bruce. *Literatures of the World in English*. London: Routledge & Kegan, 1974. 1-21.

Kristeva, Julia. *Revolution in Poetic Language*. Trans. Margaret Waller. New York: Columbia University Press, 1984.

Lim, Shirley Geok-lin. "Semiotics, Experience, and the Material Self: An Inquiry into the Subject of the Contemporary Women Writer." *Women's Studies 18* (Summer 1990): 153-75.

Ling, Ding. *Miss Sophie's Diary*. Trans. W.J.F.Jenner. Beijing: Panda Books, 1985.

O'Sullivan, Vincent. "Whose Voice is Where? On Listening to Kamala Das." Syd Harrex and Vincent O'Sullivan. 179-94.

Rahmin, Anisur. *Expressive Form in the Poetry of Kamala Das*. New Delhi: Abhinav Publishers, 1981.

Rich, Adrienne. *Of Woman Born: Motherhood as Experience and Institution*. New York: W. W. Norton, 1976.

Rao, Vimala. "Kamala Das — The Limits of Over-exposure." A. N. Dwivedi: 87-96.

Sharma, Mohan Lal. "The Road to Brindavan: The Theme of Love in Kamala Das' Poetry." A. N. Dwivedi. 97-111.

Varna, Monika. "Gauri Deshpande." A. N. Dwivedi. 65-75.

Who Do We Name When We Say "Diaspora"?:
Race, National Identity, and the Subject of the Subject in Timothy Mo's Novels

Part of the appeal of the concept of "diaspora" lies in the way it is able to wedge an interrogation of given unequal positions between a hegemonic state authority and individual "selves." Homi Bhabha, valorizing the counter-hegemonic, anti-colonialist, postmodern intellectual, inserts the notion of the diaspora in the idea of the marginal:

> It is one of the salutary features of postmodern theory to suggest that it is the disjunctive, fragmented, displaced agency of those who have suffered the sentence of history, subjugation, diaspora, displacement — that forces one to think outside the certainty of the sententious. It is from the affective experience of social marginality that we must conceive of a political strategy of empowerment and articulation, a strategy outside the liberatory rhetoric of idealism and beyond the sovereign subject that haunts the "civil" sentence of the law. (*Cultural Studies* 56)

In addressing the issue of "cultural incommensurability," Bhabha argues that the liberal ethic of tolerance and the pluralistic frame of multiculturalism are no longer adequate perspectives. Instead, because the historical moment is "caught in an aporetic, contingent position, in-between a plurality of practices that are different and yet must occupy the same space of adjudication and articulation," intellectuals must begin to speak from the perspective of the "edge," a "liminal form of cultural identification" for "non-ethnocentric, transcultural judgments" (57).

Bhabha's position is problematic for a variety of reasons. First, the cultural moment he speaks of is not so much a postmodern moment as a historical repetition. The history of humans at a macro and micro level is the history of "a plurality of practices that are different and yet must occupy the same space for adjudication and articulation," the history of colonialism, of religious and national wars, of race, class, and gender struggles. Moreover, the non-ethnocentric and transcultural judgments he appeals to, arguably, have been identified with those social values articulated by an international, cosmopolitan elite, whose cultural productions elide their class and metropolitan bases.[1] Inserting the experience of "diaspora" into his reinscription of the cosmopolitan argument, Bhabha's statements appear to suggest an empowering strategy of origin-as-identity on a global basis to move beyond the idealization or "liberatory rhetoric" of the "sovereign subject" at exactly the moment when more and more totalitarian systems are forced to take account of the desires of their populations for this "liberation."[2]

Indeed, the work of some "diasporic" writers, such as Maxine Hong Kingston and Timothy Mo, can be seen to contest Bhabha's notion of "diaspora" as a social phenomenon subverting the ideal of the individual ("sovereign subject") and illuminating the irrelevance of national legislated, secured borders. While Maxine Hong Kingston, a second generation American, born in Stockton, California, and Timothy Mo, born in Hong Kong and now living in Britain, are both of Chinese descent, their works come from and refer to very different national affiliations. Of the two, only Mo can be considered a migrant. However, as a child of Hong Kong, Mo was already a British subject before coming to London in his teens and working as a newspaper man in the eighties.[3]

Kingston has never been considered anything but an American. In fact, in her various interviews, she positions herself within an American literary canon and locates her own work in the tradition of Gertrude Stein and Walt Whitman.[4] In her second book, *China Men* (1980), for example, the narrator confesses her complete dis-orientation from the geographical nation state called China:

> I'd like to go to China if I can get a visa and — more difficult — permission from my family, who are afraid that applying for a visa would call attention to us: the relatives in China would get in trouble for having American capitalist connections, and we Americans would be put in relocation camps during the next witch hunt for Communists . . . . I want to discern what it is that makes people go West and turn into Americans. I want to compare China, a country I made up, with what country is really out there. (87)

The passage triangulates a settled position between the writer and her relation to the United States ("we Americans"), and this fused American identity with two "Chinas." The first "China" has been constructed in the discourse of political economy as a geographical identity "out there," separate, Communist, and antagonistic to the United States capitalist system Despite the narrator's identification with the American state, the United States, like Communist China, is also critiqued as authoritarian and repressive: thus, the fear that "We Americans would be put in relocations camps during the next witch hunt for communists."[5] In contrast to the Communist state, the second China is constructed as a cultural imaginary, and only in this imaginary can the subject's relation to China as "homeland" be situated. The relation of the narrator to a geopolitical China is projected as a restrictive antagonism between capitalist and

Communist state membership, unless "China" is displaced into the Imaginary, a country the narrator has "invented." Signaling that her writing belongs to United States national discourse, the narrat or denies an identity between herself and a Chinese national, *except in the domain of the Imaginary that does not participate in the political discourse of China*. Thus, although categorized under the truth claims of history and biography, *China Men,* according to the narrator, is a work of American fiction, excused from and defended against the competing claims of Chinese national politics.

If the "diaspora" in Kingston's texts is negotiated as United States national with China as Imaginary, we should not lose sight of the other side of the argument, that in Kingston's work, America is also another Imaginary. Kingston's United States Imaginary, however, includes United States history and law, discourses that legitimatize the narrator's claim to an American identity. Hence the chapter, "The Laws" (152-159), constructs an authorial position within United States constitutional rights, locating the subject not as diasporic but as immigrant national. United States identity in Kingston's writing is continuously claimed, while the political and state elements of a China identity are disclaimed. Even apparent race-specific materials are negotiated as a symbolic transformation of Chinese "race" into American "culture", as in the chapter, "The Making of more Americans."

American identity politics, taken up in these passages and chapters in *China Men,* are folded into a different diasporic perspective in the book's concluding chapter. "On listening" thematizes the global dispersal of Chinese immigrants in a brief epilogue that quotes scholars discussing the Chinese presence in the Philippines, Mexico, California, and Spain. This conclusion deliberately avoids closure; instead, it follows an "open end" strategy [6] — "Now I could watch the young men who listen" — with the narrator observing the process of subject formations for young "Chinese Americans" (308). The final sentence suggests that, while the stories of global Chinese immigration, of the Chinese diaspora, must affect the young male listeners, the authorial subject — Kingston herself — is distanced from the discussion. Differentiated by gender and generation, the narrator paradoxically is both embricated yet passive in the closing narratives on the Chinese diaspora.

This overtly non-diasporic quality of Kingston's work, its insistence on a United States site, is perhaps most clearly viewed against the work of another writer of Chinese descent, Timothy Mo. Mo's four novels, *The Monkey King* (1978), *Sour Sweet* (short listed for the prestigious Booker Prize in 1982), *An Insular Possession* (1986) and *The Redundancy of Courage* (1991), set in Hong Kong, Britain, Portuguese Timor and the Americas, range the Chinese diasporic subject as a geographically unrooted individual.[7] The diasporic individual's ambiguous or unsettled national identity catalyzes the fictions' dramatic conflicts. Such identity ambiguity provides the materials for ironic and dystopic interrogations of Sino culture, colonialist structures, neocolonialist depredations, and the individual's struggles to maintain an autonomous dignity among hegemonic state powers. Ien Ang describes the overseas Chinese' relation to China as a double bind, producing a "continuous ambivalence" that "highlights the fundamental precariousness of diasporic identity construction, its positive indeterminacy" (4). However, arguably, the "content" of the diasporic Chinese identity in Mo's novels is always already culturally overdetermined. These overdeterminations constrain and locate the individual in a life-and-death struggle against the diasporic collectivity of race and culture, and within and against the host society, the non-Chinese Other. Indeed, the subject's identity is configured and reconfigured within these constrained conditions of cultural overdeterminacy.

Mo's novels demonstrate a collapsing of the boundaries of fiction and non-fiction. Kingston's collapsing of these boundaries privileged the Imaginary in non-fiction genres, and secured the authorial subject and the author's subjects in a United States national base. Mo's novels, however, move toward a greater and greater transgression of the novel as a discourse of the Imaginary. They repoliticize the novel form as a vehicle for sociopolitical critiques on the ways in which non-secured individuals are threatened, manipulated, swallowed up, colonized, erased, and extinguished by powers of the collective, whether of family, race, or state.

In Mo's novels, the imagined homeland is never simple territoriality, a geopolitical space or original home. His novels show no trace of the diasporic nostalgia and yearning, inseparable from the myth of pure race, that results in ethnocentrism, found in Overseas Chinese cultures.[8] Mo's protagonists do not participate in an Overseas Chinese community as much as they resist being subsumed by it. A transnational writer owing loyalty to neither China nor Britain, the two nations that can be said to have biographical contingency for him, Mo treats a diasporic Chineseness disarticulated from nationality or territory[9] — but tied to a collectivity whose power encompasses race and culture. Surrounded by a diasporic collectivity, the individual never gets to leave this "homeland", which operates, like ideology, to ironize, eviscerate, and cannibalize the individual who presumes to escape it. In order to preserve the tatters of a sovereign subject condition, indeed, to preserve his physical life, the individual must abandon his homeland, must unbecome Chinese.

The failed resistance to the homeland/culture of Chinese collectivism forms the major thematics in *The Monkey King.* In *Sour Sweet,* the collectivity, in the form of the criminal Triad society, destroys Chen, and survives in the form of the more benevolent matriarchal family of Lily, represented in the person of Son. In *The Redundancy of Courage,* Chineseness remains as a trace that overdetermines Ng's positionality as a citizen-outsider in the nation state of Danu. A social construct and category, "Chineseness" operates as a sensitized double-layered perspective of multiple diasporas, producing in Ng, the diasporic Chinese, the marked status of the refugee/witness to the horrors of genocide. Now euphemized as "ethnic cleansing," genocide denotes the extermination of subjects under the rule of territoriality, occurring when the ideology of a homeland erases the human rights of individuals.

The Monkey King's examination of this thematics is perhaps the lightest among Mo's novels. A domestic novel set in Hong Kong of the seventies, it critiques Sino culture through situating the novel's point-of-view in a putative non-Chinese character. Wallace Nolasco's "Portuguese" Macao ethnicity serves to bracket "Chinese" as a race. The novel's opening passage deconstructs both Portuguese and Chinese ethnicity as unstable identities: "Centuries of mixed marriages with the Cantonese had obliterated whatever had been distinctive about their shadowy buccaneer ancestors" (3). Wallace enters into an arranged marriage with May Ling who, as daughter of Mr. Poon and his second concubine, "was lucky not to have been sold into a brothel" (7). The match testifies to Mr. Poon's genius in negotiating the values of Chinese civil society to achieve a very communal goal: "What Mr. Poon wanted was posterity, the more the better. . . . Even a concubine's grandchildren could venerate an ancestor" (8). Wallace enters the Poon family as a commodified object whose value lies in his potential usefulness to the Chinese family [10]: "It would be possible to economise on the initial capital outlay of the dowry to balance out defrayments on an additional mouth. . . . And while not a celestial, Wallace was not a real *faan gwai lo,* a foreign devil. Compromise was at the centre of Mr Poon's political system, and in securing Wallace he had achieved such a balance" (8).

The novel's comedy lies in tracing Wallace's resistance to the Poon political system, whose eccentric economies coupled with hidden wealth are lambasted: "The quantities of food served would have been sufficient for three hungry adults. Eight, and in the school vacations the adolescent grandsons as well, sat down to the round wooden table" (13). Wallace's outsider position in the family, dramatized as domestic battles over food and minor privileges, affects his marital relationship: "Mr. Poon had not exactly welched on his obligations but Wallace had voluntarily turned his back on the dowry; he would not give something for nothing. Mr Poon could expect no grandsons from him in the future" (58). Wallace resists the domestic economy of the

Confucianist family. Rejecting the dowry, and therefore getting nothing, he also ethically could give nothing. Male sexuality, necessary for the continuance of the patrilocal and patrilineal system, is reduced to a commodity; but Wallace's refusal to exchange it asserts his rights as an individual over and against the rights of the collective.

However, as the novel proceeds to demonstrate, the individual cannot withstand the hegemonic pull of the Chinese family. Exiled to a village in the New Territories after being manipulated into a civil act of corruption by his father-in-law, Wallace falls into the community burial grave, an accident that sets a series of incidents into motion, and that stirs up trouble between the Cantonese villagers and British authorities. Averting a bloody war between the Cantonese and their Hakka neighbors, Wallace causes a lake to form, then leads the villagers to exploiting the lake as a weekend resort for Hong Kong urbanites. His rejection of May's early suggestion — "You thought I could make myself boss of your father house just like you were saying? Things just didn't ever happen like that" (116) — proves incorrect. As the Monkey King of the novel's title, his intelligence, wit, and audacity result in his assuming the patriarchal position in the Poon household after Mr. Poon's death, displacing Ah Lung, the spend-thrift legal son.[11] Mr. Poon's will, repeating the Confucianist ideal of the "supreme man," "kept [Ah Lung] in perpetual tutelage . . . a concrete, persistent reminder of his unevolved condition" (199). Forming a part-nership with Fong, his sister-in-law, Wallace becomes the economic manager for Mrs. Poon, and has a son, whose "wrinkled, simian features," suggesting the patrilineal continuance of the Monkey King, signifies the Chinese family's triumphant survival: "If anything, it looked like Mr. Poon, reincarnated" (210).

The conclusion, therefore, subverts the plot of resistance and under-lines the syncretic power of the Sino familial community as it absorbs the resisting individual into its collective maw. Wallace's rebellion against the Confucianist patriarch, which concludes in his becoming "boss of your father [sic] house," is thoroughly ironized. The subject's revolt ends with the cooptation of that individual into the Confucianist structure. Wallace's dream of a banquet where diners feast on a living monkey's brains symbolizes his unconscious recognition that his ascendancy to Monkey King marks the loss of his status as an individual subject; indeed, his intelligence becomes merely a commodity to be consumed by the Chinese family. The image of cannibalistic sacrifice of the individual to the Chinese socius shades *The Monkey King* as a darker novel that its comic texture would suggest.

This critique is further developed in *Sour Sweet*, a novel which continues to be misread as a comedy.[12] In *Sour Sweet*, Mo charges the world of the English novel, set in London, with a diasporic perspective that unsettles the traditional notion of British nationality and polity. Paul Gilroy's remarks on the concept of the African diaspora are enlightening in relation to the horizon of intercultural expectations in which *Sour Sweet* operates. Speaking of "some new intermediate concepts, between the local and the global," Gilroy argues that such concepts "break the dogmatic focus on national cultures and traditions which has characterized so much Euro-American cultural thought. Getting beyond this national and nationalistic perspective is essential," he adds, because of "the postmodern eclipse of the modern nation-state as a political, economic, and cultural unit" (188). Concepts of diasporic perspectives question the integrity of cultures and the relationship between nationality and ethnicity. Following on Gilroy's diasporic framing of the Afro-American experience, I argue that the Chinese British experience constructed in *Sour Sweet* must be read as "continuous with a hemispheric order that is . . . explicitly anti-ethnic," and that the identities of Chinese in Mo's novels must be read as "a matter of politics rather than a purely cultural condition" (196).

Just as there are two civil societies in the novel, the British and the Chinese, so the novel treats two families, Chen's extended family — composed of his wife Lily, her sister Mui, their child Mun Kee, and later his father — and the Hung Triad "family," whose international network of diverse individuals knitted into an economic collectivity offers a criminal mirroring of the Confucianist family. The novel's structure interpellates one family with the other (chapters 2, 4, 6, 8, 13, 16, 18, 20, 24, 30, 33, and 35 specifically treat the Triad family), a device that shadows, juxtaposes, and imprisons the domestic family within the criminal family. The Triad family is not strictly an imagined family. Based on Mo's research, information on the Triad's hierarchical structure, initiation rituals, global criminal links, and so forth, is taken from two works on Hong Kong Triad societies.[13]

John Rothfork has argued that *Sour Sweet* dramatizes "the rectification or renewal of an authentic Confucianism leading to [an] authoritatively human life" (64). But, as *The Monkey King* intimates, Mo's criticism of Confucianist forms of social control in *Sour Sweet* abjures a recuperation of "authentic Confucianism."[14] Immigrating to the United Kingdom, Chen, the diasporic male subject, has been emptied of cultural and social significance. While "Chen had lost his claim to clan land in his ancestral village," he has gained no identity in the United Kingdom except as "an interloper," "a foreigner," "a gatecrasher who had stayed too long and been identified" (1). His life is a calculated servitude: "seventy-two hours in the restaurant, slept fifty-six, spent forty hours with his wife," and so forth. His marriage further strips him of any autonomy. Lily, a watchful, controlling wife whose actions are governed by Chinese cultural beliefs in "dualistic male and female principles of harmony" (2), permits him no space for his individual responses.

Lily is associated significantly with the Triad society that finally kills Chen. Her "masterful" personality comes from her childhood training in Chinese boxing with her father, a famous practitioner of *sui lum* temple boxing (11). The leader of the Hung Triad society in London is Red Cudgel, who had been a fellow fighter of Lily's father.   Thus, even as he was manipulated out of his leadership position in the Triad, he "was most insistent that reparation should be made to [Chen's] widow and family. . . . [because of the] community of feeling between fighters" (264). This "community of feeling," a construction of social dutifulness within a Confucianist-ordered hierarchy, is ironically called upon by the assassin after Chen's murder. The Triad society's use of the Chinese kinship system as its principal form of organization (the officers call each other "Elder Brother" or "younger sister" to signify hierarchical status and power) reproduces Confucianist values in which the individual is subordinated to the group. This doubling narrative device, paralleling Lily's control of her husband and sister and the Triad ringleaders' control of their criminal organization, underlines the similarities between domestic and public spheres in Confucianist-ruled communities. Chen's eventual entrapment in the Triad's machinations, his murder, is a. fate only a degree more extreme than his entrapment in Lily's machinations and his psychological withering.

To Lily, Chen is only "Husband" without an individual name; and a husband, moreover, in whom she is disappointed. She finds him "uninspired" (7), but maintains towards him a proper ritualized attitude: "Whatever her well-stifled misgivings, she intended to be a good wife to him. All these new characteristics she incorporated into a revised assessment of Husband — one which remained loyally high" (198). To Lily, Chen's humanity as an individual is erased in his role as "Husband." In contrast, Lily's relationship with her sister Mui comes from an emotional intimacy that humanizes the two women. As Chen noticed, "those two sisters were rather obviously good friends. Life had been going on behind his back; life of a gay, irresponsible, female kind" (108). The women on this Confucianist stage are presented as vital. Their intimacy affords them a vitality denied to Chen, whose only escape is in gardening, an expression of his peasant roots and his immigrant condition: the flourishing garden showed "Chen's skills as a farmer were not lost. At home in the New Territories vegetable growing was an ignominious mode of agriculture, practised by refugees and immigrants. It was fitting he should grow them here in alien soil" (168).

Chinese diasporic culture, in reproducing those Confucianist state and social controls that arguably form the core of Chinese culture,[15] is critiqued as a social economic system in which the individual subject is violently consumed (as in Wallace's dream in *The Monkey King)* or violently exterminated (as with Chen in *Sour Sweet)*. Chen's death, therefore, leaves no emotional aftermath for Lily, as long as "the remittances kept coming" (278). In fact, Lily forgives his supposed abandonment of the family, the ultimate Confucianist sin, in the light of his supposed economic caring of the family. The conclusion suggests that the patriarchal construction of the Chinese family is ironically a matriarchal conspiracy to preserve what is of primary importance to women, the future of their off-springs. Far from being devastated by the loss of the male, Lily is set free by his disappearance: "it was as if a stone had been taken off her and she had sprung to what her height should have been" (278). "Husband" is after all an expendable object once he has fulfilled his function in the Confucianist matriarchy: "She might have lost Husband for a while but she still had Son. Who could take him away from her?" (278).

Mo's last novel, *The Redundancy of Courage,* treats the Chinese diasporic subject in a different political world. Mo turns away from the critique of colonialism and Confucianist social organization to a representation of the place of the diasporic subject in postcolonial and neocolonial contexts. The narrator-protagonist, Adolph Ng, is a citizen of Danu, a state which is a thinly disguised version of Portuguese Timor. Adolph is self-consciously reflective of his multiple identities. However, in contrast to postmodernist fictions that play on ambiguity and instability, Adolph, like Chen, is imagined as a stolid or solid personality. He possesses a recognizable core of psychological features: worldly intelligence, sensitivity to his problematic identity as Chinese diasporic and citizen of a non-Chinese state, loyalty and affection to friends, and a strong will to survive. In naming himself "Ng," he names his identity as Chinese: "You know I am of the Chinese race" (24). Race, he suggests, is not the most important feature of his character. He is "a citizen o the great world," a cosmopolitan, and his "modernity" makes him, like Wallace and Chen, an outsider in his home country, which is "a desolate place" (24). Adolph's race, nationality, and subject are three different constructs that are straddled by the force of a cultural value, "Chinese pragmatism" (24).

The novel demonstrates the operation of Chinese pragmatism as a survival mode, first when Adolph's security is threatened by a civil war between contending Danuese nationalist forces that are racially divided, then by the neocolonialist invasion of the "malai" forces. Mo does not valorize Chinese pragmatism; in fact, the narrator establishes a critical distance from this cultural mode which is criticized as simultaneously producing and produced by an economic rationality that subordinates all political systems: "Most Chinese didn't give a damn about politics, independence or dependency, it was all one and the same to them. . . . Exploitation was the name of the game. We'd always done it and were cheerfully continuing the tradition of our ancestors. Rip-off didn't begin to describe it" (7).

The novel opens with a chapter describing the malai invasion of Danu, "parachutes dropping" (3), the massacre of women, children, and civilians, and the brutal murder of an Australian journalist. The malais,[16] we are told, have a history of massacres: "They'd killed hundreds of thousands in their own country: communists, socialists, liberals even" (20). The neocolonialist moment, presented as a fascist genocidal scene, is almost unbearably particular in its reportorial strategy, while verging on the macabrely lyrical. The novel moves through two extreme visions, of humans' hateful destruction and nature's indifferent beauty. Thus, at the conclusion to the litany of murders and mayhem, Mo contrasts the corpse of the Australian journalist "shrinking into a semi-foetal position and quite black now in the middle of the flames" with "the shoals of giant white jelly fish" that "hung in the clear water like ghostly canopies, suspended . . . in a fall they suggest but would never make" (23).

As narrator and protagonist, Adolph distinguishes himself from the "'blind' Chinaman with his eyes in the trough along with his snout" (54). He is a politicized, articulate consciousness serving as commentator on decolonizing and neocolonizing dynamics of collapsing and new empires (55). Tracing the course of rising nationalism, Adolph follows the Danuese "autonomists" as they are drawn into civil war through greed and power politics (56). Adolph understands that in this nativist/nationalist drama, he "didn't have a piece of the action," "that I was Chinese and treated as such" (58).

But it is the non-native nationalist who is entrusted with telling the story of the Danuese, with keeping alive the political memory of an incipient nation. Adolph begins the narrative: "I didn't want them forgotten: Rosa, Osvaldo, Raoul, Maria, Martinho, Arsenio" (3). Ironically, the diasporic subject, rejected by native Danuese as non-national, must carry the weight of moral authority and national history, both threatened by the supranational history of the malais, whose assault on central human morals concerning the value of individual lives and respect for others' freedom demonstrates the evil of neocolonialist ideology.

Adolph flees into the jungle with the Danuese resistance forces, and when he is captured by the malais, survives by serving as a domestic slave to the malai general's wife. When he finally buys his freedom, he leaves for "the Home Country" in Europe — evidently Portugal — thence to Brazil. Adolph is three times denied a community: first from China, the country of his ancestors; then in Danu, among his nationalist friends who deny him a national identity; then by the malais who reduce him to the ultimate *subjectless* condition, of slavery. The survivor of colonialist and neocolonialist violence, Adolph is eager to leave the past behind and begin a future someplace else: "I didn't care if . . . the pangs of birth were ugly; I wanted to be somewhere I wouldn't be defined by what I'd been, where I could fashion a new notion of myself and impose it on others as the truth" (402). The diasporic desire carries the individual toward the hope of an imagined subject identity in a new country.

However, the novel does not conclude on this birth of a new subject. The old subject persists and cannot be rewritten. In this way, Mo's novel is unambiguously modernist rather than postmodern, for it asserts the identity of the individual as the value by which history, civilization, and morality are measured. Adolph recognizes,

I could not terminate Adolph Ng so conveniently. I was trying to accomplish within my own small person what the malais hadn't been able to do to a nation. An identity and a history cannot be obliterated. I arrived in the vastness of a new country as what I thought a *tabula rasa* but there was writing underneath, the coded determinants of what I was and always would be inscribed. (406)

The inextinguishable identity of the individual resists the evils of totalitarianism. "One woodchuck" is always left in the torched field, a trope for the innocent and weak creature of nature, the unprotected human, that will persist in defeating the fascists' project of genocide. Stripped of the protective group status of race and nation, Ng nonetheless receives this saving illumination.

The novel concludes with these modern interrogations of the individual's identity within the competing categories of nation, race, and world. For a diasporic character like Ng, his "story"/history as Danuese citizen is no "regnant cliché" of race and identity politics[17] but the very ground on which the totalizing obliteration of genocide is combated. Mo's novels do not complacently enthrone the subject as sovereign; in fact, they represent this subject condition as historically contingent, entrapped, threatened by erasure, and fragile. But they speak for the necessity for the preservation and liberation of this subject as the only defense against the violence of the collectivity, whether it is the collectivity of the Confucianist family, the Triad society, or the totalitarian state.

1992

Notes

1. See Timothy Brennan, "Cosmopolitans and celebrities," *Race and Class*. Brennan reads in the post-war Western sociologists' and historians' criticism of nationalism an attack on the project of decolonization in the Third World. While Brennan's term, "cosmopolitanism," and Bhabha's term, "transnational," are different, Brennan's deployment of "cosmopolitanism" suggests an analogue to Bhabha's notion of the intellectual who speaks from a "liminal form of cultural identification": "spokespersons for a kind of perennial immigration, valorized by a rhetoric of wandering, and rife with allusions to the all-seeing eye of the nomadic sensibility" (2).

2. Bhabha's ideas on the transnational are more complex and contradictory than are expressed in this one particular essay. In "DissemiNation," he argues that the established "liminality of the nation-state" transforms the threat of cultural difference from "outside" to "within," and quotes approvingly Foucault's description of "the marginalistic integration of the individual in the social totality" (301-2). Minority discourse, however, "contests genealogies of 'origin' that lead to claims of cultural supremacy and historical priority" (307). It is only by "living on the borderline of history and language, on the limits of race and gender, that we are in a position to translate the differences between them into a kind of solidarity" (320). In arguing for "culture's transnational dissemination," Bhabha appears to assume a depoliticized/demilitarized transnational cultural dynamics that Mo's novel, *The Redundancy of Courage,* demonstrates in the historical decolonizing moment, albeit through fiction, as impossible.

3. Mo was born in 1953 in Hong Kong and attended Oxford University; he is over a decade younger than Kingston (*Contemporary Authors* 301).

4. According to Kingston, her "books are much more American than they are Chinese. I felt that I was building, creating myself and these people as American people to make everyone realize that these people are American people. Also I am creating part of American literature. . . . The critics haven't recognized my work enough as another tradition of American literature" (Rabinowitz 182).

5. See Kingston's interview with Paula Rabinowitz where she distinguishes between her "memories" of a China she has never seen and China itself. She had avoided visiting China because "Going off to China would have meant the creation of, and the beginning of, another memory" (178).

6. Spivak in *The Postcolonial Critic* speaks of the practical politics of the open end, when "some kind of massive ideological act" and "the everyday maintenance of practical politics" each "brings the other to productive crisis" and "neither is privileged" (105). In Kingston's concluding chapter, one can read the notion of the Chinese diaspora as a massive ideological act and the conversations of various nationals of Chinese ancestry as "practical politics."

7. This essay does not discuss Mo's third novel, *An Insular Possession* as it offers other challenges not within the scope of the essay.

8. Lynn Pan defines the pioneering Overseas Chinese community unproblematically as synonymous with the Chinese diaspora: all those people who can trace their origins to Chinese ancestry and who maintain the speech and customs of the provinces from which their forefathers had come (1-22).

9. As a British subject originally from Hong Kong, Mo's diplomatic status may be said to figure the transnational condition. "Transnational" is a currently preferred term that underlines the mobility, instability, and porous national borders that characterize the movements of global populations.

10. The novel's construction of an insider/outsider liminal position through Wallace's resistance to and eventual absorption into the syncretic Confucianist familial unit can be read as an analogue to Hong Kong's position vis-a-vis China and Mo's satirical stance on post-1997 when Hong Kong will revert to the People's Republic of China.

11. The novel's title and metaplay refer to the Chinese classic, *Monkey,* in which the protagonist, Monkey, creates havoc among the hierarchical levels of gods and goddesses. An epic comedy as well as a religious text, *Monkey* underlines Buddhist valuation of cosmic harmony and right living at the same time that it valorizes the energy and subversive transgressiveness of its lowly hero.

12. *Sour Sweet* has chiefly been constructed as a comedy by its Anglo-American reviewers and publishers; the paper back version of the novel carries a blurb from *The Listener* praising Mo's "delicious gingery sense of humour." Overlooking the lurid psychological and physical violence enacted within the diasporic Chinese cultural system, Peter Lewis in the *Times Literary Supplement* misses the level of Mo's expose of the Chinese Triadic global crime network in *Sour Sweet* and focuses on the text as a late twentieth-century Austen social comedy: "He has a very sharp eye indeed for the nuances of behaviour in close-knit social units" (cited in *Contemporary Authors* 302).

13. For example, Stanton 1900; Morgan 1960. Similarly, Mo tells us that he "supplemented personal knowledge with sociological and anthropological studies" in his representation of the rural community in *The Monkey King.*

14. A notion that indicates Rothfork's essentializing move as coming out of a Western tradition of "orientalizing" Chinese society.

15. See Perry Link's "China's 'Core' Problem" for a sympathetic summary of the hegemony of Confucianism ruling "most of China's imperial history of the last thousand years" (192). As Link notes, the "answer" to the fundamental question of how society in China should be organized was "originally a Confucian one, but after centuries of custom now so deeply rooted in Chinese culture that it tends to appear almost reflexively" (191).

16. A fictional term to suggest the Indonesian forces that invaded the island nation of Timor in 1975. Declaring Timor to be Indonesia's 27th province, the Indonesian state has put down the Timorese resistance; between 100,000 and 200,000 people have been killed. The national language of Indonesia is Malay, coincidentally the national language of Malaysia

17. A phrase used by Gates and Appiah in their editorial introduction to the special issue of *Critical Inquiry* devoted to Identities.

Works Cited

Ang, Ien. "Migrations of Chineseness." *SPAN* 34 & 35, Oct. 1992/May 1993: 3-15.

Appiah, Kwame Anthony and Henry Louis Gates, Jr. "Editors' Introduction: Multiplying Identities." *Critical Inquiry* 18 (Summer 1992): 625-29.

Bhabha, Homi K. "DissemiNation: time, narrative, and the margins of the modern nation." In *Nation and Narration,* edited by Homi K. Bhabha. London and New York: Routledge, 1990. 291-322.

———. "Postcolonial Authority and Postmodern Guilt." In *Cultural Studies,* eds. Lawrence Grossberg, Cary Nelson, and Paula Treichler. New York: Routledge, 1992. 56-68.

Brennan, Timothy. "Cosmopolitans and celebrities." *Race and Class* 13:1, July-Sept. 1989: 1-19.

Contemporary Authors. 117. Detroit: Gale Research Co., 1986: 301-2.

Gilroy, Paul. "Cultural Studies and Ethnic Absolutism." In *Cultural Studies,* eds. L. Grossberg, et al. 187-198.

Kingston, Maxine Hong. *The Woman Warrior.* New York: Knopf, 1976.

———. *China Men.* New York: Knopf, 1980.

Link, Perry. "China's 'Core' Problem." *Daedalus* 122:2 (Spring 1993): 189-205.

Mo, Timothy. *The Monkey King.* London: Sphere Books, 1978.

———. *Sour Sweet.* New York: Vintage, 1985, 1st pub. 1982.

———. *An Insular Possession.* London: Chatto & Windus, 1986.

———. *The Redundancy of Courage.* London: Chatto & Windus, 1991.

Pan, Lynn. *Sons of the Yellow Emperor: A History of the Chinese Diaspora.* Boston: Little, Brown, 1990.

Rabinowitz, Paula. "Eccentric Memories: A Conversation with Maxine Hong Kingston." *Michigan Quarterly Review* 26 (1987): 177-87.

Rothfork, John. "Confucianism in Timothy Mo's Sour Sweet." *Journal of Commonwealth Literature.* 1990: 49-64.

Spivak, Gayatri. *The Post-Colonial Critic.* Ed. Sarah Harasym. New York: Routledge, 1990.

Wu Ch'eng-en (c.a. 1500 - c.a. 1582). *The Monkey King.* London: P. Hamlyn, 1965.

PART THREE

MALAYSIAN / SINGAPOREAN WRITING IN ENGLISH

The English-Language Writer in Singapore
(1940s - 1980s)

In this chapter, the term "local" or "Singapore literature" includes all "Malayan" English-language writing of the imagination from the 1940s to 1965, and, from 1965 onwards with Singapore's separation from Malaysia, only such writing as comes from the newly established state of Singapore.[1]

"Ideology" refers to a set or sets of beliefs, either formally established (as in a nation's constitution or pledge of allegiance) or having a fairly conscious and formulated existence (Eagleton 1976). According to most observers of the Singapore scene, there are two major ideological frames in Singapore. One is that of nation-building, which includes pursuing a pluralistic or multi-ethnic policy and the specific language policy of bilingualism, meaning proficiency in English and in the mother tongue — whether Mandarin, Malay, or Tamil. The other is modernization, which includes changing traditional social characteristics to those more amenable to industrialization, internationalism, high technology; for example, attitudes of efficiency, rationality, high achievement, flexibility and so on. In the directions prescribed by these major ideological orientations, specific institutions and policies have been modified or created; for example, the Housing and Development Board program to break down ethnic separations, "purposive" education to achieve a scientific and technocratic labor force, and National Service, to create national identity, patriotism and virtues of ruggedness, preparedness and total defence, all of which support the "survival" mind-set of the ruling party.[2]

The English-language writers' position vis-a-vis these politically articulated ideals appears generally fairly simple and clear. It is difficult to find in Singapore any writer who has explicitly accepted these ideologies and made it his business to be a spokesman for them. Whether or not the writer individually and privately, as a citizen, supports the push for nation-building and modernization, most evidence up to date shows the English-language writer adapting an aesthetical ideology, that the writer is, above all, committed to his art.

The oppositional nature of literary debate in Indonesia, in contrast, where the quarrel between writers who maintain the autonomy of literary values — an art for art's sake attitude — and those who believe "literature has a mission," that is, between aestheticians and the socially committed, is still as vital today as when President Sukarno banned the Manifes

Kubudayaan in 1965.[3] In the Philippines, a similar quarrel between the followers of Jose Villa, the arch-aesthete, and Salvador Lopez, the 1940s self-styled socialist spokesman for socially committed literature, is practically over. During the Marcos regime, writers either went underground or spoke openly on political issues, with some of them working for the Marcos Administration as press secretaries and palace spokesmen. Filipino writers not only feel that it is their duty to be politically involved, they expect that they have important roles, as writers, in the nation's destiny.[4]

In Singapore, however, the English-language writer (who is frequently an employee in the Civil Service) seems to hold hard to his special status as artist. By appealing to the Western liberal tradition of the autonomy of the artistic domain, he appeals to features of objectivity, creative freedom and the absolute nature of literary standards which effectively separate, protect, and insulate the writer from external social forces and pressures. In 1984 Arthur Yap, one of Singapore's foremost poets, said in an interview, "I don't think it's a poet's business to be a spokesman of any kind. . . . I'm not a person who wants to write poems with a political basis or a social basis, commenting upon society as such. As a writer my commitment is to writing" (Sullivan 8).

Such a statement is neither shocking nor new in the Singapore literary scene. In 1969, Edwin Thumboo, a leading literary figure in the nation, said:

> I have always thought the poet is an individual aware of, if not actually guarding, his freedom. His position in the consciousness of his society is fluid. He is seldom the norm, working out of what is 'doctrinal to the nation.' Nor does he reflect the ethos of his community for either our convenience or as a primary purpose of his poetry. . . . Indeed, we should be surprised if he were not wise enough to avoid dealing with National Identity. To take to it would be to risk his personal identity, his own image of himself. For National Identity implies a summing up of attributes, a levelling off. And what profiteth a man if he gaineth National Identity, but loseth the power of his poetry? (Goodwin 195)

Earlier, in 1963, D. J. Enright, then Johore Professor of English Literature at the University of Malaya in Singapore, criticized the Malay and Chinese writers who had spoken up for a socially committed literature during the 1962 Malayan Writers Conference. "At the moment the Malayan writer's head is likely to be so full of what he has been told about his duty, his role, his obligations, that he may never be able to work out his own artistic destiny." Literature, he added, was not "simple instruction, the teaching of ethics, of religion, of civics" but "only exists by virtue of being true art and conforming to the severe but indefinable laws of art." Prior to this expatriate Englishman's defense of the autonomy of art, a local writer, Choo Liang Haw, wrote in 1962, "If a writer will say anything because of the Government's command and not out of his personal conviction, then he is no more than 'a venal hack'. . . . [The writer] must expose the pernicious implications . . . about identification with the masses, the need for political commitment, and the invincibility of the historical process" (29).

The majority of Singapore English-language writers, likewise, see the domain of art as separate from the domain of the state (that is, expressed as the government, as national identity or as the public), and reject any attempt on the part of the state to take literature under its sphere of influence. This autonomy, this rejection, in almost all cases, has meant a separation of the themes and content of the work from the themes and content of state ideology.

Such a separation of the writer from political and social involvement was absent from pioneering efforts of the first undergraduates to try consciously to create a Malayan literature. The most important figure in the early period was Wang Gungwu whose 1950 collection of poems, *Pulse,* is the first English-language publication in the country. As Wang (1950) tells us, he was then deliberately using Malayan images and Malayan subjects in order to create a Malayan consciousness. In his twelve poems, he explores Malayan landscapes and local color:

> The crowds wait their share of the steaming fun
> at the kuey-teow stalls of the kerosene glare.
> ("Three Faces of Night" 14)

and attempts to discover Malayan themes and experiences: the young illegitimate girl raised by a greedy aunt, "A barren bag of nerves," to be a prostitute ("Investment" 6); the adolescent play during a beach party ("Mata Ikan Laughter" 10-11); and Chinese New Year celebrations ("Add One" 5). Wang was conscious throughout his innovations, was perhaps freed to innovate because of this consciousness, that "we persisted . . . not so much for the art of poetry as for the ideal of the new Malayan consciousness. The emphasis in our search for Malayan poetry was in the word 'Malayan'" (Wang 1958, 6). In short, Wang saw his literary efforts as subsumed by a larger effort to discover a national identity. Prophetically, even then, Wang's idea of national identity correlates very closely with the present ideology of pluralistic cultures to form one nation. "What it was that we called 'Malayan' was no less difficult to determine than it is now," he wrote in 1958. "Most of the time we were merely hopeful that the three major communities would throw up from their native or imported civilizations the material for a new synthesis. . . . This synthetic product would then be infused with the stuff of European poetry and bound firmly in the English-language. This was cosmopolitan art and we had come around to thinking that Malayan poetry would have to be cosmopolitan" (7).

Why did this first impetus, the tradition of the writer as involved, committed to the evolution of national identity and national destiny, fizzle out? And why has the counter-tradition, of the writer as solely committed to his art and jealous of his freedom from historical process and social forces, developed so strongly in its place?

One reason is that English-language writing has never freed itself from the overwhelming effects of British colonialism. The continued dominance of English literature in the school curriculum, the official support of standard English which is both respectable and prestigious internationally, and the continued authority of British-liberal-educated leaders in decision-making positions — all have implications for the writer. One is the exonomous nature of literary standards and criteria for achievement; hence the continued emphasis on the 'absolute' nature of literary values (by which obviously is meant the dominance of the British canon). The pressure on the local writer is to demonstrate his ability against an external, cosmopolitan standard — which pushes him away from nationalistic social concerns and values. Ee Tiang Hong representatively expresses this distinctly international orientation implied in the "art for art's sake" stance as a higher and nobler universalistic concern:

> the poet . . . is responsible only for his art and to himself. . . . To these questions [of nationalism], I would suggest that the writer has no part to play, not consciously and directly, anyway. . . . it is not only the immediate society or circumstance he is concerned with, but the larger society of man, a society composed not only of Malays, Chinese and Indians but of the countless variety of peoples spread over all the breadth and corners of the world. The whole world is his fountain. (1971, 120-21)

Moreover, the continued influence of English literature also signifies the continued acceptance of Western liberal ideology concerning the freedom of the artist from social constraints, a belief expressed so frequently as to be *ipso facto* an article of faith for any self-respecting writer in the English-language world.

Paul Tabori notes in *Solidarity* (1972) that, "To speak of the writer's 'obligation' to society is itself an insult. He has obligations, certainly, as a tax payer or as a voter — but not in the practice of his craft. *There* his sole obligation is to his talent and his ideas" (57). E. M. Forster said of poetry, "We have entered a universe that only answers to its own laws, supports itself, internally coheres, and has a new standard of truth. . . . A poem points to nothing but itself. Information is relative. A poem is absolute." And the dominant schools of literary criticism from the appearance of the New Criticism movement in the 1930s onwards have spoken for an intrinsic rather than extrinsic approach to literature, to move away from contextual — except for the most limited biographical — readings to a purely textual analysis.

Yet in other societies that possess similar features to Singapore, writers have not so wholeheartedly adopted the aesthetical line nor so totally abandoned the possibility for the writers to have a stronger, firmer relationship to their society. In Nigeria, Chinua Achebe's career and powerful novels demonstrate that it is possible for writers to write from "a social basis," to articulate social obligations, and still to produce high literature with significance for their nation and the international community. Derek Walcott, for all his international reputation, keeps returning to his island sources and searching for more ways to include social concerns in his work. His dramas are politically and socially assertive, nativized technically and linguistically.

What are the consequences, if any, of this aesthetical stance? It seems to me that at least two related consequences are perceivable. One is the confusion of social with institutional or political (and therefore partisan) spheres. In so much as writers value their freedom from political and institutional objectives, their definition of art tends to constrict to exclude any reflection or representation of political and institutional concern and activity. In small, modernizing Singapore, political and institutional bureaucracies have intruded and to some extent taken over the public and social spheres (Busch 1972), and to that extent must these writers be deprived of the motivation to write about these spheres. There emerges the danger for the writers that in insisting on their separation from social and political concerns, that is, in attempting to "depoliticize" their work in a society where many social features have become imbued with political significance, they will find themselves further and further alienated from that society in which their choice of a non-indigenous language and their Westernized education have already marked them as different. The ironic tragedy lies in the strong possibility that that society that they remove themselves from, in consequence, will find them irrelevant.

Finally, of course, it becomes a chicken-and-egg question. Does the larger society find no function, no role, for writers because writers have removed themselves from social involvement, or do the writers, outcast and disempowered by society which finds them irrelevant, reject social claims as pernicious, pedestrian and damaging? The perceived reality depends on who is doing the talking.

A young Singaporean poet, Simon Tay, condemns the purposive approach to education that, by emphasizing the importance of the science and technologies, works against interest in literature. "Our best minds," he laments, "are not drawn to the role of the writer because the writer is not recognized and accepted; because the writer in our society is no one's hero" (58). "Literature in Singapore is not recognized as a source of vital, vigorous and possible change-bringing elements but as a simple auxilliary to life" (59). Yet this conclusion is almost inevitable when writers insist that to impute social obligation to them is insulting. One cannot be a hero to a society one refuses to join. Tay's anger, while directed against social forces hostile to the relevance of writers for the nation, recognizes that social indifference has actual implications for the writer's art, for the writer "may suffer an otherness" so complete as to render his talents useless to society. It may also "impoverish him of ideas and ideals and leave him with little else but a biting and ultimately shallow disregard for his society" (58).

The writer's separation from immediate social concerns is an idea almost totally accepted by Singapore's political leaders. Unlike President Soekarno, who, in banning the Manifes Kebudayaan, was rejecting the writer's right to autonomous artistic concerns and insisting that politics was part of literature and literature part of politics, Singapore's politicians generally reflect the attitude that, as Simon Tay tells us, literature is "a simple auxilliary to life." Koh Tai Ann tells us that, "Because of the intimate link between literature and language and the seemingly gratuitous nature of the former, associated as it often is with a private enlightenment and pleasure, literature has either been deemphasized for political reasons or disregarded for pragmatic economic reasons" (Koh 1980, 303). In support of her argument, she cites these examples: in 1968, the Prime Minister, Mr Lee Kuan Yew, in an address at the University of Singapore said, "Poetry is a luxury we cannot afford." In 1978, he elaborated further, "Literature and heritage or tradition are different altogether. What is important for pupils is not literature, but a philosophy of life . . . a value system. . . . This is an important matter which is concerned not with poetry or literature, but with relationships — the relationship between brothers and sisters, and between friends" (304). Koh disagrees with these statements, adding that "the Prime Minister for political reasons was downplaying the function of literature in education and culture" and that "above all, literature is concerned with values and therefore with human relationships" (304).

Yet, are her objections well-founded? Could not the Prime Minister be simply reflecting, indeed accepting wholly, the Singapore writers' own doctrinal "art for art's sake" position? It is difficult for a public official properly to include literature as educationally useful for the teaching of moral and social relationships when he has been told by the writers themselves that "The writer's only responsibility is his art. . . . I myself am too busy to care about the public" (William Faulkner, quoted approvingly by Choo, 25); "Literature . . . largely conceived of as simple instruction, the teaching of ethics, of religion, of civics, is [a world] in which there would be no place for the truly original, truly imaginative writer" (Enright 1963, 21); "A poem points to nothing but itself" (E. M. Forster); "To speak of the writer's obligation to society is itself an insult . . . his sole obligation is to his talent and his ideas . . . the best society can do for the writer is to leave him alone . . . all creative artists must be fundamentally anarchist — certainly in their attitudes to the community, to the crowd" (Tabori 68); the poet "is responsible only to his art and to himself" (Ee 20); "I'm not a person who wants to write poems with a political basis or a social basis, commenting upon society as such. . . . as a writer my commitment is to writing" (Yap, in Sullivan 8). Compare these attitudes with the Singapore Chinese writer whose aim "is usually to air his views on certain issues but more often than not it reflects the contemporary thinking of society in general" (Kock 42). If English-language writers in Singapore find that literature and writers have no "function" in the nation, could it be that perhaps they have succeeded only too well in their ideological persuasions for the aesthetic position, and so have helped to dig their own graves?

The separation of writer from society, however, is not necessarily a corollary of the belief in the autonomous nature of the aesthetic domain. The alienation of the English-language writer from the public, that is, from his potential audience, has been exacerbated by the confusion of state with society. A writers' defence of artistic freedom does not signify the absence of social themes and interests but rather the absence of state or government-dictation in choice of themes and interests. Literary production is a social phenomenon, and is acted upon by economic, political, and cultural forces. Writers can and should demand freedom from social or political coercion, but this freedom is not synonymous with detachment from social or political concerns. While a work's artistic achievement is evaluated on literary criteria, the work is embedded in a social context. Flaubert's *Madame Bovary* — a literary triumph — reflects and expresses the views of a nineteenth-century bourgeois French world, and can be said to succeed partly as the reflections constitute a deeper (therefore more convincing) apprehension of characters, motivations and relationships of that particular society. When a defence of authors' freedom against external authorities and state intrusions (for example, as in the Soviet Union or in the People's Republic of China, where the state attempts to dictate writers' themes and styles) is confused with an unyielding insistence on total separation of art from society and a rejection of community and social involvement, writers may find themselves without a place in their own culture and country. The redundancy of English-language writing in Singapore, as Tay described it, reminds us that "The arts cannot cut themselves off from life. What they are in their essence, they can also be in the framework of the historical reality which gave them birth, and not in some shadow realm outside it" (Hartmann 46).

Although other societies have found places for the very private, individual, subjective, anarchic creators, the indigenous traditions of Singapore's immigrant peoples have little experience of such a tradition. The Malay writer, as Ismail Hussein pointed out, had always been perceived as a community and religious or moral teacher (94); Tamil poets wrote from a strong Hindu and Hindu mythological source; and Chinese poets, even in the contemplative and reclusive tradition, were rooted in their social world.[5] Western cultural traditions, as many sociologists have demonstrated, are only weakly grafted onto this Asian stock (see, for example, Gopinathan and Clammer).

The English-language writers' position in the evolution and formation of a Singapore destiny is further vitiated by the ideology underlying language policy in Singapore. After separation in 1965, Malay (although officially the national language) diminished in importance. English swiftly became the working language, the language of dominance. It was perceived as a bridge language (Thumboo 1977, 1984), capable of breaking down ethno-linguistic communal barriers among the Chinese (76 per cent of the population in 1986), Malays (15 per cent), Indians (7 per cent) and others (2 per cent). It was a neutral language, acceptable to all ethnic groups since it did not mean the language and culture dominance of any one group. It was conveniently a world language, essential to the modernization process in Singapore, a small country with hardly any natural resources and therefore wholly dependent on international trade, commerce and industrialization. For all these reasons, and because of Singapore's British colonial history and continued acceptance of British-style education policies and curriculum, English became the language of prestige and of elite professional groups (Kuo 1985). A mastery of English was deemed essential for economic success and social mobility. Although the government supported a policy of education in the three so-called mother tongues (Tamil, Mandarin, and Malay), these primary schools and even the powerful Chinese Nanyang University lost enrollment drastically.

The present language policy of bilingualism (meaning proficiency in English and a mother tongue) is meant to arrest the decline of proficiency in the mother tongues. The rationale behind this bilingual policy is that the mother tongues are the repositories of "Asian" values — associated with the positive attributes of thrift, industriousness, stable family life, respect for authority, heritage and so on — so providing an essential ballast to "Western" values — associated with the negative attributes of individualism, selfishness, hedonism, promiscuity, and social disintegration. It follows that, while the English-language can be promoted as a neutral and bridge language, it is also, although less openly so, feared as a language conveying Westernized debased values, whose use would lead to the eventual destruction of "Asian" identity and virtues (see Kuo and Gopinathan).

Obviously there exists a contradiction in the language policy as officially explained. English cannot be both a neutral and a Western-value-loaded medium; it cannot both help to bridge ethno-linguistic communities and destroy the integrity of these communities. In short, English is not in actuality either a neutral or a bridge language except in a rather simple-minded use of the terms. The English-language carries with it British and Western traditions and ideals; it is a strong transmitter of cosmopolitan values. Especially if it is used as a first language (as opposed to a second language with a limited function), it will break down ancient ethno-linguistic identities and threaten what Clifford Geertz called the "primordial sentiments" of the community that shape the individual's attachments to a larger social unit.[6] The obvious danger in this loss of traditional social identity is that of anomie, the condition in which individuals lose their traditional points of references and do not know who they are, where they belong, what their position and role in life are. According to Tham Seong Chee, "The fact that, in Singapore, the language of mobilization is an ethnic language and the language of participation is English may have resulted in a certain amount of alienation" (quoted in Kuo 37).

Many Singaporeans have suffered and will continue to suffer from this condition. In 1956, for example, Mr Lee Kuan Yew said of his own experiences: "There is a sense — I would not say of humiliation, but definitely of inadequacy — that I have not the same facility and control over my own language [as over English]" (quoted by Gordon 41). In 1978, at a National Day Rally Speech, Mr. Lee said, "A person who gets deculturalized — and I nearly was, so I know that danger — loses his self-confidence. He suffers from a sense of deprivation" (quoted in Clammer 22).

The English-language writer is faced with this bilingual ideology: that English cannot be a "mother tongue"; it expresses Western debased values; it is useful only for international trade and technological purposes (Jonathan Malicsi praises the Singapore language policy as one that "serves the purpose of technological development in the production, distribution, and consumption of technological products, as well as in learning from foreign technologies"); and not having mastery of his mother tongue (whether Mandarin, Tamil or Malay) signifies inadequacy, deprivation and deculturalization. He or she thus faces a severe handicap in legitimizing his or her place in the national culture.

Yet it is a fact, lamentable or otherwise, that many English-language Singapore writers have been monolingual. A. L. McLeod, in 1966, recognized that "the generation who acquired their university education in the 1950's. . . generally regarded English as their first language" (313). Ong Teong Hean in 1975 pointed out that since he was educated in the colonial period between 1935 to 1959, he was "monolingual [in English]" (Ong 1975a, 64). And Simon Tay, speaking of writers of the 1980s, notes that the English-language writers "have little choice . . . a generation, my generation, is emerging, of which many have little or no knowledge of another language" (57). In fact, a recent Singapore *Straits Times* survey on the Speak Mandarin Campaign found that "the younger generation prefer English to Mandarin, speaking more of the former to their children, spouses, and brothers and sisters,"[7] which points to an increasing proportion of the population favoring English as its first choice for communication at home.

However, this first language (if not yet a mother tongue) is ideologically upheld as separate from an Asian (that is, Singapore) identity. The very act of writing in English (even apart from writers' choice of message, subject or mood) must already be associated with "otherness," "alienation," and "Westernization," which raises a prime question: Can one write in English and still reflect Singapore (that is, Asian) values and identity? Can there be a Singaporean English-language writer?

At some level, the hardening of such confused, even primitive sentiments concerning language and mother-tongues into official ideology is counter-productive. Not only have few English-language writers emerged to flourish in Singapore's exciting, energetic and dynamic last twenty years, but even Mandarin, Malay and Tamil writing have suffered a decline or failed to take off. Wong Yoon Wah tells us, "Singapore's Chinese literature has a very small size of readership today." Reporting that there has been a decline in the sales of Chinese literary books, he adds that among Chinese readers "The general feeling is that literature as a whole has little or no role to play in modernizing countries like Singapore" (36). The once active Malay Writers Association now has a meagre membership of perhaps 50 writers, who are reduced to publishing and selling their own works (*Asiaweek* 5 July 1985, 51-54). In short, there has been no competition among the literatures of the various languages in Singapore — only a parallel decline in the readership and role for the writer.

But the English-language group, which is the only group to have significantly increased its members in the last two decades (in terms of speakers, literacy members, sales of books and across ethnic groups) still faces an ideology officially hostile to or skeptical of its integrity, identity, and creative power. As S. Gopinathan concludes, "The rather simplistic identification of English with the values of a technological, modernizing culture and of the various mother tongues with more enduring moral and social values which are seen as uniquely Eastern, does not offer sufficient help in the establishment of either conditions or directions with which to guide linguistic and cultural development" (292).

Singapore, as a new nation composed of an originally immigrant and pluralistic population, possesses no tradition of an indigenous, national literature. Writers in the mother tongues have to refer to traditions, styles and forms from their original mother cultures, that is, to Chinese, Indian, or Malay (including Indonesian) literary cultures, just as English-language writers generally take their criteria, styles, forms and references from the traditions of British and American literature. There has not yet been created in Singapore a sense of national literary tradition. One may point out skeptically that since 1948, according to one critic, there has been only eighty volumes and collections of Singapore English-language poetry, fourteen novels, sixteen biographies, twenty collections of stories, and a handful of plays (Koh Tai Ann 1985). Still, as a body, it is sufficient for a degree of self-consciousness about its national character to emerge.

Edward Shils, discussing the place of intellectuals (among whom he includes writers) in developing countries, points out that too often the "location of the intellectual center of gravity is foreign," a "displacement [that] arises from xenophilia," which is a pernicious element because "it manifests and fosters a severely deficient empathy for the states of mind of one's fellow countrymen, a lack of intimacy with the society" (1958a, 238). However, elsewhere, he is more optimistic about the anomic conditions to be found in such societies, for, he argues, "since . . . *anomie* and creativity are closely related to each other, the very situation which stimulates *anomie* also releases creative potentialities. Both consequences may co-exist in the same individual; in any case, they are certainly likely to co-exist in the same society" (1958b, 15). He pointed out that "the daring imagination, the readiness to enter into *terra incognita* where the lessons of the past are insufficient, the deep conviction and the unrelenting persistence and intensity of effort would appear to make the achievements of the great businessman as creative as the achievements of a great ruler or a great captain" (15). If we accept the notion that anomie, while it can disable, can also result in creative achievements in business and politics (achievements which are visible in Singapore today), we would again have to ask ourselves why English-language writers have not made as visible a mark on the nation's cultural and material face as have the politicians and businessmen. In a passage that still appears to be pertinent to Singapore writers today, Wang Gungwu explained that the Malayan English-educated group of the 1930s to 1950s failed to be intellectually creative "because they were too hurriedly and superficially westernized, too few in number, too busy or comfortable, drawn into prestigious and well-paid jobs." Moreover they did not have a large enough local audience, they could not compete with Malay and Chinese intellectuals for the Malay and Chinese-educated public, and their Western education, while it potentially gave them the largest audience in the world, ironically demanded high standards and a cosmopolitan sophistication which they could not cultivate (Wang 1981, 243-244). Kirpal Singh explains the paucity of novels in Singapore on "the exigencies of living in a very small, pluralistic society [that hinder] the frank expression of views and ideas. . . . One is, therefore, constantly on one's guard. In these circumstances, the writing of a good novel becomes virtually impossible. . . . The writer therefore, always conscious of his role and more of his duty, hesitates, becomes necessarily cautious, or resorts to the writing of a kind of novel that will inevitably prove unconvincing" (Singh 1984, 9). It would seem that the writers' lot in Singapore is made even less tenable by these material circumstances, of too much comfort or of too much closeness. Yet surely similar difficult circumstances have prevailed elsewhere, without necessarily suppressing literary achievement.[8]

There seems to be a consensus among literary and sociological observers that not enough Singapore literature has yet been produced to give rise to a sense of a national literary tradition. Interestingly enough, a UNESCO study shows that, while in proportion to Malaysia's population Singapore publishes a respectable number of texts and books on language and philology, there is an enormous disparity in numbers of books on literary history and criticism. In 1982, for example, seven such books (in all the official languages) were published in Singapore compared to Malaysia's 212. The figures indicate that while in Malaysia there has already developed a strong sense of literary history and therefore an independent literary identity, Singapore has yet to develop a sense of its own literary history or self-consciousness about its literary culture.[9]

I would argue that there is in fact a literary tradition of English-language writing in Singapore, much of which is being overlooked because both writers and the sophisticated English-educated elite have focused too narrowly on external, Western ideals of aesthetic and grammatical standards, stylistic and formal achievement derived wholly from the canon and traditions of British and American literature. The dominant tone of this Singapore English-language writing is that of an international English-language variety, often in relation with more "universal" themes of individualism, love, disillusionment, personal conflicts, and so on, and in less identifiable, more metropolitan settings.

This attempt, as we have seen, comes from the writers' ideology of "art for art's sake;" from the ideology of English as a world language, with its own set of Western, cosmopolitan values and removed from Asian identity associated with the mother tongue and from the consequent ideal of the writer as writing within the mainstream of British (and American) literary traditions based on the canon of English literature.

Yet, as every ideology contains within it the seeds of a counter-ideology, so this prevailing tradition has its double, its counter-tradition, based on an acknowledgement of the social nature of writing. This counter-tradition is seen in the attempt to use English in its local varieties (the three varieties of *Singlish* based on Chinese, Malay and Indian idiolects — and code-mixing), often with an emphasis on local color, social observations, and socio-political comments or criticisms.

Some writers belong unequivocally to the dominant tradition: Oliver Seet, Rebecca Chua, and Wong May, for example. Among other writers, such as Chandran Nair and Wong Phui Nam, even when they attempt to write of personal and subjective feelings or larger social conflicts, their choice of diction, images and rhythm — heavily influenced by such English masters as Dylan Thomas and T. S. Eliot — demonstrates their orientation in the aesthetic tradition of English literature.

A few writers clearly write from the counter-traditions — the young Wang Gungwu and Ee Tiang Hong, Catherine Lim, and dramatists such as Robert Yeo and Stella Kon. Wang Gungwu's experimentation with *Engmalchin* (a synthetic invention of a poetic diction incorporating words and phrases from Malay and Chinese in Malayanized English variety) in the late 1940s was more than an attempt at poetry; it was, as said earlier, tied up with his attempt to help create a Malayan identity. Similarly, Robert Yeo, in his two plays, *Are You there, Singapore* (1974) and *One Year Back Home* (1980) was trying, he said, "to reflect, to mirror reality." "I've been panned," he added, "[but] now is the time, I feel, to start writing about the things around us . . . not symbolically or metaphorically, but realistically" (*Straits Times,* 20 November 1980, Leisure 1). In contrast to Singh's portrait of the cautious writer, "always on one's guard," Yeo believes that the artist "should speak out on sensitive issues. . . . Speak up, be bold about what you have to say and don't be afraid that, just because you speak out, critically or otherwise, the government is going to come down hard on you."

In *One Year Back Home,* the major conflict is between two friends who run against each other for political office — Chye, a People's Action Party (PAP) candidate, and Fernandez, the Opposition. While the play has a romantic subplot, the most passionately written passages are the explicitly political arguments between Fernandez and the standard PAP line: debates over materialism, high property prices, and the manipulation of symbols for national purposes:

> and when they are paraded before the electorate they
> will all be preening in white while the PAP elders cluck
> their pious endorsements. Like I said to Chye, white is
> the colour of political whitewashing. Do you see why I
> wear colourful kurtas?

Anyone who has been exposed to the irreverent and contentious nature of political commentary in Britain and the United States would find such passages little more than mildly amusing, but in a country where the traditional Asian respect for authority and government is still very strong, the play created a sensation.

In fact, Singapore English-language writing in this counter-tradition, although generally unappreciated by the academic and critical community, is accessible to a larger group of Singaporeans and more popular. Yeo's dramas played to full houses, as did Stella Kon's *Emily of Emerald Hill,* a dramatic monologue about the life of a *peranakan*[10] woman that mirrors the history, changes and values of that particular local-born society. Kon's play was received with ovations and rave reviews from the local press, showing that a real audience exists in Singapore for such literary production — a fact perceivable also in the very high sales of Catherine Lim's collection of short stories, *Little Ironies.* The lack of a large audience appears to be only for writers writing in the dominant, cosmopolitan, English-literary tradition. Many Singapore English-language writers appear to oscillate between the two traditions. In fact, Edwin Thumboo, who in 1967 was so adamant about the separation of writer from community and nation, by 1970 was disturbed by "the other half of the problem," that is, the social half, and this "lack of audience." In Singapore, he avers, the English-educated, "although we have had the language for 150 years," "continue to be embarrassed by the fact that we have not produced any writers of the first rank" (1970, 2). He sees the dearth of high literary achievement as a direct result of the absence of a social role for the writer — of "the gap between the writer and society" which produces peripheral work in English "not contributing to the growth of sensibility." Thumboo suggests the writer can enlarge his audience (and, it is assumed, therefore produce first-rank literature), by changing "his attitude" and accepting "a number of functions": "the writer must explain his society, bring into focus the forces, whether healthy or pernicious, which move society" (1970, 3-4). This didactic role, quite different from Yeo's aim "to reflect, to mirror" Singapore society and to "speak up" on issues, springs from an elitist view that "There is a need to demonstrate to the ordinary people the relevance of what is written," and that the audience's "quality of thinking must be raised and refined." Moreover, the writer chooses to write on social concerns because "social comment and the like will have a better chance of being understood, will more likely succeed in generating interest."

To sum up Thumboo's argument: in order to enlarge his audience and to write really well, the poet must instruct the ordinary people, improve their minds, and write on subjects they can understand and will be interested in. This argument has a mixture of writer's self-interest, elitism, and shrewd social insight in it. "The early [Malayan] poetry in English," he notes, "was not truly creative [because] it had too much regard for 'poetic' elements" (1970, 5). After this imitative period, poetry came out of "growing political consciousness," at which time literature then "had to identify itself with nationalistic impulses and help directly in nation building" (1970, 6). The rejection of *Engmalchin*, Thumboo rightly observes, was part of the drift away from political themes. He warns that complete freedom in choice of subjects, notable about Singapore poetry today, can widen the gap btween poet and audience.

In his own poetry, Thumboo can be seen to oscillate between the tradition of subjective and obscure poems on universal themes of love, self-identity, and personal emotions, using the literary techniques and stylistic diction associated with an international style of poetry (for example, free verse, imagistic techniques, and Western-based myths) and this reformed tradition of the poet as teacher, commenting on social issues and explaining his society to itself in order to uplift and refine its consciousness. The poems in his first volume, *Rib of Earth* (1956), belong strictly to the first tradition, for example:

> O Abel, Rima's chords are lost:
> The serpent bites,
> Green mansions, a scarecrow of steel
> To hang our automatic greetings
> ("Steel" 26)

In *Gods Can Die* (1977), his second volume, Thumboo is writing from a public position. He comments on social phenomena, stripping his diction of British-style literariness, and attempts to find an acceptable diction combining Standard English decorum and local references and colloquialisms. For example:

> The Executive beams
> From plush Diethelm chair,
> Table priced to match
> Cigar in the air,
> Large
> I came for a drink
> To spin the past and let it sing
> The goodies spread:
> Adelphi cakes, Bacardi rum,
> Cheese cookies in the breeze
> of Collyer Quay. . . .
>
> Proud, uncouth, man,
> Is this the tapper's son
> Six years away from Jemaliang
> Beneath this slim executive tan?
> ("Plush" 24)

In moving ideologically from a purely aesthetic or "poetical" position to a balancing of art and social "commitment" — and in Thumboo's case, commitment meaning to the higher, more refined aspects of social consciousness rather than to political propaganda or opposition — Thumboo has created a poetry of general statement, social comment, moral exhortation, and civic instruction. In his later poems in *Ulysses by the Merlion* (1979), he has modified his earlier techniques, adhering to economy of words, antithetical neatness, a balance of abstractions with specificity of images, and an unobtrusive free verse form. He is the closest Singapore has to a poet laureate, chiefly because he has the most public style in a profession notorious for private, if not obscure, voices.

Generally, Singapore poets display a similar oscillation between the two literary traditions coming from two different ideologies. Even that seemingly inaccessible and private poet, Arthur Yap, shares more of the counter-tradition than he would admit. Kevin Sullivan tells us that Yap "eschews the line of the poet as a public figure" (3). The standard critical perception of Yap's poetry is that "the poetry is essential, all else secondary" (Singh 17). And Yap himself distances his work from the second tradition, saying of *Engmalchin*, "it was really such a laugh," "I don't think [the trend of reflecting the community] is terribly important," and "I don't think that that development [of the very public aspect of poetry] is particularly good" (Sullivan 8-18). His four volumes of verse are filled with sophisticated, literate and literary, self-conscious concerns with the English language, descriptions of experiences in foreign countries (England, Wales, Japan, Indonesia) and subjective musings on private events, emotions, and observations that cannot be tied down to a particular society or nation:

> On reading a current bestseller
> the naming of parts, never direct,
> is nevertheless carefully alluded to, the lovers
> anatomised, have their parts, if not their roles,
> served up to the eye: proxy voyeur
> a paragraph's a huff,
> a page a pant
> (who was it ran a mile under 4 minutes?)
> (*Commonplace* 5)

Yap is in the difficult position of a poet without an audience, chiefly, it has been said, because his themes and concerns are so idiosyncratic, eccentric even, as to leave him unappreciated locally, despite such well-known admirers as Anthony Burgess and Enright overseas *(Straits Times,* 9 August 1983, 8; *Times Literary Supplement,* 24 November 1978, 13).

Yap's neglect has something to do with his ideological stance, although it is a stance not consistently reflected in his poetic practice. In many poems such as "letter from a youth to his prospective employer" *(Commonplace* 10), "statement" *(down the line* 5), and "two mothers in a HDB playground" *(down the line* 54-55), Yap's poetry is rooted in the counter-tradition. "Everything's coming up numbers," for instance, satirizes the national mania for betting:

> the death of the prime minister of china
> left a wake of sorrow and a flock of numbers,
> the death of the prime minister of malaysia
> left a similar sorrow and a different set of numbers
> in market place, coffeeshops,
> the communal privacy of homes,
> telephone and pencil were relaying numbers:
> do we add 3 to his age?

put 6 at the end, or as the third digit?
do we follow the same for him as well?
the betting-booths displayed a list of numbers,
numbers already oversubscribed by collective certainty.
everything's coming up numbers:. . .
what, where, somehow, who says so;
what figures, where, add which, whom,
you saw what time, how many, good or not

(Commonplace 2)

In "two mothers in a HDB playground," while it may be true that Yap is concerned with poetic craft, he is also concerned with expressing "a genuine feeling." Such poems, he admits, are "rooted in a particular area . . . reflect the life styles and the folk ways and the mores of a particular area" (Sullivan 4). But these poems also do more than reflect Singapore social fissures and folkways. Their sharply ironic and comic observations form an implicitly critical commentary on money-mentality that presents, by negative example, an opposing set of values and morality.

Both Robert Yeo and Arthur Yap use the term "reflect" to explain the relation between their writing and society, subscribing to the notion that every literary work has its source in material reality and perforce reflects this reality. Every short story, poem or play, even while insisting on an autonomous, aesthetic set of criteria, reflects social reality and the ideological attitudes ruling that reality. Each is, in fact, itself a material product of that set of ideological and social forces. In choosing to write in the English-language and, more importantly, in accepting the standards, forms and traditions of British and American literature, the English-language writers, especially those in the first tradition, are exhibiting a certain colonialist and/or cosmopolitan mentality not always consonant with nationalistic or indigenous identity and values. Looking more closely at writers' themes, one can point to the reiteration of certain humanistic qualities (importance of emotions, of the individual, traditions, nature) in conflict with dehumanizing tendencies (the effects of technological development, rapid urbanization, metropolitan anonymity). Identifying largely with international mainstream literary movements, many of these same writers chose further to identify with the liberal, oppositionist tradition in this mainstream. Nair (1972) in "Ceremony" expresses the conflict between individual romanticism and social conformity and the resulting loss of feelings:

Love is a burnt-out diary
or at best a squirrel fixed in alcohol
squirming a little as you killed it
(*Once the Horsemen and Other Poems* 5)

Goh Poh Seng, in praising the spontaneous, simple and natural life, is also anti-urban and anti-commercial, and sees himself as generally opposed to the values of modern Singapore:

Towards the sea's fresh salt
the river bears pollution
whose source was simple hills
whose immigration was tainted
when man
decided to dip his hand
Nourishing his wants
a commercial waterway
greased with waste
("Singapore" in *Seven Poets*, 97-98)

Generally, the stories that appear in the collected volumes also reflect the writers' unease with the rapid political and material changes in their society, from 1959, when Singapore received self-government, to 1965, when it became an independent nation, to the 1980s, when the leaders are set on the course of transforming the city into a "global village". As Yap puts it in his poem "Now":

Nobody sells sea-shells on the seashore:
only defence bonds
(*The Second Tongue* 93)

The relationship of the writer to ideology in Singapore is perhaps most aptly characterized as one of "contradictions." Gopinathan points out that some of these contradictions are inherent in the larger cultural situation.[11] The writers who insist on their autonomy but are in danger of becoming irrelevant to society are situated within these larger cultural contradictions. Writing in English, they are inevitably identified with a colonialist heritage, and are seen officially as working in a second tongue, alien from Asian identity, and transmitting dangerous, Westernized, cosmopolitan, and technological attitudes. Yet they are consciously trying to recover past Asian traditions and cultural values and are generally critical of the encroachment of cosmopolitan and technological attitudes. As Wang Gungwu perceived in 1958, there exists a basic contradiction "between our search for Malayan [that is, national] poetry and our decision to base that search on English forms." Singapore writers who reject a purposive or utilitarian definition for their art reject the notion of the writer's obligation to society in producing literature as instruction, civics, or moral education. Yet they are taken aback when governmental authorities displace literature as part of moral education in the school curriculum. They appeal to British and American literary traditions and to exonomously established forms, styles and standards. But they insist on the validity, integrity and independence of local literature. These writers seek autonomy and freedom of artistic concerns from state-dictated aims. Yet, because they are almost always university-educated and working in the Civil Service or in government-controlled institutions (as teachers, professors, journalists, doctors, and administrators), they belong to the small, English-educated elite whose interests are inextricably bound up with governmental, bureaucratic aims and whose independence of action and thought consequently is constrained.

Both Jan Gordon and Harry Aveling, two foreign critics, sharply characterize the ideological bond between English-language writers and the ruling elite. Gordon argues that Singapore poets "enjoy a privileged relationship with the government in power, while at the same time the very marginality of the language in the Singapore 'living' context restrains any adversary political venturesomeness" (39). Such a position, he concludes, makes the creative endeavour peculiarly susceptible to direction from outside. Thus, it is not surprising that a well-known Singapore short-story writer, poet, critic and academician, Dr Kirpal Singh, could in all sincerity offer the opinion that, "Whether or not a distinct Singaporean English will flower depends considerably on how such powers that be see the question"[12] (Singh 1984, 11).

If, as Koh Tai Ann pointed out, "cultural development" in Singapore has become part of the nation-building ideology (culture subsumed to government policy), it must follow that literature also will be taken over as a contribution to this state ideology. As far back as 1969, D. J. Enright had already pointed out that the concept of a national culture to be created in Singapore was "a political concept with a political objective — to homogenize a very mixed bunch of people" (1969, 183). Singapore writers appear to welcome the prizes and publishing opportunities given them by the Ministry of Community Development, going so far as to ask for even more state support in terms of publishing and grant subsidies, while at the same time insisting on their independence from state concerns. But for the coming years, despite the contradictions inherent in their role in society, it will be difficult to see how English-language writers, whether in the first or second tradition, can establish a fully autonomous existence from the dominant ideologies of the state (that is, nation-building and modernization), whether in reflecting these concerns or in conscious and material links with the state. The major concerns, after all, for both writers and state, coincide remarkably well, in process if not in ends — that is, that "a literature in English . . . be created quickly so as to give the different races a sense of cultural identity" (Singh 1984, 9).

1986

Notes

1. This definition was also accepted by Koh (1981).
2. See Chan Heng Chee, Geoffrey Benjamin, John Clammer, S. Gopinathan, Tham Seong Chee, and Wang Gungwu among others for background on this subject.
3. See Margaret Agusta (30 September 1985) for a summary of this history; also Oemarjati (1979).
4. See Lopez (1940) for the first full expression of the writer's social role. This committed stance is continued in more contemporary and radical Filipino studies, for example, Teodoro, Jr. and San Juan, Jr. (1981), and Cruz, Jr. (1984).
5. See T. Wignesan's discussion of Tamil poetry in *Bunga Emas* and Wong Lai Peng's analysis (1984) of the Chinese writer's social role.
6. According to Malisci (1977), there are at least ten different ethno-linguistic groups in Singapore.
7. While 82% of Chinese Singaporeans can speak Mandarin, 44% fluently, only 25% use the language regularly with their children, compared with 28% who use English regularly.

The language most often used when speaking		
	Mandarin	English
To children	25%	28%
To spouse	17%	26%
To siblings	17%	25%

Straits Times, "Dialect Used Less, But English More," 5 October 1985.
8. Compare, for example the rather mild social/political constraints in Singapore with the PEN International's Writers in Prison Committee report that in 1984 at least 441 international writers were in jail and that "arrest, imprisonment, physical maltreatment, disappearance and death must all be included among the risks that writers are obliged to undergo today in the pursuit of their vocation", UPI Report from N.Y., 16 January 1986.

9.

1982	No. of Titles	Languages and Philology	Literary History and Criticism	Literary Texts
Singapore	1,530	148	12	254
Malaysia	2,801	379	212	242

1982	No. of 1st Edition Titles	Languages and Philology	Literary History and Criticism	Literary Texts
Singapore (not counting government publications)	961	104	7	190
Malaysia	2,778	371	212	242

Source: *Statistical Yearbook 1984* UNESCO

10. The *peranakan* or *baba* appear to be principally of Hokkien descent, and their "*peranakan/baba*-Malay language" has a great deal of Hokkien in it. The *peranakan* or *baba* version of Malay, a mixture of Chinese and Malay with the latter predominating, was until recently the language commonly spoken in *peranakan* or *baba* homes. The majority could not speak Chinese, although they still retained their Chinese customs and manners and brought up their children as Chinese. They tended to marry within their group. Today, *peranakans* form a substantial and distinctive part of the Chinese population of Melaka.

11. Gopinathan noted that the education system "has both sustained ethnic separation and provided — mainly through the use of a metropolitan language, English — an opportunity for the erosion of communal barriers." Contradictions in the cultural situation encompass "how traditional Asian values are to be sustained and reconciled with other important values in the face of a rapidly changing socio-cultural environment. [But] public housing patterns promote a nuclear family structure . . . meritocracy and achievement orientation are more likely to be effective when the individual is given scope to innovate . . . the pursuit of rationality and meliorism could lead to a devaluing of religion" (293). Moreover, the continued emphasis on ethnic cultures makes cultural integration more difficult, while "the nation-building effort itself may be affected by the disruption of these sentimental attachments" (294).

12. Kirpal Singh elsewhere characteristically argues for the teaching of science-fiction in Singapore on pragmatic and technological grounds, very much in keeping with state ideology: "the most important use of science fiction for Singapore is the way in which it will prepare us and our children for the new Singapore tomorrow. And I want to suggest that science fiction be introduced into the school curriculum so that young Singaporeans can become better informed and better equipped to understand the changes that are rapidly taking place" (Singh 1982, 13).

Agusta, Margaret. "The Role of Art in Development Remains Issue." *Jakarta Post* 30 September 1985: 5.

Anonoymous. "Some Suggestions for Malayan Verse Written in English." *New Cauldron* (Raffles Society, University of Malaya, Singapore), November 1958: 27-28.

Asiaweek. "Literary Magazines: Blue Skies and Red Ink." 7 June 1985: 59-62.

Aveling, Harry. "Towards an Anthology of Poetry from Singapore Malaysia." In *South Pacific Images,* edited by C. Tiffin. Queensland: South Pacific Association of Commonwealth Languages and Literatures,1978. 81-92.

Ban, Kah Choon. "An Introduction to Undergraduate Poetry." *Focus,* no. 8 (July 1976): 26-35.

Benjamin, Geoffrey. "The Cultural Logic of Singapore's 'Multi-racialism.'" *Singapore Society in Transition,* edited by Riaz Hassan. Kuala Lumpur: Oxford University Press, 1976. 115-33.

Burgess, Anthony. "Too Much Eliot and Alas, no Ulysses." *Straits Times,* 9 August 1983: 8.

Busch, P. "Political Unity and Ethnic Diversity: A Case Study of Singapore." Ph.D. dissertation, University of Michigan, 1972. Michigan: University Microfilms, 1972.

Chan, Heng Chee. "Nation-building in Southeast Asia: The Singapore Case." Paper presented in seminar on Southeast Asia in the Modern World, 1970, at the Institute fur Asienkunde, Hamburg.

——————. *Singapore the Politics of Survival* 1965-1967. Singapore: Oxford University Press, 1971.

——————. "Nation-building and Nation Identity in Southeast Asia. "*Building States and Nations,* vol. 2, edited by S. N. Eisenstadt and S. Rokkan. Beverly Hills, California: Sage Publications,1973. 301-19.

——————. "The Role of Intellectuals in Singapore Politics." *Southeast Asian Journal of Social Science* 3 (1975): 59-64.

Chen, Peter S. J. "Elites and National Development in Singapore." *Southeast Asian Journal of Social Science* 3 (1975): 17-25.

Clammer, John. *Ideology, Society, Culture* Singapore: Chopman Press, 1985.

Choo, Liang Haw. "The Writer's Commitment." *Focus,* nos. 1-2 (1962): 24-29.

Crewe, William. "The Singapore Writer and the English Language." *Regional English Language Centre Journal* 9 (1978): 77-86.

Cultural Value and Modern Singapore. Ministry of Education, Singapore, 1979.

Eagleton, Terry. *Criticism and Ideology.* London: New Library Books, 1976.

Ee, Tiang Hong. "Language and Imagery in Malayan Poetry." *Malayan Writers Conference.* Kuala Lumpur, 1962. 126-129.

——————. "The Poet and His Role." *Focus,* no. 5 (1971): 120-131.

——————. "Experiments, Prospects, Encounters." *Centre for Regional and National Literatures in English Reviews Journal,* no. 2 Flinders University, Australia (1980): 74-77.

Enright, D. J. "Necessary Conditions for the Creation of Literature." *Malayan Writers Conference.* Kuala Lumpur 1962. 130-134.

——————. "Reflections on the Malayan Writers Conference." *Focus,* no. 2 (1963): 19-21.

————. *Memoirs of a Medicant Professor*. London: Chatto & Windus,1969.

————. "Beyond Responsibility." *Times Literary Supplement,* 24 November 1978.

Fernando, Lloyd. "Literary English in the Southeast Asian Tradition." *National Identity,* edited by K. Goodwin. London: Heinemann Educational Books, 1970. 57-65.

Goodwin, K, ed. *National Identity.* London: Heinemann Educational Books, 1970.

Gopinathan, S. "Singapore's Language Policies: Strategies for a Plural Society." *Southeast Asian Affairs 1979.* Singapore: Heinemann for Institute of Southeast Asian Studies, 1979. 280-294.

Gordon, Jan B. "The Second Tongue Myth: English Poetry in Polylingual Singapore." *ARIEL* 15 (1984): 41-65.

Hartmann, Nicolai. *Aesthetik.* Berlin: W. de Gruyter, 1953.

Ho, Chin Beng. "Dialect Used Less, but English More." *Straits Times,* 5 October 1985: 1.

Hope, A. D. *Native Companions, Essays and Comments on Australian Literature 1936-1966.* Sydney: Angus & Robertson,1974.

Ismail Hussein. "Obstacles to the Development of a New Literary Culture in Asia." *Solidarity* 9 (1978): 94-102.

Jameson, Fredric. *Marxism and Form, Twentieth-Century Dialectical Theories of Literature.* Princeton: Princeton University Press, 1971.

————. *The Political Unconscious, Narrative as a Socially Symbolic Act.* Ithaca: Cornell University Press, 1981.

Kock, See Hai. "Singapore Chinese Literature, Chinese Writers and their Readers." *Solidarity* 5 (1984): 42-46.

Koh, Tai Ann. "The Singapore Experience: Cultural Development in the Global Village." *Southeast Asian Affairs 1980.* Singapore: Heinemann for Institute of Southeast Asian Studies, 1980. 292-307.

————. "Singapore: The Novel in English; a Brief Survey." Paper presented at Workshop on the Southeast Asian Novel at the Institute of Southeast Asian Studies, 1985, Singapore.

————. "Singapore Writing in English: The Literary Tradition and Cultural Identity." *Literature and Society in Southeast Asia,* edited by Tham Seong Chee. Singapore: Singapore University Press,1981. 160-186.

Kuo, Eddie C. Y. "Language, Nationhood and Communication Planning: The Case of a Multilingual Society." *Southeast Asian Journal of Social Science* 4 (1976): 31-42.

————. "Literacy in Singapore, 1970-1980." *Regional English Language Centre Journal* 14 (1983): 1-17.

————. "Language and Social Mobility in Singapore." *Language of Inequality,* edited by N. Wolfson and J. Manes. Mouton: Merlin, 1985. 337-354.

LePage, R. B. *The National Language Question: Linguistic Problems of Newly Independent States.* London: Institute of Race Relations and Oxford University Press, 1964.

Lim, Shirley. "Edwin Thumboo: A Study of Influence in the Literary History of Singapore." *The Writer's Sense of the Contemporary,* edited by B. Bennett, Ee Tiang Hong, and R. Shepherd. Western Australia: The Centre for Studies in Western Australia, 1982. 30-34.

——————. "Notes Towards a Local Fiction." *Commentary* 6 (1985): 82-87.

Lopez, Salvador P. *Literature and Society*. Manila: University Publishing Co., 1940.

Malicsi, Jonathan. "For a New National Language Policy." Paper presented at the Association of Southeast Asian Nations, 1977, Kota Kinabalu.

McLeod, A. L. "Malayan Literature in English." *Literature East and West* 10 (1966): 314-324.

Modernization in Singapore: Impact on the Individual. Singapore: University Education Press, 1972.

Oemarjati, Boen S. "Social Issues in Recent Indonesian Literature." *Southeast Asian Affairs 1979*. Singapore: Heinemann for Institute of Southeast Asian Studies, Singapore, 1979. 134-141.

Ong, Teong Hean. "A Story of Singapore Poetry." *Prospect* 7, no. 5 (1975a): 64-65.

——————. "A Story of Singapore Poetry." *Prospect* 7, no. 9 (1975b): 32-34.

——————. "A Brief Survey of Singapore Poetry in English." *Singapore Book World* 13 (1982): 15-17.

Ooi, Boo Eng. "On Versing, Poetic Integrity, and a Singapore Poet." *Journal of International Education and Development* 1 (1976): 1,107-21.

——————. "Poetry and Poetics, and Some Asian Verse in English." *Southern Review* 9 (1976): 139-50.

——————. "Malaysia/Singapore Literature in English: Towards a 'Real Estimate'." *Pacific Quarterly Moana* 6 (1981): 157-68.

——————. "Singapore/Malaysia Poetry: At Least Something and Less and More." *Southeast Asian Review of English* (1980): 41-51.

——————. "Singapore/Malaysian Poetry: At Least Something and Less and More," *Southeast Asian Review of English* (1981): 44-62.

Platt, John, Heidi Weber, and Ho Mian Lian. *The New Englishes*. London: Routledge & Kegan Paul, 1984.

Pre-U Seminar Report 1979. *Cultural Values and Modern Singapore*. Ministry of Education, Singapore, 1979.

"Seminar on Developing Creative Writing in Singapore." Proceedings of the seminar held in Singapore on 6-7 August 1976, Singapore.

Shils, Edward. "Intellectuals, Public Opinion, and Economic Development." *World Politics* 12 (1958a): 232-255.

——————. "The Concentration and Dispersion of Charisma." *World Politics* 11 (1958b): 1-19.

——————. "The Intellectuals in the Political Development of the New States." *World Politics* 12 (1966): 329-368.

——————. *The Intellectuals and the Powers and Other Essays*. Chicago and London: University of Chicago Press, 1972.

Singh, Kirpal. "Singapore Malaysian Fiction in English." *South Pacific Images*, edited by C. Tiffin. Queensland: South Pacific Association of Commonwealth Languages and Literatures, 1978. 68-80.

——————. "A Checklist of Critical Writings on Singaporean and Malaysian Literature in English: 1956-1976." *Journal of Commonwealth Literature* 14 (1979): 138-144.

——————. "The Long Haul for Writing in English," *Solidarity* 3 (1983): 52-59.

————. "Singapore and the Uses of Science Fiction." *Singapore Book World* 13 (1982): 12-14.

————. "An Approach to Singapore Writing in English." *ARIEL* 15 (1984): 5-24.

Statistical Yearbook 1984. Paris: United Nations Educational Social and Cultural Organization, 1984.

Strelka, Joseph P., ed. *Literary Criticism and Sociology.* University Park, Pennsylvania: Pennsylvania State University Press, 1973.

Sullivan, Kevin. "Achievement: The Poet with an Artist's Touch." *Southeast Asian Review of English* 8 (1984): 3-20.

Tabori, Paul. "Society and the Writer." *Solidarity* 7 (1972): 48-69.

Tay, Simon. "The Writer as a Person." *Solidarity*, no. [sic] 99 (1984): 56-59.

Teodoro, Luis V., Jr. and Epifanio San Juan, Jr. *Two Perspectives on Philippine Literature and Society.* Philippine Studies Occasional Paper no. 4. Hawaii: Center for Asian and Pacific Studies, University of Hawaii, 1981.

Tham, Seong Chee. "Literary Response and the Social Process." *Southeast Asian Journal of Social Science* 3 (1975): 85-106.

————. "Values and Modernization in Southeast Asia." *Southeast Asian Journal of Social Science* 8 (1980): 1-11.

Thumboo, Edwin. "Some Notes on the Question of Form." *Malayan Writers Conference.* Kuala Lumpur, 1962. 180-184.

————. "Malaysian Poetry: Two Examples of Sensibility and Style." *National Identity,* edited by K. Goodwin. London: Heinemann Educational Books, London, 1970. 187-196.

————. "The Role of Writers in a Multi-Racial Society." *Singapore Writing.* Singapore, 1977: 5-13.

————. "Singapore Writing in English: A Need for Commitment." *Commentary* 11 (1978): 20-25.

————. "The Writer and Society: Some Third World Reminders." *Solidarity,* no. 99 (1984): 24-32.

Tongue, R. K. *The English of Singapore and Malaysia.* Singapore: Eastern Universities Press, 1974.

Wang, Gungwu. "Trial and Error in Malayan Poetry." *Malayan Undergrad* (Singapore) 1958: 6-8.

————. *Community and Nation Essays on Southeast Asia and the Chinese.* Hong Kong: Heinemann Educational Books, 1981.

Wang Gungwu, ed. *Self and Biography. Essays on the Individual and Society in Asia.* Sydney: Sydney University Press for the Australian Association of the Humanities, 1975.

Wignesan, T. ed. *Bunga Emas: An Anthology of Contemporary Malaysian Poetry (1930-1963).* Malaysia: Anthony Blond with Rayirath Pub., 1964.

Wignesan, T. "Malaysia and Singapore." *Journal of Commonwealth Literature* 13 (1978): 81-82.

Wong, Lai Peng. "The Writer and His Audience." *Solidarity,* no. 99 (1984): 51-52.

Wong, Yoon Wah, "The Impact of Urbanization on the Recent Development of Singapore Literature in Chinese," *Solidarity,* no. 98 (1984): 36-41.

Yap, Arthur. *A Brief Critical Survey of Prose Writings in Singapore and Malaysia.* Singapore: Educational Publications Bureau,1971.

—————. "The Use of Vernacular in Fiction in English in Singapore and Malaysia." *Regional English Language Centre Journal* 7 (1976): 64-71.

—————. "The Singapore Writer and the English-language." *Regional English Language Centre* 9 (1978): 87-88.

Yeo, Robert. "University Verse: 1949-1959." *Malayan Writers Conference.* Kuala Lumpur, 1962. 191-199.

—————. "Poetry in English in Singapore and Malaya." *Singapore Book World,* 1 (1970): 14-19.

—————. "Who's Afraid of Edwin Thumboo?" *Solidarity* 3 (1983): 29-42.

—————. "Towards an English-language Singaporean Theatre." *Asian Writers on Literature and Justice,* edited by Leopold Yabes. Manila: Philippine Center of International PEN, 1982. 67-85.

Periodicals

Cauldron: Medical College Union Literary and Debating Society, Singapore, vols. 1-3 (1947-1949).

Commentary: University of Singapore Society, Singapore (1968-   ).

Focus: Literary Society of University of Singapore, Singapore (1962-   ).

New Cauldron: Raffles Society, University of Singapore, Singapore (1949-1959).

Poetry: Singapore, nos. 1-2 (1968).

Tenggara: University of Malaya, Kuala Lumpur (1967-   ).

Write: An independent student publication of the University of Malaya, Singapore, nos. 1-5 (1957-1958).

Poetry: Individual Works

Goh, Poh Seng. *Eyewitness.* Singapore: Heinemann, 1976.

—————. *Lines From Batu Ferringhi.* Singapore: Island Group,1978.

—————. *Bird With One Wing.* Singapore: Island Press, 1982.

Lee, Tzu Pheng. *Prospect of a Drowning.* Singapore: Heinemann, 1980.

Lim, Thean Soo. *The Liberation of Lily and Other Poems.* Singapore: Singapore National Printers, 1976.

Muhammad Hj. Salleh. *Time and Its People.* Singapore: Heinemann, 1978.

Nair, Chandran. *Once the Horsemen and Other Poems.* Singapore: University Education Press, 1972.

Singh, Kirpal. *Twenty.* Calcutta: P. Lal, 1978.

Tay, Simon. *Prism.* Singapore: S.H. Tay, 1980.

Thumboo, Edwin. *Rib of Earth.* Singapore: Lloyd Fernando, 1956.

—————, *Gods Can Die.* Singapore: Heinemann, 1977.

—————. *Ulysses by the Merlion.* Singapore: Heinemann, 1979.

Wang, Gungwu. *Pulse.* Singapore: Beda Lim, University of Malaya, 1950.

Wong, May. *A Bad Girl's Book of Animals.* New York: Harcourt, Brace, Jovanovich, 1963.

—————. *Reports.* New York: Harcourt, Brace, Jovanovich, 1971.

—————. *Superstitions.* New York: Harcourt, Brace, Javonvich, 1980.

Yap, Arthur. *Only Lines.* Kuala Lumpur: Federal Publications, 1971.

—————. *Commonplace.* Singapore: Heinemann, 1977.

—————. *down the line.* Singapore: Heinemann, 1980.

Yeo, Robert. *Coming Home, Baby.* Kuala Lumpur: Federal Publications, 1971.

—————. *And Napalm Does Not Help.* Singapore: Heinemann, 1978.

Poetry: Anthologies and Collections

Centre 65, Poetry Festival, 1967 Singapore, 1967.

Chung Yee-chong, Sng Boh-khim, Arthur Yap, Teo Bock-cheng, and Robert Yeo. *Five Takes*. Singapore: University of Singapore Society, 1974.

Evocations. Singapore: University of Singapore Literary Society, 1971.

Litmus One: Selected University Verse, 1949-1957. Singapore: Raffles Society, University of Malaya, 1958.

Tan, Han-Hoe, ed. *30 Poems: University of Malaya Poems, 1957-1968*. Singapore: University of Malaya, 1968.

Thumboo, Edwin, ed. *The Flowering Tree: Selected Writings from Singapore/ Malaysia*. Singapore: Educational Publications Bureau, 1970.

——————. *Seven Poets*. Singapore: Singapore University Press, 1973.

——————. *The Second Tongue: An Anthology of Poetry from Malaysia and Singapore*. Singapore: Heinemann, 1976.

Prose (Novels, Autobiographies, Short-story Collections) and Drama.

Chua, Rebecca. *The newspaper editor and other stories*. Singapore: Heinemann, 1981.

Goh, Poh Seng. *If We Dream Too Long*. Singapore: Island Press, 1972.

——————. *The Immolation*. Singapore: Heinemann, 1978.

Hochstadt, Herman, ed. *The Compact: A selection of University of Malaya Short Stories, 1953-1959*. Singapore: Raffles Society, University of Malaya, 1959.

Kon, Stella. *The Immigrant and Other Plays*. Singapore: Heinemann, 1975.

——————. *Emporium and Other Plays*. Singapore: Heinemann, 1977.

——————. *Emily of Emerald Hill*. London: Macmillan, 1989.

Lim, Catherine. *Little Ironies*. Singapore: Heinemann, 1978.

——————. *Or Else, the Lightning God*. Singapore: Heinemann, 1980.

——————. *The Serpent's Tooth*. Singapore: Times Books International, 1982.

Lim, Janet. *Sold For Silver: An Autobiography*. London: Collins, 1958.

Lim, Thean Soo. *Southward Lies the Fortress*. Singapore: Educational Publications Bureau, 1971.

——————. *Destination Singapore: From Shanghai to Singapore*. Singapore: Pan Pacific Books, 1976.

——————. *Ricky Star*. Singapore: Pan Pacific Books, 1978.

——————. *Fourteen Short Stories*. Singapore: Pan Pacific Books, 1979.

——————. *Bits of Paper and Other Short Stories*. Singapore: Pan Pacific Books, 1980.

Low, Ngiong Ing. *Chinese Jetsam on a Tropic Shore*. Singapore: Eastern Universities Press, 1974.

Tan, Kok Seng. *Son of Singapore: the Autobiography of a Coolie*. Rendered into English by the author in collaboration with Austin Coates. Singapore: Heinemann, 1972.

——————. *Man of Malaysia*. Rendered into English by the author in collaboration with Austin Coates. Singapore: Heinemann, 1974.

Yeap, Joo-kim. *The Patriarch*. Singapore: M.P.H. Distributors, 1975.

Yeo, Robert, ed. *Singapore Short Stories*. 2 vols. Singapore: Heinemann, 1978.

Yeo, Robert. *Are You There Singapore?* First performed on 27 July 1974.

——————. *One Year Back Home*. First performed on 20 November 1980.

Centers and the Fringe :
Novels in English from Malaysia and Singapore

Many critics, using tropes from history — early dispossession and postcolonial empowerment, conflict and vision, victim and plangent instruction — figure postcolonial writers and their fictions as markers on the road to national identity and as symbols and evidence of evolving cultural independence. Western and Western-trained critics tend to judge postcolonial works against a canon defined by Western texts and usually produce theories of systemic progression.[1] But the twentieth-century history of political "independence" in Third-World countries and the productions of economic explanations, national myths, and literary canons in these countries often assume a different track from the Western-dominated, globally-circulating explanation of cultural development that these critics privilege.

Countering theories of evolutionary progressivism, Abdul Jan-Mohamed, in *Manichean Aesthetics: The Politics of Literature in Colonial Africa,* targets the shifts and slippages that constitute the historicities of colonial and postcolonial writing. Offering "allegorical manicheasm" as the conceptual frame generating colonial and African literature, he subsumes the antagonistic relations between colonial and African literature under Jameson's notion of "the dialogic structure of class discourse" (277). Twentieth-century world literature, according to Jameson, has to be conceived in its Third-World manifestation as a cultural struggle between First-World imperialism and newly decolonized national states.[2] Other critics have picked up on Jameson/Jan-Mohamed's reformulation of allegory as the type closest to explaining those features in Third-World writing that mark them as foreign to the "global American post-modernist culture" (Jameson 65).[3] For Stephen Slemon, "Post-colonial allegory is changing not only our ideas of history but the concept of allegory itself, and the challenge of criticism is to learn to read this new, "revised" mode of representation in all of its diversity, its plurality, its cultural and political difference" (166).

Jameson's attempt to confront global fragmentation ironically produces a globally systemic text capable of "explaining" these bodies of national literatures; that is, yet another example of hegemonic theory.[4] His analysis of national literatures under a single conceptual grid reduces the multi-fragmentary, multi-phantasmagoric, hydra-headed mythologies that compose the politics and poetics of postcolonial national literatures, and so transforms "non-hegemonic," excluded, uncentered, fragmented, piece-meal, marginal, autonomous and remote literatures into a hegemonically constituted world literature. His thesis does not account for the centrifugal force of "local" events; the rapidly multi-plying rivalries of linguistic, tribal and ethnic identities, many ancient and long thought contained, others freshly awakened; the tensions between competitive economic systems made intolerable by increasing populations and climactic disasters; the break between the scientific and secular spirit associated with First World countries and the continued emphasis on religious superstructures in many Third-World countries; all of which and more form the dynamic context in which Third-World writers are producing.[5] In countries such as Sri Lanka or Uganda, ethnic or tribal groups are seemingly more intran-sigent and resistant to national convergences. Violent political fragmentation mirrors global fissures and paradoxically appears to deny the technological advancements and capitalist penetrations that have made national boundaries collapse into an international corporate and media market.

Novels in English from two small newly-formed nation states, Malaysia and Singapore, call into question Jameson's, and like critics', attempts to forge a totalizing, hegemonic theory of Third-World literature. English, as a foreign language used for colonial administra-tion, is under stress in both postcolonial nations. In Malaysia, English has drastically down-shifted from colonial pre-eminence to its present position as a second language enabling participation in a global economic system. In 1969, Lloyd Fernando argued, "The Malay language is used with a kind of 'grass roots' force by more than a hundred million people in South East Asia in a way that English has never been and probably never will be. . . . The comparatively small body of indigenous writing in English in Malaysia does not warrant more than a few preliminary observations" (129).

Since then, however, Fernando went on to write a novel in English, *Scorpion Orchid,* and two other novels have appeared, one by Lee Kok Liang, whose *Flowers in the Sky* was also his third literary work in English, and by K.S.Maniam, a well-known short-story writer, who completed *The Return* in 1981. What kind of sociopolitical significance is there to the publication of these novels, in the space of five years, when English had lost prestige, users and institutional validation in Malaysia?

These novels were produced by an ethnic Eurasian, Chinese and Tamil, suggesting English is an ethnic-neutral instrument whose international character counters a national-language/cultural dominance to express fragmentations resulting from exclusions and suppressions. In a mono-lingual, monocultural situation, minorities delegitimatized national-language processes use the former colonial language's "otherness" to give themselves a voice and identity. In oppressive national cultures, writers may turn to the strongly metropole function of English to criticize their societies' provincialism and chauvinism. International English, associated with rationalism, secularism, scientific thought, individualism, and skepticism, becomes the margin from which writers in unsettled national societies assert their counter-identities.[6] For Malaysian minority ethnic writers whose participation in the national literary scene has been severely marginalised, English serves as a counter-identification with a more accepting international culture. in Singapore, English-language novels have a different complication.[7] In a 1986 Institute of South-East Asian Studies Seminar, the Singapore novel was discussed separately under four categories, as Malay, Tamil, Chinese and English-language novels. No attempt was made to read these categories synthetically or cross-culturally. The parallel yet fragmented approach to novel production in the four official languages reflects local critical response which reads the national novel as four distinct species, competing for resources and prestige, but with little in common.[8]

Singapore has enjoyed almost unprecedented stability since its emergence as a city state in 1965 and presents a different literary model than the death-and-life struggle between First-World imperialism and Third-World nationalism that Jameson envisions. Instead its national debate between class struggle and class striving reflects the dialogics of the (personal) value of the individual against the (economic) value of an ever-more-technological global market-place.[9] The novelists come from the English-educated elite, and their versions of national identity present subtly nuanced reflections and social criticism crossed by complicity in dominant state and class interests. Goh's *If We Dream Too Long,* Lim Thean Soo's *Ricky Star,* and Jeyaretnam's *Raffles Place Ragtime,* for example, construct partial critiques of societal structures that can be subsumed under the success motif. The criticism of the success motif, expressed as a form of class struggle, is itself undermined and contradicted by a concern with class striving, in which, consciously or unconsciously, bourgeois characters and values pervade and/or triumph over working class protagonists.

The essay will consider eight contemporary Malaysia/Singapore novelists to interrogate how national identity is problematized through explorations of ethnicity, history, language, and social success.[10] Singapore's English-language novelists, like the Malaysians, are non-Malay. The Malays are generally rooted in their language-culture, and their novel-productions are usually limited to their mother tongue. A study of English-language novels from these contiguous, historically merged nations is perforce skewered in its omission of the prolific and (as read in translation) thematically separate Malay novels that form the national literature in Malaysia and a separate body in Singapore.[11]

Because both nations share common immigrant, colonialist and national histories, in fact having for the first few years of independence been merged as one nation and only separating in 1965, English-language novels share common themes and characteristics. Their production can be traced to colonialist English-language education policies and postcolonial vestiges of British cultural superiority. However, the novels are not unselfconscious productions. Novelists such as Fernando, Lee, Maniam, Goh, Lim Thean Soo, and Jeyaretnam show a preoccupation with social identity other than as British colonial subject. Together they cover a range of modern identity strategies (which is one reason why postmodernists who have moved beyond *Dubliners* to *Ulysses* would be out of sympathy with their aims).[12]

K. S. Maniam's *The Return* and Catherine Lim's *The Serpent's Tooth* are almost ethnographic in their fidelity to ethnic surface and social interactions. In nations, where individual experience is almost always ethnic-identified and partial, development of a national, non-ethnic-based identity may threaten valued communal bonds and beliefs. Their novels examine immigrant cultures in a period of modernization, that signifies assimilation into a quasi-Westernized, state-controlled national culture. Both writers use South Indian and Chinese cultural materials to portray that initial stage of identity conflict of the first-generation and second-generation Tamil and Chinese immigrants in South East Asia.

In Maniam's *The Return*, the richest resonances come from South Indian religious symbols.[13] Reading the opening chapter, the reader is immediately aware that she is in the presence of something at once new and old: a fiction that recreates the ancient "thick spiritual air" of some remote district in India in the new "most undeveloped part of Bedong"; a literature in English in which the exhausted colonialist adaptations of the master's tongue and master's culture are abandoned for a longer reach into an original racial past. The opening image, of the grand-mother arriving "suddenly out of the horizon, like a camel, with nothing except some baggage and three boys in tow," offers, as Ooi Boo Eng noted in his preview, "a major underlying motif . . . of some deeply felt human urge driving a displaced person to strive not just for survival but for a survival that leaves something of the person's past — call it identity or roots . . . — intact" (13). To Ravi, the first-person protagonist, the grandmother Periathai is the link between himself and the old world of India, "a land haunted by ghosts, treaded lightly by gods and goddesses" (10). She survives in the new world on "her Indian skills and heritage," as a peddler, a religious healer, and a hawker of Indian goods. More than ancestress, she functions as a priestess, instructing her children on the spiritual values of their racial past.

The theme of an immigrant culture's persistent vitality and its erosion in the second generation is suggested in the Nataraja symbol. Nataraja, the patron god of Hindu Tamils, functions as the most evident representation of immigrant Tamil culture. In the opening paragraph, Periathai is pictured "brooding" over her tin-trunks in which she keeps the Nataraja statue and other religious Indian artifacts. The children are instructed "to witness, even to participate" in her worship which is also a worship of racial origins (6). Despite Periathai's failures to thrive in the new land, her spirit, closely identified with the energy of Nataraja, is never broken. As she lies dying of a cancerous tumor, the townspeople remember only "the deft hands that had danced to a certain rhythm as she wrapped their *vadais*," and "her eyes never lost their vitality" (11).

The grandmother bequeaths her spirituality to her children. Naina, Ravi's father, repeats the pattern of economic striving. Much of the novel's action is composed of a description of the entire family in the primal dance of work. Naina is described as "a modulated series of self-sustaining movements" who would finish ironing eighty pieces of laundry in a single evening "when the rhythm took him" (113). Through Ravi's alienated eyes, Naina's gradual withdrawal from the naturalistic world of material struggle to the spiritual world of Hindu faith, abandoning "work, comfort and security for a hut almost at the fringe of the jungle" (161), is condemned as "backward," caused by Naina's fear of a competitive, modern, Westernized society, "where you are always tested."

The Nataraja motif runs counter, in ironic opposition, to the first-person commentary. Naina with a broad *thurnuru* mark covering his forehead, contemplating the Nataraja statue lighted by "Periathai's silver and copper lamps" (161), is an ancient, familiar Hindu ideal of the ascetic who practices tapas, rituals, and worship to purify himself of material illusion. On one level, Naina's actions are of a man who "had lost touch with reality completely" (177). The son's understandable impulse was "to keep out of whatever mess (the family) might create" (163). But on the level of symbolic action, Naina's apparent irrational practices testify to his intense spiritual life. His tragedy is yet another aspect of the cosmic dance of life and destruction symbolized in the flames surrounding the Nataraja figure.[14] As Ananda Coomaraswamy explains it, the dance of Shiva in Chidambaram forms the motif of the South Indian copper images of Shri Nataraja, the Lord of the Dance. The plot and psychological action parallel the five activities symbolized in the Dance: *Shrishti* (creation); *Sthiti* (preservation); *Samhara* (destruction); *Tirobhava* (illusion); and

Anugraha (salvation). In Hindu mythology, the burning ground is the place where the ego is destroyed, signifying the state where illusions and deeds are burnt away. Appropriately, Naina dies in the conflagration that destroys his house.

The novel's social action is plotted on a broadly South Indian hinterland. The conflict between Ayah, supervisor of the Tamil hospital workers, and Ravi's family can only be understood in a Hindu caste context. In the first section, Ayah humiliates Naina's family because he is of a superior caste. Naina's upwardly mobile move, out of the hospital compound to his own laundry shop in town, is a defiant rebellion against his social place. Although the narrative is not explicit on the castes the major characters belong to, the conflict suggests that Ayah belongs to the Kshatriyas, the executive warrior caste, and Naina and his children to the Vaishyas, the caste of merchants. Ravi's rapid progression through the colonial educational system is the first sign that the family is breaking away from traditional communal structures, and his success encourages his father to follow suit. Ayah abuses Ravi's accomplishments but continues to patronize Naina's business, typifying the upper caste Indian's reactions to a lower caste's upstart activities. The conflict between Ayah and Naina is not randomly hostile; rather it is embedded in and plays out traditional Indian relationships.

But these ethnographic materials offer only one source, albeit significant, of the novel's cultural location. Novels of identity, treating a character's education or mis-education, tend to be *bildungsroman*. The conflicts are constructed dialogically, as relations between Ravi's Asian base and a Westernized self experienced as *individual*, separated from his community. The Western self is phantasmagoric, absorbed in fantasies insidiously propagated by an aggressively colonizing culture.

From the primordial, integrative society figured by Periathai, Ravi is ejected into the foreign world of the English School. The two societies are represented as worlds of language. "The lines of curving, intricate Tamil writing unfolded an excitingly unexpected and knowable world" (22). In contrast, Miss Nancy, the English teacher, "transported us into a pleasant, unreachable land" (25). Enacting English children's stories of Snow White and Little Red Riding Hood with the help of dolls, she seizes the children's imagination: "at her altar, everything or nothing seemed possible." Derek Walcott reminds us in his poem "Codicil," "To change your language you must change your life." The concept of infinite possibility breaks the Indian rhythm of contained communal bonds. Ravi learns the notion of individualism: "Miss Nancy made me feel I was a discovery in myself" (32). The infancy of Hindu myth and community, symbolized in the Tamil language, gives way to the magic, in the Burkean sense, of the English language: "Magic, verbal coercion, establishment of management by decree, says in effect: 'Let there be — and there was" (118). In this sense too, if English is the language of magic (mastery of environment), Tamil is the language of religion. In Burke's formulation, "If magic says, 'Let there be such and such,' religion says 'Please do such and such.' The decree of magic, the petition of prayer" (119).

Ravi's educational progress, including a scholarship to England and entry into the middle class by way of school-teaching, marks the success of nineteenth-century British liberal positivism and rationalism, but at a psychological cost. More than a foil, Ravi's father appears to take an opposing destiny. At first an economically striving character, he gradually withdraws from the town of competition to a house at the fringe of the jungle. Ravi's meditations on his father's career failures are shown to be partial. Naina's death resacrilizes for Ravi a world that, while private and middle-class, has become empty and passionless. Only at the concluding ritual purification and burial ceremony does Ravi arrive at a moral recognition of his psychic estrangement, expressed in an authorial-voiced poem: "Have you been lost/ for words?. . . . Words will not serve. . . . You'll be twisted by them. . . buried in a heart that will not serve" (183).

In representing the violence of characters still in the grip of powerful religious beliefs, motivated by centuries-old attitudes anchored in highly systematized philosophies that dictate appropriate behavior for human and divine, Maniam constructs the possibility for depth in his fiction. Shiva's dance and the Nataraja motif unite the novel's various sections, paralleling and deepening the actions. Naina's life becomes meaningful only if it is interpreted through Hindu symbolism. His withdrawal from his laundry business follows the classic Hindu pattern of movement, from the pursuit of *artha* (wealth) as a valid way of life for the man in the householder stage of life to a withdrawal to seek the ultimate goal, *moksha* (release from rebirth). The son who escapes/ abandons/loses his working-class Hindu roots through the adoption of British culture must still confront the psychic separation between spiritual resources and material rewards, inherent in the choice between languages, between the Tamil sacred (grand)mother-tongue and the secular and fantastically foreign English language. The novel gestures towards the possibility of moving from estrangement to spiritual renewal through a return to Hindu values.[15]

Catherine Lim's *The Serpent's Tooth* also focuses on one race and family — in this case, the Chinese extended family. Like Maniam, Lim uses family frictions, religious beliefs shading into superstitions, and racial myths to give density and significance to action. The novel is rich in local color, representing the varied materiality of immigrant Chinese culture in its wealth of details related to community-centered activities and kinship systems concerning the education of the young, economic support structures, and communal possessions such as heirlooms and artifacts. For example, its actions include seventy-fifth and fifteenth birthday celebrations, two deaths and burials, and one birth.

However, the novel's interest in character is weak. Centering on the conflict between Angela, a modern Singaporean woman, and her mother-in-law, the novel foregrounds the differences between an older immigrant generation, still attached to Buddhist, extended-familial values, and a Westernized, secular generation, driven by the success/money code of twentieth-century Singapore. Characters fall neatly into the two partitions of Chinese (old) culture and Westernized (new) society.

Because the prologue and epilogue are written in first-person, the novel begins and ends in Angela's voice. The rest of the novel, told through Angela's point-of-view, has a limited, unreliable third-person narrator. The strategy of an unlikable narrator masking authorial values permits the novel's didactic themes to be expressed indirectly; but there is little dialogical tension between narrator's and implied authorial intention, for the novel's pointed satire is too predictably aimed at the transitional second-generation.

Angela's struggles with ancient customs are allegorized as a moral fable, pitting the modern woman against an "Old Mother" culture. While Angela presents herself as angelic in intention and action, her actions ironically typify her as shallow and unethical. The major conflict occurs over the affections and identities of a younger generation. Angela's chief preoccupation is to raise her children free from "the dreadful irrationalities and wierdnesses of [their] forebears" (83), and for this cultural erasure she is visited by a series of nightmares, the irrational she disdains erupting into her unconsciousness. Literally a struggle between interfering mother-in-law and possessive mother, the action symbolizes a contest over the cultural future of one diasporic Chinese community. While Mark and Michelle, the older children, reject Old Mother's practices, Michael, Angela's youngest child, loves her stories. Old Mother, attempting to cure Michael, feeds him a herbal medicine, providing Angela an excuse to send her away to another son's home. Old Mother, acting out the intention of Angela's actions, runs away with an idiot servant as a companion. In this Lear-like invention, she is discovered, falls sick and dies with her children around her, leaving Angela free to keep Old Mother's property for herself and her children despite Old Mother's last wishes.

Such a plot offers rich material for portrayals of bicultural miscommunications and subversions, but The Serpent's Tooth does not rise fully to the satirical challenge. Satire has an utopianist vision against which the represented society is cruelly inadequate. *The Serpent's Tooth* is severely regressive, at the same time as it constructs nostalgia as social faith. "Old Mother" culture, despite its domineering manners, is still the best; "new mother" culture, although it hopes to nurture through education, control and reason, is selfish and grasping. The brother-in-law, "a true shifty-eyed grasping Chinaman, down to the absurd Chinaman haircut" (5), whom Angela detested in the opening chapter, is later acknowledged as the frugal, filial branch of Singapore society. To Maniam's *bildungsroman,* the Indian/Hindu and English/secular voices are dialectically related, representing the bewildering complexities of bicultural, colonial experience. In Lim's didactic work, however, the two poles are static, and the narrative is narrowly communal. The "Chinaman" brother-in-law is given the dominant position: "'Those who follow Western ways are those who eat Western shit,' he once said to nobody in particular. 'Western followers, Western shit-eaters!'" (6). As a Western-follower, Angela clearly represents the novel's shit-eater.

In Lloyd Fernando's campus novel, *Scorpion Orchid,* young characters become embroiled in political action against the state. Like Su-Chen Christine Lim's later novel, *Rice Bowl*, it traces character development through initial idealism based on friendship bonds across social and class lines to disillusionment. In *The Scorpion Orchid,* male bonding is firstly presented optimistically, as a vision of a future intra-ethnic society. Four undergraduates, the Malay Sabran, the Tamil Santinathan, the Eurasian Peter D'Almeida, and the Chinese Guan Kheng, each attempt to solve the mystery of a holy man who is causing racial unrest in the country. The sacred figured as racially indeterminate, appearing to each individual only as his racial other, is perhaps the core message of Fernando's fiction.

What Tok Said represents in spiritual terms is also repeated in a prostitute figure. Sally is raped during the race riots. Visiting her in the hospital, Santinathan discovers her racial ambiguity: "Her name is Sally Yu alias Salmah binte Yub. That shook me. I thought she was Chinese" (109). The formation of a new nation in which racial origin will have to be abandoned, according to the fiction, will always be attended by violence. The medium tells Sabran, "Birth is bloody. Do not lose heart" (56). Fernando's choice of author omniscient allows him to flesh out the four racially distinct responses to a multiracial nation's birthpangs; to trace this birth in his characters' changing psyches.

Only the Eurasian Peter abandons the new society for Australia. A product of numerous colonialisms, he criticizes the new order as just another form of colonialism. Attached to the English language, he will not and cannot change further. To Sabran, Peter would rather have a white colonial master than an Asian one (132-33). This vignette dramatizes the language positions in Malaysia after 1957. While the novel makes no overt commentary, the conclusion drawn from the dissolution of youthful intra-racial bonds is the tragedy of race separation (133).

Grounded in the tradition of realism, these narrative chapters are interlayered with a more experimental fiction. A mixture of invented history and imagined asides, these fragments burst into the stream of realism almost as hallucinatory effects, deepening what Jameson would call the novel's allegorical dimension. The first fragment enacts the fate of the individual in a colonialist history. "When he was brought facing the master he was ordered to bow, but he remained standing. A man came forward and struck him ten or twenty times with a bamboo cane. Then he was asked, "Do you wish to join this society or not?" (10). The opening fragment is picked up again in the final chapter. We learn that the prisoner, Peter's uncle, was tortured by the Japanese to force him to collaborate. The torture scene explains and forgives Peter's decision to immigrate, for it dramatizes the kind of psychic violence dealt to individuals who resist forced social formations.

The figure of torture as the colonized experience is picked up in chapter 10, first in the legend of the Raja of Haru, who, hearing of "the beauty of Raja Puteh. . . conceived a great desire for her" (93). 'Raja Puteh' in Bahasa translates as King or Queen White. The legend alludes to the fatal attraction that the white race holds for the native subject, so much so that he would deny his mother culture (the mother opposes the Raja of Haru's plan to marry the White Queen). This tidy allegory is juxtaposed with an indeterminate stream-of-consciousness passage. The tortured prisoner's voice returns in Sabran's subconscious thoughts as he is chased during the riots. In this passage, a surrealistic moment of fear penetrates a Malay pastoral when Sabran learns from the holy man that "I was going to die this year, die because I refused to live by the cool bank under the cool trees. . . " (95). The theme of coerced social formation is again located in the next passage: "The surprise was how swiftly his own childhood memories flowed back, suggesting by the ease with which they repossessed him that there had been a synthetic quality in that hope [of interracial friendship]" (97). The fiction constructs the "synthetic hope" of interracial harmony, then deliberately subverts the first figure with the other construction of racial origins or "childhood memories" (97). The novel's stylistic polarities, the dissolution of realism juxtaposed with the inventions of surrealistic fiction, underline the thematic dualisms, that youthful idealism invested in the hope of racial forgetfulness must dissolve in the "fire" of racial hatred.

The novel does not end with this bleak rupture. The major protagonist, Sabran, freed after two weeks detention, marvels "how hate could have vanished so completely" (124) and weighs the racial rift against an early utopian vision. The criticism of Malaysian society encoded here is not that it is guilty of communalism; rather the criticism rests on the perception of man opposed to man, each isolated in his private self.

The final chapter epitomizes the novel's competing stylistics and thematics. One fragment dramatizes the condescending colonialist attitude of Ellman, the university lecturer who had seduced and abandoned Santi's sister, as he expounds European cultural superiority to the four friends and predicts the most dire outcome for the national future. Through Ellman, the corrupt seducer of young minds and innocent bodies, the novel satirizes a British interpretation of Malaysian history. Ellman, portrayed as a supercilious, barren character motivated by racism and cowardice, is symptomatic of authorial cynicism concerning British colonial rule. Similarly, this cynicism is again expressed in the flashbacks to historical and invented documents that encapsulate the rapacious attitudes of the British toward the indigenous peoples.

Another fragment describes a visit to a Chinese temple that commemorates the Japanese massacre of five hundred Chinese. The trip suggests a rapprochement among Guan Kheng, Santi and Sabran, just as the third fragment explicitly expresses a move on the part of Peter to a reconciliation. Written in epistolary form, this third narrative fragment traces Peter's alienation in England and recognition that he does belong "back home" (146). These fragments move in an ever increasing arc of optimism to Peter's final statement of his "return passage."

But they are embedded in eight pseudo and actual historical narratives that set up dialogical tremors, offering two versions of history. One is grounded in local legend in which the colonizers are portrayed as rapacious murderers, the other offered by colonial historians in which the colonizers are rescuers of the native rulers. The ironic gaps between colonial and colonized perceptions imply the "bogusness" of historical explanations and further suggest the thematics of mistrust as the inevitable consequence of a colonized history.

The last two fragments allegorize the fiction's final thematic, concluding with the birth of Hang Tuah, the legendary hero adopted by Malay nationalism as its historical figure embodying a heroic nationalistic future, and with the report of a traveller on the conditions of the interior of the country into which Malay and Chinese chiefs have gone. The interior homesteads which can only be reached through crocodile-infested streams (147) is the closing figure in Fernando's novel of the birth of a nation. The figure balances the hope of a home against the perils in attaining it. Multi-leveled, multi-voiced and densely experimental,

Scorpion Orchid is perhaps the most ambitious novel from Malaysia/ Singapore to speak from and of the fringes on the swirling vortex of the phenomenon called Third-World nationalism.

Su-chen Christine Lim's first novel, *Rice Bowl,* attempts to represent a totality of Singaporean society. It moves beyond the single communal entity to question the what and why of an evolving national identity. An identity novel and a *bildungsroman* like *The Return,* it has a broader sweep, moving to issues of social cohesion and national identity formation. In its nationally inclusive portrayals, political and historical approach to the question of identity, and its use of religious motifs and themes to give resonance to conflict, it forms a pair with Fernando's first-generation novel, *Scorpion Orchid. Rice Bowl* is also a campus narrative. The major character is a Westernized idealist who constructs an individualist's version of Singapore identity. Marie challenges students to think for themselves: "Scared of being wrong? Young Singaporeans like yourself?" (12). Her ideological position is recognizably liberationist: "Education is freedom from fear, especially the fear of being wrong. It is a liberating process" (13).

Against this charismatic figure, the novel portrays a skeptical, cautious male whom Marie rejects as an "inarticulate Singaporean male, limiting and rigid" (17). The clash of ideological positions is figured in their eventual developments. Paul criticizes Marie as an extremist incapable of compromise. The continuous debate between them constructs two antipathetical versions of Western-influenced national identity. Paul, as the male Harvard-trained elitist, is the mouth piece for the standard establishment realist's argument. He sees his responsibility as contributing to his nation's economic survival and growth; he values practicality, conformity, stability, obedience to the state. As he tells Marie, "Singapore is a small nation. We cannot afford defiance, rebellion and constant questioning of government policies" (20). The figure for the government ideology of pragmatism, he becomes appropriately an Assistant Superintendent of Police whose authoritarian position brings him into further conflict with Marie. Leading her undergraduate fans, who call her Sis, in protest against Singapore's social conditions, Marie's political activities get her emotionally involved with an American pastor, and she leaves the Convent to marry Hans just before they are to be deported for their activism.

The novel does not present a simple dialectic between democratic idealism and state pragmatism, between humanistic values and economic necessities. From the very beginning of the novel, Marie is a complex character whose appealing idealism masks egotistical drives. Her revolutionary rhetoric attracts followers, but her individualist vision ends in her abandonment of her country for a more selfish future in

America. Her followers are eventually disillusioned, and Yean learns the truth in Paul's pronouncement, "Marie celebrates the greatness of the great individual — herself" (261).

The fiction constructs and subverts simultaneously both ideological positions. Marie's manipulation of her students and Paul's pragmatic sacrifice of individual, subjective concerns for state goals are dramatized as inadequate definitions of national identity. In the midst of this debate are suffering individuals who need rescue. Ser Mei, for example, is forced into prostitution by a greedy mother and dies as a possible suicide; Mak, the Chinese chauvinist and Communist agent-provocateur, goes crazy in his attempts to radicalize the students-workers' protest activities; Yean, rich and confused, is unable to stop her father from moving his entire family to California.

While race is foregrounded in Fernando's novel, it does not intrude in *Rice Bowl*. Instead, economics, the class struggle between worker and bourgeoisie, forms a major conflict in the second-generation of Singapore's fiction. Conflicts arise between individual and state needs, religious and secular principles, idealism and realism. The novel ends with the recognition that, for all its dangers, the ideology of individualism requires humanism as part of economic pragmatism. The concluding scene, when Paul leaves behind the avenue of consumerist vulgarity for a quiet war-memorial park, is one of separation and loss. It figures the State's patriarchal victory and suggests the banishment of the female, subjective, and individualist principles from the ideology of national identity as a irremediable loss, an ideological victory the State won, and lost.

Three Singapore novels deal specifically and urgently with the relationship between the individual and the economic, material world. Goh Poh Seng's *If We Dream Too Long*, Lim Thean Soo's *Ricky Star*, and Philip Jeyaretnam's *Raffles Place Ragtime* have as their protagonists ambitious yet thwarted characters who are defeated by their own weaknesses and by the cruel competition of a cut-throat mercantile society. All three novels are *romans-a-clef*, portraying the mis-education of a male protagonist in his attempt to survive and succeed in a material(ist) context, in order to educate their readers on a moral apprehension of the just society. The dialectic between character and social/material ideology allows these novels a sharpness of social criticism that involves them in a debate on national identity.

In the earliest novel, *If We Dream Too Long*, the working-class non-hero, Kwang Meng, hates his meaningless clerical job, yearns to escape through upward mobility or emigration, finds sex and alcohol as compensations, and is trapped finally in his dead-end position by his father's illness and family responsibilities.[16] The young Kwang

Meng's frustrations permit Goh to write a classical critique of the postcolonialist society. The novel begins with Kwang Meng taking a sick day off from work and observing the activities of the colonialist English, a class so removed from him that he can only approach them in ironic imagination: "the same English masters were seen going in for their Whiskey Stengahs and their Brandy Drys. He caught a glimpse of the white uniformed Chinese 'boys'. It's funny how the English can unselfconsciously call these old Hainanese men, 'boys'" (4).

Kwang Meng lives at home with his parents and two younger brothers. Privacy is a middle-class luxury he cannot afford, and he finds it only in his stolen swims. In early postcolonial Singapore, limited economic opportunities signified class-identified destinies: "Those with well-to-do parents did not worry: they could afford the university, or failing that, go abroad. The rest of the class. . . . knew what was to come. . . . Most saw themselves become like their fathers, fated to their fathers' lives" (9). Kwang Meng is more sensitive, indeed, more morbid than his cohorts. Still, his future is already imaged in the figure of Balthazar, the role he played in his school production of *The Merchant of Venice*. Balthazar is a character with only one line, "Madam, I go with all convenient speed," and the line is for an exit. Goh portrays Kwang Meng as that insignificant player in society, whose only role is to exit expediently.

The novel ends with a refiguration of the Balthazar motif. His affair with the bar-girl Lucy over, his hopes of moving to Sarawak for a more adventurous life ended, and even the beginning of a romance with middle-class Anne nipped because of his father's illness, drunk and distraught, Kwang Meng takes on the role of Balthazar one more time in response to an elderly English lady's request for directions to Raffles Hotel. This single irrational act completes the implicit authorial frame of social commentary. Kwang Meng's tentative attempts to move out of his working-class existence having failed, the novel ends as he abruptly exits. In short, the character is vivid so long as he maintains the sensitivity and dissatisfactions that drive him to escape his class origins. Once escape is closed off, he becomes only a bit player. *If We Dream Too Long* is a middle-class fiction, critical of narrow proletarian interests (portrayed in Kwang Meng's parents' obsession with security and money), valorizing middle-class mores and aspirations (in the pleasures in books and classical music of the paragon couple, Boon Teik and Mei-I) and presenting in Kwang Meng's entrapment in poverty the truly bourgeois nightmare.

Lim Thean Soo's *Ricky Star* has a more malevolent protagonist. Coming from a mercantile family (his father was a fast-dealing middle-man), Ricky struggles to educate himself in order to succeed as a business executive. Following his rise and fall, the novel foregrounds a modern, urban society in which the emphasis on money and social success results in family and individual deterioration. Socially ambitious, Ricky measures everything and every individual in material terms. He approaches paintings as consumer items exhibiting material status. Similarly, he courts and marries a middle-class woman as part of his campaign to move out of his lower-class position: "He never felt endearingly towards his wife, as some husbands did, and always measured his wife in material terms. . . . He had unjustly concluded that she was, all in all, a marginal liability" (3).

Ricky's obsession with success and his manipulative dishonesty are explained by his psycho/cultural anomie. He finds his father's (ancestral) values distasteful at the same time as he is insecure with Western customs. The novel provides a number of sharply detailed instances of the protagonist's identity crisis. Contemptuous of his father's racial thriftiness, figured in the old man's one shabby pair of pajamas, Ricky indulges in expensive although uncomfortable bathrobes (4). Moreover, the patriarchal oppressiveness of his childhood home sets the destructive model for his adult life. "There had never been a fixed time for meals at home. . . . It was rare that father, mother, and children had any meal together, even on Chinese New Year's Eve" (39). The father has a mistress and an illegitimate son, the mother withdraws into a catatonic state and kills herself, and Ricky abandons his loveless paternal home to pursue his own career.

Ricky Star portrays a society in material transition. Unlike the economic dead-ends that Goh's novel indicts, *Ricky Star* reflects a dynamic society in which fortunes can be readily made. The authorial frame, however, is stringently didactic. The dishonest are always punished (Ricky's father dies a penniless penitent, Ricky is last seen "a social pariah"); the good rewarded with success. Teck Soon, "an honest, sober man with hidden talent for business," marries the boss's daughter, and the narrator tells us, "One day, he would be immensely rich and he could look back without bitterness to the early years" (185). The fiction is predictably structured with less of psychological and moral complexity and more of straightforward social instruction. If the fiction has allegorical resonances, it is not that Ricky is the Singapore Everyman. Minor characters such as Teck Soon or Ricky's business antagonist Jimmy or his brother-in-law, Graham, are held as the model Singaporean businessman. In fact, Ricky is the dark side of this figure, the morally deficient, inadequately cultured, business failure whose life teaches by dis-exemplar.

Philip Jeyaretnam's *Raffles Place Ragtime* is the most recent expression of this peculiarly Singaporean moral vision, the fear of corruption and of emotional bankruptcy brought on by the social pressure to succeed. In *Raffles Place Ragtime,* this society is no longer static, as in *If We Dream Too Long,* nor is it merely dynamic. Instead, it is a supercharged society, running on high technology in the workplace; luxury Western consumer items such as Mercedes Benzes and French wines and cuisine; and a multi-national-coporation network. But the class/moral outlines remain the same. That is, under the enormous material changes in Singapore reflected in the three novels' changed material descriptions, the thematic focus on the success motif as a problematic affecting individual happiness and social/moral coherence remains unchanged.

In Jeyaretnam's novel, the protagonist, Vincent, comes from a working class family. His parents are food hawkers, and he shares a bedroom with a younger brother in a public housing apartment. Vincent is on the fast track. Working for the Singapore Monetary Exchange, he courts Connie Lim, the daughter of a socially prominent family. Like Ricky, Vincent's drive to economic and social mobility distorts his moral vision. Every one and every event is perceived only in terms of its material outcome for him.

Vincent's point-of-view is shared by others. His best friend, Yeow Khoon, who functions as a choral commentator on the action, is equally cynical about human relations. About Connie, he tells Vincent: "You have rung up the jackpot, Vincent. . . . Don't waste time. Dig in" (4). Even Mr. Lim, Connie's father, whom Vincent admires, is morally reprehensible; he keeps a mistress on the side. The novel draws a more damning portrait of Singapore society than is found in the earlier works. Vincent's ambitions, after all, coincide with and reflect national aspirations: "He alone truly appreciated the magnitude of Mr. Lim's rise from carpenter's son to stewardship of a banking empire. . . . It was Vincent's vigor and his ability that would propel Singapore forward in the twenty-first century, building on Mr. Lim's achievements a generation earlier" (24).

Raffles Place Ragtime demonstrates a greater self-consciousness about national identity and the place of the individual in the socio-political process. This self-consciousness is expressed in satirical and ironic mode, so that the moral dimension to which the fiction is pinned is not always simply addressed as it is in *Ricky Star.* Instead, for the greater part of the novel, the interrogation of social/national identity is subtly carried out through the portrayal of the protagonist's contradictions. Vincent works long hours and is sober and ambitious. His personal ambitions are often elided with national ideological aspirations, as in the passage above, so that selfish careerism is equated at points with nationalistic idealism. The fiction satirizes the national drive for success at the same time as it satirizes the individual who dramatizes it. Vincent is also an insecure, manipulative character who has an affair with a secretary at the same time that he is courting Connie. He denies his feelings in order to climb the slippery ladder of mobility, and is finally betrayed by his own working-class lack of *savoir-faire* , losing both his job and his rich girl.

The novel's didactic dimension is more sophisticated and stringently bourgeois in its socio-politcal reflections than either Goh's or Lim's novels. In all three novels, the working class protagonist fails to rise out of his class origin. But only *Raffles Place Ragtime* specifically assigns the anti-hero to a class resolution; Vincent loses his rich girl/future but discovers happiness in his true working-class girl's arms. He is only punished for desiring a social position that is not for him. Connie rejects Vincent because he is a loser: "Go back to your HDB flat," she taunts him. "Mother always said you were not good enough for me" (77). Depressed, she spends the next day shopping and drives home, "exhausted but happy. . . . she would survive" (102).

Strangely, the novel concludes with this shallow materialist as its moral center. Released from her proletarian lover, disillusioned by her father's marital infidelity, Connie is given the privilege of moral re-cognition. "She felt suffocated in here with this crowd of people in a rush, a rush for degrees, jobs, careers, spouses, houses. . . . She needed once and for all to escape" (123). The claustrophobic existentialist nausea that afflicted the working class Kwang Meng affects the upper-class heroine here. The escape is both moral and physical, to escape the nation's geographical confines for a larger, more adventurous location: "perhaps teach English in Papua New Guinea. . . . Travel round India" (124). Ironically, the character who *has* the resources to succeed in Singapore turns her back on success in search of a more meaningful life: "'But what sort of life will I have had? . . . And what about the rest of Singapore? Is everyone to sit around comparing husbands like motor cars?" (125).

Raffles Place Ragtime concludes on this diminutive allusion to *Paradise Lost:* "The world was all before her, but Connie was in no hurry" (125). Interestingly, the fiction has slipped from the opening male anti-hero to the closing female heroine, from an examination of working-class pressure to climb up the social-economic ladder to an expression of bourgeois dissatisfaction and idealistic rejection of the success motif. The novel's unacknowledged slippage demonstrates the split between working-class and bourgeois consciousness in the same fiction. While working-class striving for material success is satirized, the bourgeois revolt against such crass materialism is taken seriously. The fiction, even as it expresses this revolt in Connie's closing mood, does not successfully depict it. Her sudden moral growth is unearned; in the early depiction of her shallow concerns and her equally crass rejection of her crass lover, nothing prepares the reader for the epiphany that falls upon her in the conclusion like a spiritual mantle upon a Pauline convert. Connie is a creature of the author who uses her to express his own bourgeois position once the protagonist, Vincent, has collapsed into his working-class origin.

The fascination with the social/national drive for material development and success coupled with a revolt against the kinds of individual/moral costs such a drive exacts takes different expression in the Malaysian novel, *Flowers in the Sky*, one of the finest novels to come out of the region. Unlike the three *romans-a-clefs*, it does not have a simple didactic agenda. More explicit in its use of religious and moral themes, the social message is less obvious or primary. While the novel's examination of "the meeting and clash of different religions and their resolutions [in Southeast Asia]" (Harrex 6) includes some jibes at Christianity, its major concern is the characters of two immigrant types. While the Venerable Hung, a Chinese Abbot, struggles to overcome his physical drives, the Indian surgeon, Mr. K, interrogates the monk's spirituality. The Venerable Hung represents Buddhist consciousness, other-worldly, monastic, celibate, seeking escape from the Karmic world of sensuality through meditation, in contrast to Mr. K, worldly lover of women and material goods, an unbelieving Christian. The action oscillates between these dualisms, suggesting a universal drama of sinfulness, guilt and retribution. Preparing for this interpretation, the novel opens with two quotations from the *Lotus Sutra* that directly touch upon a central Buddhist belief, that the sin of fornication is subject to karmic retribution.

The novel's dualistic form is loosened by a non-linear construction (the action moves from Hung to K. to the comic sub-plot, and from present to past at will); however, it is also structured by the division of the book into six days. The number six is a controlling motif, for it is enlarged in the conclusion in the ironic vision of Hung leaving the Marvellous Cure Clinic after his surgery in a chauffeur-driven Mercedes carrying the license-plate '666.' While Mr. K., the subtle skeptical Christian, is amused by the unwitting allusion to Satan in Ch. 13 of the Book of Revelations, the authorial voice intrudes at this point to remind the reader that '666' in Cantonese approximates to 'Joy, joy, joy,' that is, to beatific vision. In leaving the reader at this conjunction of cross-cultural misreadings, the novel underscores religious/cultural relativism as its major thematic.

This relativism, even an ambiguity of valuation, is strongly suggested in the portrayals of the monk, the spiritual healer, and the surgeon, the physical healer. Both men, representing other-worldly and worldly striving, are two sides of the same coin. Hung's career from a youth in South China to become the foremost Temple Abbot in Penang, the growth of his spiritual self, is vivified by sensual conflict, symbolized in the carp image that disturbs his meditation as an apprentice and that is recalled later in his sexual attraction to the mute girl, Ah Lan. The horrible act of stigmatization, when Hung burns charcoal on his chest, is to be understood as retribution for his sensuality.

Conversely, K., who "had given up all this rigmarole" of religion (27) and settled for an earthly paradise, is continuously disturbed by longings for the transcendental. As much as Hung, his greatest consciousness is of what is absent: "The warmth and the tradition seemed to have been sieved off, leaving only struggling maggots of resentment and emptiness where the flesh should have been" (26). While Hung struggles to empty his consciousness of all sensation, K. struggles to keep his senses from ennui, the existential horror of nothingness. The possibility of faith deepens the novel's focus on race as defining character types and makes it a different fiction from the Malaysian and Singapore novels discussed so far.

The novel's minor characters are also representative of racial types in Malaysia, including Gopal, the Tamil police inspector, who finds in the Indian maid Nila his religious Shakti, or the union between flesh and spirit; and Hashim, the Malay Riot Squad inspector, whose political ambitions and intelligence are bent on "crowd-control." These sub-plots treat religious concerns in a more facetious manner, approaching religious sources less for sacramental value than for sociological content. The comic narratives also enlarge the novel's social range beyond the primary East-West dialectic to accommodate the Hindu and Malay aspects of Malaysian society. The novel shows a radical split in conception, when it moves from the interior drama of Buddhist/ Christian attitudes, materials into which the author has breathed his own ambivalences and psychic tensions, to the external drama of Hindu action and Malay crowd-control.

In the context of Malaysian racial divisions, the novel's attempt to overcome the suspicions and rigidity of one-race consciousness through a focus on cultural relativism, expressed in both serious and comic terms, is admirable. Emerging from the tragi-farcical elements is a composite identity of a Malaysia of many gods, a land in which individuals act within the confines of their ethnocentric societies, bumping now and again into each other with curiosity, tact, or the absence of it, and with only partial understanding of the others' motivations and perceptions. The novel succeeds as a subtle rendering of a polyglot society that stops short of the conventional twentieth-century thematic of alienation.

What larger thesis on twentieth-century world literature do these eight English-language novels, written on the fringes of their societies, illuminate? For one thing, although these novelists and other English-language writers continue to publish, the phenomenon of English-language novel-production appears as sporadic, discontinuous cultural activity. Using a fringe language (in Malay-dominant Malaysia), producing a fringe product (in pragmatic, mercantile Singapore), centering themselves in fringe cultures and ideologies (for example, immigrant ethnic communities or Westernized mentalities), these novelists are largely ignored by their societies and almost totally unknown in metropolitan centers. T. Wignesan, editor of the first English-language Malaysian literature anthology, *Bunga Emas,* argued English as a "neutral tongue brings with it another culture, tradition, style, and, more significantly, a means of escape from the reality of the Malaysian socio-political cleft-stick" (18).[17] Reading these Malaysian and Singapore novels disabuses us of the illusion that any tongue can or should be "neutral." Rather, the English in these novels encode and call upon multiple cultural systems, constructing fictions that delineate ethnically differentiated, ancient and modern, Asian and Western, proletarian and bourgeois societies. Whether early or late, little paradigmatic progression of national or social identity can be discerned in these examples. Instead, they repeat questions of identity from a variety of positions, individual, economic, moral, spiritual, national. They are identity-haunted books spiralling from their fringe locations. If literature from the West prides itself on its postmodernist liberation from the old questions of nationalism, literature from the fringe is in some ways pre-nationalist, anterior to twentieth-century national categories. In the groping for a match between identity and destiny, these novels are very much a product of the postmodernist collapse of geographical/cultural boundaries into global fragmentations.

1989

Notes

1. See A. D. Hope's three-stage model for all colonial literature, the first being an imitation of the homeland's literary tradition; the second that of provincialism; and the third, of authentic and confident expression. Fanon's theory of postcolonial literature also provides a systemic thesis: that it will move from an aping of the colonialists' literature to a stage of provincialism to a national and finally international identity. Fanon's progressive theory was based on the social reformer's utopianist vision of liberated societies.
2. Fredric Jameson has noted among American intellectuals an "imprisonment in the present of postmodernism" (66) that results in their reading of Third-World literature as "outmoded stages of our first-world cultural development" (65). He suggests in place of "this particular mirage of the 'centered subject' and the

154

unified personal identity, we would do better to confront honestly the fact of fragmentation on a global scale; it is a confrontation with which we can at least make a cultural beginning" (67).

3. To Jameson, "Third-world texts, even those which are seemingly private and invested with a properly libidinal dynamic — necessarily project a political dimension in the form of national allegory: *the story of the private individual destiny is always an allegory of the embattled situation of the public third-world culture and society*" (69) (italics the author's).

4. Aijaz Ahmad argues against Jameson's totalizing of national literatures and asks for a different premise that will "encompass all the fecundity of real narratives in the so-called third world" (9). S. Gopinathan's "Intellectual Dependency and the Indigenization Response" makes a similar case against the hegemonic tendencies of Western intellectual thought.

5. See Mochtar Pabottingi for a South East Asian perspective on the sociopolitical material base for culture. Also see Chinweizu, et al., and Neil Lazarus for critiques of Eurocentric interpretations of non-Western literature. Also Bruce King, *The New Literatures* and King, ed. *Literatures of the World in English,* for examples of nation-bounded readings of Third-World texts.

6. As Margaret Atwood summed up the position of Ee Tiang Hong, a Malaysian emigre poet in Australia, "In his view, English in ex-colonies is not always the language of oppression; at the moment, since its use is almost forbidden by an extremely nationalistic government, it is practically a language of political protest" (303).

7. R. K. Tongue provides a useful introduction to the functions and localized usages of English in the region. Afendras and Kuo offer a more sociologically nuanced analysis of the complex language situations in Singapore.

8. According to Koh Tai Ann, only eight English-language novels of serious worth had been published up to 1986. In the last few years, many more English-language novels have appeared. Koh Tai Ann calls Goh's *If We Dream Too Long* "the first serious novel (in English) set in Singapore' by a Singaporean" *(Tropic Crucible* 163). Elsewhere, she contends that "the existing prose work in English is generally lacking in literary merit" and that such prose is better studied as sociological documentary" (*Literature and Society in Southeast Asia* 177).

9. See Peter Chen for a sociological view on the place of elites in Singapore's development.

10. This chapter will focus on K. S. Maniam, *The Return* (1981); Catherine Lim, *The Serpent's Tooth* (1982); Lloyd Fernando, *Scorpion Orchid* (1976); Christine Su-Chen Lim, *Rice Bowl* (1984); Goh Poh Seng, *If We Dream Too Long* (1972); Lim Thean Soo, *Ricky Star* (1978); Philip Jeyaretnam, *Raffles Place Ragtime* (1988); and Lee Kok Liang, *Flowers in the Sky* (1981). Page references to these novels will be given in the chapter.

11. Shannon Ahmad's novel, *Srengenge,* exemplifies the rural, agarian, and Islamic concerns of many Malay-language novelists.

12. Nicholson and Chaterjee, *Tropic Crucible,* and Tham Seong Chee, *Literature and Society,* contain useful essays on the literature of the region.

13. Maniam's essay, "The Malaysian Novelist: Detachment or Spiritual Transcendence," offers his views on the novel's themes.

14. Coomaraswamy explains Nataraja as an iconic figure signifying Shiva as "Lord of Dancers . . . the manifestation of primal rhythmic energy."
15. See Anne Brewster, "Linguistic Boundaries: K.S. Maniam's *The Return*," and "The Discourse of Nationalism and Multiculturalism in Singapore and Malaysia in the 50's and 60's," for further discussions on the novel and on the interrelations between nationalism and text in the region.
16. Michael Lowy offers a corollary to the sub-text of Romantic protest against the economic atomism of urban civilization that runs through much Singapore writing.
17. Gerald Moore's *The Chosen Tongue* similarly demonstrates the reductive view of English-language writing from the British colonies that Wignesan endorses.

Works Cited

Afendras, E. A. and Eddie C. Y. Kuo. *Language and Society in Singapore*. Singapore: Singapore University Press, 1980.

Ahmad, Aijaz. "Jameson's Rhetoric of Otherness and the 'National Allegory'." *Social Text* 17 (Fall 1987): 3-25.

Ahmad, Shannon. *Srengenge*. Kuala Lumpur: Heinemann, 1973.

Atwood, Margaret. "Diary Down Under." *Second Words*. Beacon Press: Boston, 1982.

Brewster, Anne. "Linguistic Boundaries: K.S. Maniam's *The Return*." *A Sense of Exile*, ed. Bruce Bennett. Perth: Centre for Studies in Australian Literature, 1988:173-180.

———. "The Discourse of Nationalism and Multiculturalism in Singapore and Malaysia in the 50's and 60's." *Inventing Countries*, 136-150.

Burke, Kenneth. *Perspectives by Incongruity and Terms For Order*, edited by Stanley E. Hyman. Bloomington: Indiana University Press, 1964.

Chen, Peter. "Elites and National Development in Singapore." *Southeast Asian Journal of Social Science* 3:1 (1975):17-25.

Chinweizu, Onwuchekwa Jemie, Ihechukwu Madubuike. *Toward the Decolonization of African Literature*. Washington D.C.: Howard University Press, 1983.

Coomaraswamy, Ananda K. *The Dance of Shiva*. New York: The Noonday Press, 1957.

Fanon, Franz. *Black Skin, White Masks*. Trans. Charles Lam Markmann. New York: Grove, 1967.

Fernando, Lloyd. *Scorpion Orchid*. Kuala Lumpur: Heinemann Educational Books, 1976.

———. *Cultures in Conflict: Essays on Literature & the English Language in South East Asia*. Singapore: Graham Brash, 1986.

Goh, Poh Seng. *If We Dream Too Long*. Singapore: Island Press, 1972.

Gopinathan, S. "Intellectual Dependency and the Indigenization Response: Case Studies of University Curricula in two Third World universities." Paper presented at the Institute of Education, Singapore, 1985.

Harrex, S. C. "Scalpel, Scar, Icon: Lee Kok Liang's *Flowers in the Sky*." *The Writer's Sense of the Contemporary*, ed. Bruce Bennett, Ee Tiang Hong and Ron Shepherd. Perth: The Centre for Studies in Australian Literature, 1982: 35-40.

Hope, A. D. *Native Companions, Essays and Comments on Australian Literature 1936-1966*. Sydney: Angus & Robertson, 1974.

Jameson, Fredric. "Third World Literature in the Era of Multinational Capitalism." *Social Text* 15 (Fall 1986): 65-88.

JanMohamed, Abdul R. *Manichean Aesthetics The Politics of Literature in Colonial Africa*. Amherst: The University of Massachusetts Press, 1983.

Jeyaretnam, Phillip. *Raffles Place Ragtime*. Singapore: Times Books International, 1988.

King, Bruce, ed. *Literatures of the World in English*. London and Boston: Routledge & Kegan Paul, 1974.

King, Bruce. *The New Literatures*. New York: St. Martin's Press, 1980.

Koh, Tai Ann. "Singapore Writing in English: The Literary Tradition and Cultural Identity." *Literature and Society in Southeast Asia*. 160-186.

————. "Singapore: The Novel in English; A Brief Survey." Paper presented at Workshop on the Southeast Asian Novel at the Institute of Southeast Asian Studies, 1985, Singapore.

Lazarus, Neil, "Great Expectations and After: The Politics of Postcolonialism in African Fiction." *Social Text* 13/14 (1986):49-63.

Lee, Kok Liang. *Flowers in the Sky*. Kuala Lumpur: Heinemann, 1981.

Lim, Catherine. *The Serpent's Tooth*. Singapore: Times Books International, 1982.

Lim, Su-chen Christine. *Rice Bowl*. Singapore: Times Books International, 1984.

Lim, Thean Soo. *Ricky Star*. Singapore: Pan Pacific Books, 1978.

Lowy, Michael. "The Romantic and the Marxist Critique of Modern Civilization." *Theory and Society* 16 (1987): 891-904.

Maniam, K. S. *The Return*. Kuala Lumpur: Heinemann Educational Books, 1981.

————. "The Malaysian Novelist: Detachment or Spiritual Transcendence." *A Sense of Exile*, ed. Bruce Bennett. Adelaide: Centre for Studies in Australian Literature, 1988: 167-72.

McLeod, A. L. *The Commonwealth Pen*. Ithaca: Cornell University Press, 1961.

Moore, Gerald. *The Chosen Tongue: English Writing in the Tropical World*. London: Longmans, 1969.

Nicholson, Colin E. & Ranjit Chaterjee. *Tropic Crucible: Self and Theory in Language and Literature*. Singapore: Singapore University Press, 1984.

Slemon, Stephen. "Post-Colonial Allegory and the Transformation of History." *Journal of Commonwealth Literature*: 157-168.

Tham, Seong Chee. *Literature and Society in Southeast Asia Political and Sociological Perspectives*. Singapore: Singapore University Press, 1981.

Tongue, R. K. *The English of Singapore and Malaysia*. Singapore: Eastern Universities Press, 1974.

Walcott, Derek. *The Castaway*. London: Jonathan Cape, 1965.

Wignesan, T., ed. *Bunga Emas*. Malaysia: Anthony Blond with Rayirath Pub,, 1964.

The National Canon and English-language Women Writers
from Malaysia and Singapore, 1949-1969

Introduction

Every emerging literature has its pioneering women writers. If their number has been small, this has resulted usually from the unfavorable conditions under which they wrote: absence of encouragement for their "unwomanly" efforts, lack of publishing opportunities, and the burden of domestic work and marital responsibilities.[1] As many critics have noted, pioneer women writers tended to write in forms not traditionally considered literature, such as diaries, letters, journals, stories for children, and autobiographies, and because the subjects and content of their writing tended to fall outside areas assumed to be significant, their themes have been dismissed as subjective, personal, or sentimental.[2] Indeed, because many women generally have not been present in the halls of political power and decision-making, their work has been perceived as extraneous to a national literature.[3] In colonial and postcolonial societies, women writers may face additional forces arising from the gendered or patriarchal shape of national ideologies that exclude them. Even when they do publish, their works are located outside the perspectives of critics and cultural historians of these newly emerging nation-states who are themselves involved in articulating ideologies of nationalism to counter their colonial past. The authors of *Toward the Decolonization of African Literature,* for example, argue for an Afrocentric literature that resists European and nonnative influences and that revives a pure and original tradition, leading to the corollary that value can only be attributed to works that in some way carry of a family or national identity.[4] Many examples of women's writing therefore have not been collected or even noticed, laboring as many critics do under assumed values of what constitutes a "significant" or "national" literature.

Malaysian-Singapore women writing in English today still face the crisis of which the 1958 *Litmus One* editors complained: "[the] lack of a common local and long-standing tradition."[5] (17). The major difficulty in attempting to recover neglected texts and inscribing the names of Singapore and Malaysian women writers who do not appear in the national canons is that there is little information or material on them. Their works are usually out of print and may not be found in libraries, even in special collections. They may not appear in editions of *Who's Who,* newspaper clippings, or biographies. Defining and assessing their contribution to cultural history is difficult given this absence or scarcity of materials.

This study attempts to map a tradition of women's writing, to light up an area of invisibility, as it were. The trope of uncharted territory is closely related, moreover, to that of territory that has no legal status, that needs as yet to be "chartered." Bearing in mind the significance of the Women's Charter Bill of 1961, which secured legal, professional, and economic rights for Singaporean women (Vivienne Wee 1987), the term "unchartered" has a special aptness for the women who were writing in the region before the 1961 bill. My study suggests that the works of early women writers from Malaysia and Singapore have been neglected partly because their status as individuals in newly formed nation-states was legalistically unclear, undefined, and outside hegemonic national definitions. Writing within the context of rapid identity changes fostered by cultural and language policies that are shaped by ideologies of nation-building, women writers such as Hedwig Aroozoo, Sybil Kathigasu, Janet Lim, Cecile Parrish, and Wong May manifest that "uprootedness, social displacement, even exile" charac-teristic of the lives of a number of international women writers (Shulman 18). "The phenomenon of displacement," Shulman notes, is the cause for the obscurity for many international women writers; their lives and the fate of their books reflect "the political upheavals, class warfare, and social turbulence that have characterized our century" (18). Even Aroozoo, a Singapore citizen, who appears the least uprooted of these five women, manifests the vicissitudes of postcolonial identity in her life: British subject, conquered subject of the Japanese Emperor (1941-45); citizen of independent Malaysia (1964); and citizen of the island nation of Singapore (1965 onwards).

Pioneer Women Poets

Malaysian-Singapore women's poetry in English (generally assumed as pre-dating women's efforts in prose) is usually said to begin with the generation writing in the late 1960s: "Wong May, Shirley Lim, Lee Tzu Pheng, Lee Geok Lan and Hilary Tham were the first women poets" (Lau Yok Ching 104). According to Edwin Thumboo, "Before the mid-sixties, very few women wrote creatively; there were no women among the pioneer poets. Wong May and Lee Geok Lan were about the first" (1970 xxxii). Other studies of Malaysian/Singapore writing echo the judgement that the literature was an all-male purview from its inception in the late 1940s to the mid-sixties, when Lee Geok Lan, Lee

Tzu Pheng, and Wong May began to publish (Nair 1970; Yeo 1970; Singh 1987; Brewster 1988, 1989; Lim 1989).

These studies overlook a major phenomenon: women were writing and publishing poetry and prose in Malaysia and Singapore as early as the 1950s. Koh Tai Ann's bibliography on women's writing offers a more accurate view of the tradition of Malaysian-Singapore women's writing in English (1987). Between 1950 and 1970, English-language women writers published memoirs, children's verse, and collections of serious poetry. In 1969, Hilary Tham self-published a collection of poems, *Paper Boats*. Other women writers published irregularly; for example, Lee Geok Lan, the only woman represented in *Bunga Emas*, the first anthology of Malayan English language writing (Wignesan 1964).[6] Other women who published only occasionally have received scant critical notice. These occasional pieces, read together, offer evidence of women's participation in the formation of a different kind of literary tradition, one that approaches the ideology of nationalism from a more critical and unbounded position.

Hedwig Aroozoo, who published in early student journals, will serve as an archival case in point.[7] She attended the University of Malaya in Singapore in 1949-52, and later took a course in librarianship in London from 1955-57, during which time she co-edited *Suara Merdeka*. *Suara Merdeka* was the organ of the Malayan Forum, a Malayan (including Singapore) students' organization founded in London in 1949 to discuss and study politics. Its earliest members include Tun (then Datuk) Abdul Razak, Dr. Toh Chin Chye, Lee Kuan Yew, Goh Keng Swee, Maurice Baker, and Dato' Mohamed Sofie, men who became prominent politicians in their countries (notes from the author). Aroozoo also wrote love poems in 1956, but destroyed them later, she says, as they were not intended for publication.

Patrick Anderson, a University of Malaya English literature teacher in the early fifties, documents his impressions of young university intellectuals such as Beda Lim, Wang Gungwu, and Hedwig Aroozoo in his memoirs, *Snake Wine: A Singapore Episode* (1955). Recorded in his memoirs, Aroozoo appears the more mature, sophisticated intellectual:

> . . . where Gung-wu's nationalism may strike one as no more than a chip on his shoulder, Hedwig's is worn as a mark of good breeding, a civilized discrimination and sympathy, which provides so to speak a vista back from her very obvious intelligence (some people regard her as a blue-stocking) to her equally strong, and charming femininity. She never dogmatizes. (242)

Anderson's characterization contains prophetic ironies, as well as a marked reliance on stereotypes for "femininity." Despite the noted lack of dogmatism, Aroozoo devoted her life to education and literature through her work in the nation's library systems, eventually serving as Librarian in the National Library.

Male writers by and large have not suffered from such neglect. Take the case of Wang Gungwu, born in Indonesia and educated for many years in China, who wrote a slim volume of poems, *Pulse*, and two critical essays on Malayan writing in the 1950s before moving on to make his career as a historian.[8] Although Wang removed himself from identification with the nationalistic politics of Malaysia and Singapore by emigrating to Australia in the 1960s, *Pulse,* is generally referred to as marking the beginning of Malaysian writing in English (Yeo 1970a; Brewster 1988, 1989; Lim 1989). His two essays (1958a 27-8; 1958b 6-8), on the use of English in creating a Malayan literature, are also cited as formative contributions to the evolution of a Malaysian/ Singapore literature in English. Wang's contribution is still recognized today, perhaps for the very reason that his involvement in Malayan writing some forty years ago was of a dogmatic nature in that it helped to formulate a nationalist ideology consistent with contemporary nation-building ideals.

The continued usefulness of Wang's texts to contemporary cultural commentators demonstrates how ideological considerations play a role in the construction of a national canon. This is not to say that texts are appropriated as propagandistic instruments to serve the authority of powerful established agencies. Literary texts and readers after all have their own evasive linguistic discourse strategies that resist political appropriation. However, in the constructions of canons, works that diverge from or critique the prevailing ideology of national identity can be expected to be marginalized or excluded.[9]

Wang's early interrogations into the relationship between a "foreign" language, English, and the viability of national identity expressed in English became foregrounded as Malaysia and Singapore moved into state-sponsored efforts to build national cultures. His position — that a Malayan identity had to be based on multiracialism and that Malayan literature reflected this multiracialism in its images and idioms — anticipated Singapore's pluralistic Constitution and counters the Malay-dominant, monocultural policies currently in place in Malaysia.[10] In 1968, for example, ten years after Wang's call for the representation of a pluralistic national identity in literature, Dr. Goh Keng Swee, then Minister for Finance, and Patron of the '68 Arts Festival, spoke for the necessity of a "culturally distinctive" society, and described the "national culture" as having to fuse "the cultural heritages of four ancient civilizations" (*Straits*

Times Jan. 1968); that is, the Malay, Chinese, Indian and Anglo-European civilizations that make up the major components of Singapore multicultural population.[11] The need for political stability, social cohesiveness, and communal understanding immediately upon Singapore's break with Malaysia appears to support the ideology of pluralism or "cultural democracy" (a phrase used by Mr. Lee Khoon Choy, Minister for State and Culture, and reported in the same article) that Wang expounded in his essays and poems.

In contrast to Wang, Aroozoo did not claim a "serious intention" for her work. Although she wrote poetry, she did not publish most of them as she thought them too private and did not wish exposure. Indeed, she went to great trouble to repress the publication of her poems. "Rhyme in Time," a parody written as a tutorial exercise for Anderson in 1951, appeared without her permission in *Litmus One* (1958). Aroozoo strove to have it removed, arguing that it was not "a seriously-intentioned poem" (letter from H.A. 1989).

Between 1946 and 1956, however, she did publish five parodies on sociopolitical themes in various non-literary journals.[12] The parody is a form that imitates and mocks the piece it imitates. As a strategic expression of the anxiety of influence that characterizes latecomers to a strong or classical tradition, it flatters the original while permitting some distancing from its influence.[13] The parody was a favorite form for Aroozoo, whose first published piece (1946), written as a schoolgirl, imitates the "To be or not to be" soliloquy in *Hamlet*, notorious to colonial schoolchildren by way of rote-drilling English teachers. While the protest against homework is clearly juvenilia, what surprises is the political imagination suggested in certain images. Indeed, despite the lack of control over the pentameter, the counterpointed abstractions provide a structural pleasure:

> And thus the defiant flush of revolution
> Is clouded o'er, by faint glimm'rings of commonsense,
> And enterprises born of foolish fervour,
> (Oh, headlines crying, "Schoolgirl goes on strike!")
> Are now submerged in the unconscious mind. (79)

Similarly her undergraduate poem, "Rhyme in Time," parodying the *vers libre* of The Waste Land,[14] is distinguished from mere imitation. Its theme, to fuse the unassimilated "fragments" of a colonized Singapore, leads to pastiche as structure; for example, in the opening question which plays on nursery rhyme associations. "Where has my lion's tail gone?" — punning on Singapore, the lion city, and tale, the story of the country (22) — asks, in the poet's construction of a social wasteland, where is the story of Singapore? The poem satirizes Mrs. Mildred Barrington-Smith, the colonial white woman, childless, untiring hostess, and juxtaposes Mrs. Smith's self-important social whirl in Singapore with the drab reality of post-war Britain: "Pavement-stuck queues,/ Eight-penny meat rations,/ And not many nylons" (22). Like Aroozoo's schoolgirl's effort, the poem shows a public imagination at work. Parody, in the disjointed, discontinuous, and multilingual passages in Aroozoo's poem, operates as a strategy of cultural hybridity, akin to postmodern strategies of the pastiche.[15] Aroozoo's pastiche anticipates contemporary theorizing about colonial and postcolonial productions. Homi Bhabha, for example, has characterized the uneasy and unstable relations between local cultural detail and the detail of imperial and colonial culture in these productions, and suggests a "Third Space of enunciation," a transformative "hybrid" moment that is "neither one nor the other but something else besides" (13). Bhabha's explanation for the quality of hybridity in colonial and postcolonial works acutely recognizes their construction of style as constituting a "struggle of identifications" that cannot be "sublated into an image of the collective will" (14).

In fact, Aroozoo's 1951 parody foreshadows the satirical themes, the turn to a historical imagination, and the use of local idiom that are persistent features of a more mature poetic tradition in Malaysian/ Singapore writing. For example, her poem uses local dialect, idiomatic phrases that are recognizably British colonial bureaucratese, and acronyms that are characteristic of Singapore English-language use.[16]

> Your name for an S.I.T. flat?
> An O.B.E. for your brat?
> Just count the dollar bills.
> Culture with a capital C? —
> It's yours for a moderate fee (23)

The poem contextualizes its allusions, situating itself in a colonial history that includes Malay heroes and the heroes of Portuguese and British conquest: "our fathers that begat us . . . /Alphonso D'Alburquerque, / Francisco d'Almeida . . . / The river Rajahs,/ The Hang Tuahs . . ./ And the incomparable/ Raffles." Prefiguring later post-colonial writing in English that crosses the boundaries of linguistic purity to engage the resources of other languages, Aroozoo's poem presses toward a recognition that the identity of colonized subjects cannot be contained simply within the English language.[17] Asking who Singaporeans of the 1950s were, the poem raises the issue that their identity can be best constructed in a bilingual form, and, then, ironically, only by a reader who understands the cultural nuances of both languages. In the passage,

> Who are the people?
> *Tida-apa-lah*!
> *Mana boleh-la*! -
> Let's get out of this place.

the insider will recognize two Malay sentences as favorite local ejaculations that encapsulate specific cultural attitudes. "Tidak-apa-lah" (it doesn't matter) and "Mana-boleh-lah" (it can't be done) are linguistic metonyms or tags for a nativist world characterized by apathy and social disengagement. The tension between the insider's satirical acknowledgement of these cultural negatives and the desire to escape them accounts for much of the poem's interest.

Aroozoo's three parodies published in *Suara Merdeka* (May 1956, 24-25; June 1956, 25-27; July 1956, 23) treat more topical political subjects. The first poem alludes to a popular American song that accompanied the Hollywood movie, "Davie Crockett," to satirize David Marshall, then Chief Minister of Singapore. Satire on pressing political events, as evident in Pope's and Dryden's collected works, seldom maintains interest outside that occasion. With Marshall's exit from Singapore politics, Aroozoo's piece lost its pertinence to a contemporary audience. Similarly outdated is the parody, based on a *Straits Budget* report (21st June 1956) on the question of merger between the Federation of Malaya and Singapore, when Mr. Lim Yew Hock, then Chief Minister of Singapore, replied: "Well, gentlemen, the love-making has started. As you know yourselves, once you start making love, there are always chances of a marriage." Significant as Mr. Lim's metaphor may have appeared in 1956, the poem appears as an ironic historical footnote in the wake of Singapore's separation from Malaysia in 1967. The final parody in my possession, titled "Suez Canal Blues" (July 1956, 23) treats Britain's loss of the Suez Canal to Egypt's Nasser, a theme that also has limited historical interest in the light of later events in the Middle East. The poems' limited interest underlines their similarity to the public poems produced by Wang and Oliver Seet, Aroozoo's male contemporaries.

Occasional poems by other women published before 1969 also break the boundary between subjective representation and political enunciation. For example, a 1961 poem by Daisy Chan Heng Chee, recently Singapore's United Nations representative, already demonstrates a political imagination at work (*Focus* 1) "The Safer Art" compares the non-conformist painter with the dissenting writer, to criticize the practice of censorship:

> Placed under detention, he languished,
> Were he gifted more in paints than ink
> He would have enjoyed at least
> A compromise freedom of expression.

The ambiguity suggested in the contradiction, "compromise freedom," suggests also the entangled nature of the state's relationship to the two arts. The painter's freedom is compromised because his medium is not directly political; but any form of expression permitted by a repressive state must be, perforce, already compromised. The conjunction of "enjoy" with "compromise" brackets "freedom" and indicts the "detention" of art's "free" condition.

The contributions of male writers such as Wang Gungwu or Oliver Seet are read for their historical significance and sociopolitical reflections in understanding the birth and evolution of Malaysian/ Singapore English-language literature (Yeo 1970a, 1977; Singh 1984; Brewster 1988, 1989). Arguably, therefore, the occasional poetry of women poets like Aroozoo also should be noted in an historical survey of English-language literature from Malaya/Singapore. According to Ee Tiang Hong, for example, "Rhyme in Time" "merits a place in any anthology of Malaysian poetry that has a historical import" (1987 10). Aroozoo's parodies revise the general perception that women writers from the region wrote more subjectively than men, that their subjects were private, and that their preferred forms were lyrical. The poems suggest that women writers, like their male counterparts, were engaged in issues of national identity, colonial and postcolonial tensions, and literary presence. While, like her peers, Aroozoo can be said to lack "[t]hat sustained vision and the assimilative verve of an expanding theme within which particular experiences best yield their inner significance" (Thumboo, 1976 xvi), her occasional poems are pioneering attempts to "translate their cultural identities in a discontinuous intertextual temporality of cultural difference" (Bhabha 22). Their discontinuity, intertextuality, and instability of identities challenge the assimilative and hegemonizing "vision" of a single, authentic "national culture" that native critics like Chinweizu construct as the Other to Western culture.

The evidence of political consciousness and a public imagination in Malaysian/Singapore women's writing prior to 1970 is substantial, especially in prose works. Indeed, political consciousness is foregrounded in the early autobiographies, *No Dram of Mercy* by Sybil Kathigasu and Janet Lim's *Sold For Silver*. Kathigasu's memoir presents the author as a heroine, a woman warrior, and an upholder of Western values such as individual liberty and free speech: "I have never been held back by fear of the consequences from saying what I think is right, and I refused to deprive myself of the liberty of expressing my true feelings about the Japanese" (44). Kathigasu was a well-known and well-loved community figure, a midwife and nurse, who during the war risks her life and her family's safety by giving medical assistance to the Malayan People's Anti-Japanese Army (MPAJA). Throughout the memoir she refers to the resistance group as guerillas; they were later labeled as Communists.[18] As a result of this resistance work, she was arrested by the Japanese and imprisoned. The first part of the memoir describes the Japanese occupation of Malaya as a particularly brutal suppression of the Chinese population: "Their rule was based on terror, and this was particularly so in respet of the Chinese. . . . [T]hey feared the Chinese, and gave expression to their fear in savage persecution and constant spying. . . . Hence the public executions which were a barbarous feature of Japanese rule" (52). The memoir's documentation of "savage" and "barbaric" sexual assaults, looting, and killings of innocent civilians bears searing witness to a recent history that has been suppressed by Japanese nationals and the interests of international corporate capital.

Three ideological aspects of the opening make it especially problematic from a nationalist perspective: the protagonist's unswerving pro-British stance, her sympathetic view of the MPAJA, and her Catholic faith. As a part-Irish Eurasian, born Sybil Daly and married to a doctor, Kathigasu was a privileged woman in a colonized society and counted white professionals and white women among her friends. As revealed in her memoir, her personal traits, generous treatment of poor patients, devotion to the sick, idealism in helping the guerillas, and extraordinary courage, explain the sympathy and furtive support she received from her non-Japanese captors and guards (35). She frequently seems to ignore the fact that the prison guards are collaborators, and interprets their support as an expression of covert pro-British loyalties: "Our guards made no secret of their hatred of the Japanese regime and their longing for the return of the British" (150). One incident describes Kathigasu's reply to a Japanese officer who orders her to "address a Japanese as Tuan [master]." Boldly, she declares, "I speak

English . . . and I never used 'Tuan' to the British so why should I to you?" (142). Here Kathigasu appeals to English as the language of democratic egalitarianism. The British, according to her account, operate outside the frame of fascist domination, unlike the Japanese colonizers who insist on their superior position. We glimpse how deep an ideological gulf there is between Kathigasu and ordinary Malayan people, who were treated as racial inferiors by Japanese *and* British alike. British colonialism has historically meant domination over and suppression of non-British peoples, albeit in a paternalistic manner in contrast to the Japanese colonizers' violent militarism. Kathigasu's Anglophilia emerges again and again in her memoir: "I reminded the guard of what Malaya owed to Britain, and of the amount of talent, labour, money and material which had gone to make Malaya the happiest and most advanced country in the East" (162).

Kathigasu's perspective contrasts sharply with that of Janet Lim whose war memoir expresses disenchantment. Lim, unlike Kathigasu, was not a privileged colonial subject, but an impoverished China-born orphan, an unmarried nurse having no class or race privileges and therefore no stake in British rule. Lim, therefore, approached the Japanese displacement of British colonial rule with a certain optimism: "I thought that war would solve some of our problems, especially that of the colour bar, which was very marked in those days. For instance, during the early campaign of Malaya, someone wrote to the local press asking the Government to supply a special bus for Europeans only, as Asians were filthy" (104). Kathigasu's white-privileged procolonial admiration for British paternalistic rule thus problematizes an interpretation of her work as Malaysian *national* literature when "national" is constituted as unambivalently oppositional to colonialist culture.

Similarly, Kathigasu's sympathetic account of MPAJA military activities which describe the resistance movement as cheifly Chinese (58) and the portraits of informers and collaborators, willing or unwilling, do not fit in with the accepted version of Malaysian national history. In Kathigasu's memoir, Chinese resistance fighters are national patriots. Postwar British colonial history, and contemporary histories written of Malaysia condemn these "patriots" as Communist insurgents and murderous sympathizers of the People's Republic of China.[19] Kathigasu's memoir reminds the reader that the MPAJA was an ally of "Britain and America in the fight against the Axis" (99). Her portraits of idealistic young Chinese men such as Berani, Don Juan, and Moru contradict the stereotype of the killer jungle squads popularized in the sensationalist nonfiction accounts by British ex-administrators (Miller 1954; Moran 1959). In the struggle for the minds and hearts of the people that characterized the postwar years in Malaysia, Kathigasu's memoir stands apart from the prevailing British colonial ideology and also the Malay dominant state indeology of nationalism in which Malay political practice was seen as central and the Chinese were viewed as opportunistic economic sojourners.[20]

Finally, Kathigasu's memoir testifies to her Catholic faith. Borrowing images from a long tradition of Christian martyr narrative, the text constructs her heroism and courage under unendurable torture as Christian martyrdom, and gives a literal representation of her religious beliefs: "It was during the early hours of the morning that I awoke. As I opened my eyes I was dazzled by a vision of the Sacred heart before me. . . . And His voice said to me: 'My child, you must be ready to pay the supreme sacrifice, for the glory that is to come'" (40).

Even if constructed as a fictional narrative, this passage is difficult to place in a national ideology that is strictly secular in Singapore and Islamic in Malaysia.[21] John Clammer, in his study of the culture and society in Singapore, notes that religion in Singapore "stands in a rather uneasy alliance with the secular powers: both are competing for control of the dominant symbolic system of the society" (47). In Malaysia, although Christianity is tolerated, the state has promulgated national culture as one that is Malay in customs and cultural values and religion (Hussein, 1977). Clearly the Catholic religion as a motivational and dramatic feature in a professed "true" story, complicates, if not makes impossible, the figure of the woman as (secular or Islamic) *nationalist* heroine. These aspects of the hegemony of Singapore and Malaysian secular and Islamic, anti-Communist, and decolonizing nationalisms would continue to raise difficulties in teaching Kathigasu's book in the region.

Yet *No Dram of Mercy* is a powerfully, if simply, written war memoir, which in addition to its vivid and unrelenting descriptions of brutality and corresponding courage, reveals the sources of the protagonist's survival and grace. Kathigasu may attribute her survival to her God, but the frank, straightforward narration testifies to a belief in communal sharing, communication, and interdependence in the face of physical barbarities that helped preserve her from degradation, insanity, and death. Kathigasu is a Western-informed observer, motivated by the ethos of Western-style democracy — liberty, equality, and fraternity. The highly risky effort to keep a forbidden short-wave radio in order to listen to BBC reports on the war is one instance of her resistance against the prohibition on free communication: "[The BBC news] was a constant reminder that we were not alone — that the world we knew still existed though we were temporarily cut off from it. This knowledge fortified our faith in the ultimate victory of truth and right" (51).

Kathigasu made her clinic as a clearinghouse for information, including information on Japanese troop movements that helped the guerillas, despite the threat of punishment that would follow on discovery. In prison, she continued to pass on information, using Samy, an Indian Sanitary Board laborer, to carry messages to her husband and family.

Her actions, based on these principles, provoked her Japanese captors' ill-treatment. But her drive toward democratic and communal free speech, to break the oppressive silence imposed by the Japanese military, also liberated her from her isolation in prison. Her belief in freedom of speech leads to actions that save her from the machinations of the Kempetai (Japanese Military Intelligence). More significantly, the memoir constructs a relation between Western liberal ideology and spiritual resources that preserves the individual in the face of torture and Eastern (Japanese) totalitarianism.

The narrative of torture and imprisonment is illuminated throughout by the counterinsurgent drama of "speech": "It became almost an obsession with me to make contact with as many different people and to pick up as many scraps of information as I could . . . . I took every opportunity of engaging the other prisoners in conversation and picking up from them even the slightest item of gossip" (129). The power of communication, of "free" speech practised under murderous conditions, motivated and saved Kathigasu's life and spirit. This theme gives her memoir a dimension of significant language that takes it beyond the level of simple sociopolitical documentation and into the realm of textuality.

Kathigasu died a few years after the war from septicemia in her jaw, which was broken by her Japanese guard. Her memoir, its value as a historical document, also present us with a female figure whose life and writing provide an exemplar of the Asian woman as agent in the most urgent of sociopolitical circumstances, under conditions of war.

Countering "National" History: A Feminist Memoir

Leong Liew Geok (1990), one of the few critics to examine women's memoirs from Malaysia Singapore, has pointed out that Janet Lim's *Sold For Silver* is more of an autobiography than Kathigasu's memoir, for it covers the entire life of the protagonist up to the end of the war in the Pacific. Writing a war memoir offered Lim a pretext for writing her life. Yet to read *Sold For Silver* simply as a life-story is to misread it. Lim's war experiences can be seen as the centerpiece of her autobiography, but the life-story as a whole is a feminist text that indicts not just her

Japanese captors but a broad patriarchal world, both Asian and European. Lim says in the preface that she wrote the book in two parts, the section dealing with wartime Singapore between 1949 and 1950, and the earlier part, treating her childhood, in 1955 — that is, the feminist indictments, which are almost solely confined to the first half of the book, were written almost ten years after the war ended, when Lim was older and had more distance and control over her materials.

The autobiography opens with eight-year-old Chui Mei's arrival in Singapore, then steps back to narrate the events leading to her abandoned and indentured position. Very quickly, a larger family and communal narrative is established. We learn that one of Chui Mei's sisters "was given away to a convent," and that when a brother "was born a year later . . . there was great rejoicing" (15). These details delineate the particular experience of life in a society in which value, property, and lines of descent were assigned through males: "In China, women were not entitled to inherit property; everything went to sons or, if there were no sons, to brothers and nephews" (26). In the patriarchal society, women were generally restricted to domestic roles and positions: "[O]ccupied in housework . . . Chinese wives lived almost separate from their husbands. . . . [My mother] seldom went beyond the high walls of the village" (19). For women, marriage, which offered them their only means to social position, was also an institution that secluded and oppressed them: "A village girl enjoyed great freedom before her marriage; but after a marriage had been arranged she was strictly forbidden to go out alone" (19). Thus constrained, women frequently chose the desperate way out: a cousin's wife hanged herself three months after the wedding (19).[22]

The patriarchal construction of women's identities was also perpetuated by women who, having passed through the social systems, accepted the low status of women and their marginalization in the domestic sphere. "Cooking, sewing, and looking after the house formed a girl's passport to marriage and some strict prospective mothers-in-law insisted on investigating a girl's work before they would accept her" (19). The narrator's mother, "like most village women, was convinced that daughters were of little value" (20). Lim's observations of traditional Chinese patriarchal structures are not new,[23] but together they introduce the major motif of the autobiography, the fate of women as epitomized in the life of one woman in an oppressively patriarchal society.

Although Lim's description of life in China is highly gender-differentiated, and the details are structured in terms of the asymmetrical relation between male and female roles, status, and valuations, there is no overt moral judgement: she sets down observations, not propositions. The narrative avoids a polemical feminist dimension, making it easy to overlook that the asymmetrical construction of female identity always already predicates a moral dimension. Lim's narrative, moreover, does not single out men as responsible for gender inequalities and sexist and sexual oppressions. If the conditions of women's lives in China (and Singapore) were unequal, narrow, and restrictive, the patriarchy that maintained these conditions was not solely identified as male and evil. Lim's relations with her parents illustrate the ironies in women's social enslavement. Her father "was very gentle, patient and affectionate" (20), and willed "his whole estate" to her (27). In contrast, her mother embodied the attitudes of rejection and insistence on female inferiority: "Mother was a very strict woman and never showed her love for me. Nor did she answer my endless questions; instead, I received slaps on the face for being too talkative. . . . My mother often complained that I was the ugliest child in the family" (20). On her father's death, her mother remarries and betroths the child Chui Mei to her second husband's younger nephew (33). After further unhappy wanderings, her mother and stepfather finally abandon her in a town near Swatow: "Mother gave me twenty-five cents and told me to be good and promised they would soon come back for me. . . . That was the last I ever saw of them" (36).

The structural irony of the maternal as figure for patriarchal attitudes and behavior is unconscious on the part of the narrator, however, and it becomes increasingly complex in the later part of the book, when the grown Chui Mei, now known by her anglicized name, Janet Lim, expresses her deep psychological bonds to a vision of the maternal quite unrecognizable as the mother of her childhood. The chief hurt in the protagonist's life is her orphaned or "unmothered" and "homeless" condition. After she is rescued by British women missionaries from her *mui tsai* (slave girl) position and from the sexual assaults of her elderly master[24], Janet is happy as a resident in the girls' home except during the holidays: "[P]erhaps it was when I saw the boarders go away with their parents [that] I felt most lost, unwanted and homeless" (71). Just before turning sixteen years old, she follows the advice of her beloved Miss Kilgour and takes up nursing. What troubles her is that she has to stay always in the hospital, "whereas most nurses could go back to their homes when off-duty. . . This emphasized my lack of real home and of the loving care of parents" (85). But she says she was motivated to complete her training "so that I could afford to go back to China and look for my mother, of whom I had never stopped thinking" (95). After she is adopted unofficially by a daughterless family, she feels that at last she has a home: "I always refer to Mrs. Chan as my "adopted mother.". . . I no longer had that sense of loneliness, that feeling of not being wanted, for I too could say: 'I am going home'" (96).

But her "motherless" or abandoned condition is not resolved by the appearance of an adopted mother. In the two situations when she is closest to death, she has a vision of her real mother's face: "She spoke to me and I could hear her solemn voice saying: 'Child, don't be afraid; I am always with you'" (128). The profound irony of such an ever present maternal love — "always with you" — against the truth of having been abandoned suggests multiple psychosocial inter-pretations, among them the failure of the daughter to separate herself from her mother. But as the vision disappears, she recognizes "the stark reality of her [mother's] death." In the displacement of the unacknowledged maternal abandonment to an acknowledged maternal death, the daughter receives psychological comfort and was able "to hang on grimly to life" (129).

Similarly, when she attempts to hang herself in the cell after she is captured by the Japanese, "I dreamt of my real mother. . . . I said, 'Mama, you must not leave me again, I am very lonely and everybody hates me.' But to my dismay she began to recede, growing smaller and smaller until her face became so blurred that I could see her no longer" (215). This occasion, when the experience of maternal abandonment is played out in her imagination, signals the point when her "separation anxiety" is finally internalized and integrated into the personality. Though it marks her breakdown, the lowest point of her struggle against her captors, it also marks the point when the search for the mother ends. After this revision of maternal abandonment, an independent Janet is able to work with the Japanese as housemaid and nurse, and they leave her virtue intact.

The narrative of Janet Lim's struggles to preserve her virginity from the Japanese officers forms the most gripping part of the book, but it is only a continuum of the larger narrative of women's experiences in a society that treated them as objects, "a slave, to be bargained for and sold like merchandise, to suffer shame and the whips of one's master and mistress" (42). In 1932, at the age of eight, she is sold for $250 to a Chinese family in Singapore. As is explained to the girl, her master "preferred very young [girls]"; his second wife "had suggested to him to 'import' a few girls. . . . I was to be his concubine and his slave" (46). At eight, Chui Mei learns to defend her virginity: "I cannot express my terror when I heard his footsteps. I crawled anywhere, inside cupboards, under the beds, outside the windows, anywhere, as long as I could get out of his reach" (42). Chui Mei's mistress beats her for refusing to sleep with the old man. The girl's terror of violation in this instance, under a Chinese roof and within a social economic system with legislative standing in the Straits Settlements, is perhaps more terrifying than the grown woman's flight from Japanese rapists, for it is sanctioned by men and women from her own community.

Lim's lifestory of female subjugation is legitimized and made more objective by the narrative strategy of historicizing the subjective discourse of autobiography. The personal story is placed in the context of a larger social history, and the intervention of this larger dimension into the young girl's life radically changes it. The girl's life is "rescued" and altered by external agencies; so also the "autobiography is "rescued" and altered by history. The memoir suggests that where individual rights do not matter or even exist, the story of the individual needs to be mediated by the story of society, that is, by history. Memoir, not autobiography, is produced when the value of the individual is weighted against social narratives.

Lim's memoir crosses into social history at the point when the South Seas Chinese world encounters British colonial agency, when what is personally known is taken over by the colonial unknown: "Unknown to me, changes were then taking place in Singapore which were to have a great effect on my life" (49). In 1932, the Straits Settlement Government passed the *Mui Tsai* Ordinance to control the trade in girlslaves (49). Under the ordinance, a new, Westernized, Christian influence enters Chui Mei's life. Significantly, it is European women, part of a countertradition of Victorian missionaries, who rescue her from sexual and physical abuse. Mrs. Winters is a colonial figure whose position as Lady Assistant Protector of Chinese underlines one ideological problem in many narratives of Asian women's struggles for human rights. Mrs. Winters's "rescue" of Chui Mei, after all, is a willful intervention into an "indigenous" social practice. Such Western intervention, in the context of *nationalist* struggle, can be and has been criticized as an act of colonial oppression, resulting in the destruction of the colonized culture. But a *feminist* reconstruction of Asian women's lifestories, as on Lim's memoir, may suggest a more complicated interpretation of colonial interventions, one less readily oppositional and less able to be appropriated for *nationalistic* purposes. Chui Mei is taken away from her owners to the Poh Leung Kuk Home, at that time a residence for between 200 to 300 girls, "slaves, orphans, and prostitutes" (54). Mrs. Winters, we are told, "had been the saviour of many hundreds of girls" (57). The missionary women, chiefly spinsters and educators, nurtured her; they "not only gave me my education, but also a home, security, affection and personal guidance" (61).

In bearing witness to the horrors of indigenous patriarchal societies and to the history of colonial women in effecting changes in the conditions of women in Asia, Lim's memoir interrogates national ideology that is based on the dualistic opposition of the good indigenous culture and the bad colonial exploiters, and suggests a different feminist ideology that illuminates the patriarchal aspects of indigenous culture and that can therefore be appropriated as a defense of colonialism's "civilizing" mission. In portraying political evil as indigenously patriarchal and political good as colonial agency, and in emphasizing oppression as patriarchy rather than as colonialism, a *feminist* work like Lim's contradicts, subverts, and refuses to support the hegemony of nationalism, which is constructed on the polarization of bad colonialism versus good nationalism and on the coercive power of national identity formation. Feminist accounts of colonial experience may therefore be construed as marginal if not oppositional to a dominant nationalist discourse, and they are thus more difficult to include in a canon of *national* literatures, when "national" is the governing term for a hegemonic state-articulated "culture" rationalized to support control of its citizens.

The women's movement in Singapore in the nineteenth and early twentieth centuries was chiefly motivated by Christian missionaries. Lim's memoir traces the source of Chui Mei's rescue to 1942, "when two European women . . . saw mothers forced by poverty to sell their daughters. They got permission from the Governor to start a home for such children" (60). In much of Asia, a chief attraction of Christianity for native women was its message of gender equality and human rights for women. In Korea, for example, the earliest converts and Korean missionaries came from the ranks of women who found in the Christian credo a liberationist message in contrast to the Confucianist seclusion and degradation of their sex.[25]

The missionaries' recognition of the value of women explains why it is that the authors of oral and written memoirs such as those by Lim and Kathigasu are Christianized women. Until recently, a missionary education was the only formal education available to women in Malaysia and Singapore. It gave them the English language which enabled them to record their experiences for an English-educated audience. More importantly, taught by missionary, frequently spinster teachers, the young women received models of independence, professionalism, and self-respect that offered them other visions for selfhood and life than the traditional models of wife, mother, domestic, and unvalued slave that the first chapter of Lim's memoir so graphically describes. Even the positive portrayal of the traditional positions of women in that indigenous society by Mrs. Lee Chin Koon, mother of Mr. Lee Kuan Yew, ex-Prime Minister of Singapore, cannot obviate women's subordinate and dependent status. "[The Straits-born Chinese]," she notes, "did not like their daughters to be educated in schools. It was felt that education would make daughters independent and difficult to control, and they would, therefore, have trouble with their mothers-in-law when they married. . . . And do not think that because most of us did not go to school we were not trained. No! We were being prepared for marriage at a very young age" (1974). In contrast to this traditional Straits Chinese female role, the eventual line of Janet Lim's life is non-Asian and Westernized. The narrator portrays herself as unsubmissive, resistant, and scornful of the compromises of marriage, family and domestic service that traditionally secure women's position in her society. She resists surrender of body and self to male-dominated decisions on the place of the female in society even as her women friends succumb to what appear to be easy solutions to their vulnerabilities and weaknesses. Mao, the Siamese widow who, like Chui Mei, is taken away to the Yamato Hotel by Japanese officers, withdraws into madness (169), and later happily becomes "the fifth wife of the old jeweler who tried to make me his fourth wife" (225).

Sold for Silver details numerous instances when women who place their welfare in the hands of male protectors are betrayed. Even physical beauty does not ensure male loyalty. An "unusually pretty" woman who had given birth to a baby girl "feared her husband might sell the girl when she died" (92). In order to escape the air raids in Indareong, Lim's friend Doris marries a Chinese farmer who later kills her. The killer "was told that if he behaved well he would only have to serve one year's sentence" (251). Lily, Lim's Indian friend, worries that her husband whom she had married three days before her flight from Singapore would take another woman (231). Even as Hashimoto Tada and Inou free her from her cell and find her a safe position as an unpaid housemaid in the house of a high Japanese official, Lim says, "I do not trust any men, especially men like you, with your sweet talk" (220). The dynamic of female-male relations, the memoir relentlessly asserts, is that of trust and betrayal, innocence and violation. The narrator's experiences as a victim of patriarchy lead eventually to total despair: "I hated God and all men and most of all I hated myself" (218).

In this bleak self-reflexive recoil from male tyranny, even the women missionaries are not spared. They also have been constructed by patriarchy to observe and mystify its power. To the missionary women, "men were considered superior to women. . . . We girls were told not to associate with them in any way. We were even told not to sit down on a seat recently vacated by a man since if we did so we might get a baby" (79). Even though they rescued Asian women from prostitution and slavery, these missionaries still accepted the paternalistic objectification of women as exchange value, as practiced in seemingly less abusive arranged marriage systems. "From its earliest days the school had provided wives for Chinese converts and it was a normal procedure . . . for a man to come to the school to get a young wife" (75).

Following "the traditional Chinese arranged-marriage system" (82), the "girls were lined up and walked one by one past the office and the man pointed to the girl he wanted. She had to accept or refuse on the spot. Usually it was considered worth getting married in order to get out of the home" (83). Lim's representation of European missionary activity demonstrates that while as colonial agency it intervened to correct certain abuses of women, it was itself an agent of patriarchal values.

The memoir concludes with the victory of the Allies over the Japanese and Lim's personal triumph over tremendous injustices, practised by both men and women, and by Asians and Europeans alike. The autobiographical heroine is last seen unmarried, virtue intact, and nursing career in place. Surely this is a text that should have pride of place in the evolution of a national culture? However, if Christian subjects and Western-influenced feminist themes are perceived as "non-Asian," and if "nationalism" is constructed as composed of Asian-based cultural identity, these subjects drawn from Malaysian/Singapore women's histories and war memoirs can be seen as falling outside the criteria for a *national* canon. As John Clammer argues, the idea of "Asian values" as the base of Singapore's culture — expressed in the concept of "cultural ballast," the idea of the fundamental opposition between Asian and Western values, and the notion of Western values as polluting an idealized and pure Asian society — pervades Singapore's political ideology (22), and, arguably also the Malay-dominant ideology of the Malaysian state also. A recuperation of such women's writing as contributing to a national canon must assume as its corollary, the rehistoricizing of national culture as less clearly Asian in base — as mixed, ambiguous, discontinuous, disruptive, questioning the value of indigenous social institutions, not easily assimilable to constructions of mono-Asian cultural identities. These women's contributions cannot be read simply or transparently, for they occur against a sociopolitical backdrop that has also historically privileged male cultural products and relegated women's writing to an inferior position. Kathigasu's and Lim's memoirs possess strong political voices which assert that women, in the face of condescension, persecution, and torture, hold ideological views with consequences for themselves and for their society. Although we may speculate on the reasons for their neglect, we will do even better to read them carefully. As committed women in Asian societies that have paid little attention to the tradition of women's writing, these authors can tell us much about the function of gender, class, and race in their multiethnic societies, and about the dangers of marginalization for women whose struggles for identity fall outside or resist a unitary, "true" national identity constructed by state power.

Different problems of location are demonstrated in the case of three Malaysian/Singapore women poets, Cecile Parrish, Wong May, and Margaret Leong, whose status illustrates the "unchartered" dilemma of women positioned between state-bounded identities.[26] Among non-national writers identified with the region, distinctions can be made between short-term visitors such as Somerset Maugham, expatriates who stayed for longer periods for economic and professional reasons, such as Anthony Burgess, D. J. Enright, and Han Suyin[27], and sojourners who remained in the country for longer periods and assimilated into the local culture through marriage, community relations, education and other sociocultural relations. [28] While the category, "sojourner," carries the implication of non-immigrant status, it also implies interaction with the receiving culture. Thus, although sojourners are often segregated in ethnic enclaves, their long periods of residence suggest that they are more affected by their experiences in the region than are visitors and expatriates. These distinctions, however, become less defined in the particular cases of poets such as Cecile Parrish, Wong May, and Margaret Leong, whose different positions in Singaporean literature exhibit how the discourse of nationalism overlaps the discourse of race in the formation of a national literary canon.[29] Indeed, by reason of birth and/or long residence and/or cultural assimilation and affiliation, these women's works need to be read in a Malaysian/Singapore context. An exclusionary position, arguably, is inimical to inquiry about the formation of modern Malaysian-Singapore cultures, which are characteristically pluralistic, dynamic, unstable, dialogic and creative.

In the case of Malacca-born Parrish, the issue of "loyalty" has been conflated with "authenticity" of national identity, and both issues have been raised to argue against her inclusion as a Singapore writer.[30] On the one hand, like Parrish, Margaret Leong, an American-born poet who married a Malayan, raised a family, and taught in Singapore for ten years before returning to the United States, is also usually not admitted as a Singapore writer. Although Leong's poems, steeped in local imagery and allusions, have been republished in Singapore as children's poetry, she remains unacknowledged in the Singapore canon (Lim 1991). On the other hand, Wong May, born in Shanghai, educated in Singapore, published in the United States, and now resident in Germany, has entered the Singapore canon in a way that the two Caucasian women cannot. Perhaps more ironically, Wong May has been claimed as both a Singaporean and an Asian American poet. (See *MLA Asian American Literature: An Annotated Bibliography*, 1988).

Native-born Cecile Parrish

Cecile Parrish was born of British parents who had come to Malaya in the 1930s for economic reasons.[31] Her father had a successful business in hospital, medical and surgical supplies; her mother, Rene Parrish, came over in 1934. Cecile, her only child, was born in Malacca in 1939. When Cecile was almost two, Singapore was threatened by Japanese forces, and Rene Parrish spent the war years in Australia supporting herself and the child as a nursery school teacher. Mr. Parrish was interned in Changi Prison. After mother and daughter returned to the region in 1945, the family took Singaporean citizenship, and the daughter kept her Malaysian passport. Mrs. Parrish continued to reside in Singapore after her husband's death. Cecile Parrish spent many years in educational institutions abroad, taught for a few years in Singapore and Kuala Lumpur, then at twenty-seven, left for a teaching post in Australia where she died in a car accident.

Parrish appears to have a direct claim to being a Malaysian/Singapore writer, both on the internal evidence of some of her poems and on the strength of her citizenship papers. Yet her legal status as a native-born citizen has been questioned on the grounds that her major cultural experiences — her early education and university training — had been in the West. The same question, of course, can be asked of a writer like Wang Gungwu, who received much of his education at the National Central University in Nanking, and later at the University of London, and who has not lived in Malaysia since 1968.[32] In raising these questions, critics serving as gate-keepers to a national canon have tended to conflate "national" identity with "authenticity," defined as non-Western acculturation. But non-Western acculturation is an ambiguous, unstable factor in the course of rapid, massive, and invasive Westernization of twentieth century Malaysian/Singapore society. For example, while national identity is constructed as that which is most distinguished from the Other, that is, Western culture, this Western Other, through the dynamics of modernization and global capitalism, has transformed and continues to transform Malaysian/Singapore society. Thus, "questions of authenticity" are posed even in the use of the English language as the medium of communication.[33]

"Authenticity" is a complex term in the context of indigenous, immigrant, multiracial, multicultural, postcolonial, newly national, international corporate societies and economies. The inevitable tides of external and internal historical events, intersections and separations of different ethnic and religious groups, and gaps between the experiences of generations, all these and more lead to impressions of fragmentation and individual alienation that compose the themes of pioneer

Malaysian poets, and made T. S. Eliot's *The Waste Land* a popular reference. The search for an "authentically national" idiom and identity, carried on in a non-indigenous, colonial language, immediately opened the university writers of the fifties to "foreign" (and arguably inauthentic) influences that placed their imagination outside the local community. Anne Brewster has argued that even as some Malayan writers attempted to document the local landscape and to find an analogous local idiom, their use of English and apprenticeship to Anglo-European traditions so marginalized them that their works showed instead consciousness of "absence, negativity, and irony" (1989a, 21).[34] Attempting to bypass Anglo-European cultural constructs in order to "tap an authentic national consciousness," local writers ended instead with "a cult of individualism" (Brewster 1989a, 29).

Paralleling these pioneer male writers, Parrish's posthumously published *Poems* (1966) appears as a Eurocentric collection. Five of the poems are Nativity pieces, two are translations of French poems (from Gautier and Baudelaire), and three are exercises on European art and thought ("Lines on a Portrait Miniature by Nicholas Hilliard," for example). All are crafted pieces, showing an apprenticeship in a variety of forms: the couplet, quatrain, ballad, sestet, sonnet, ode and free verse. One may argue that this interest in form (including translations) exhibits the concerns of a native English-language writer, which Parrish was; but, as writers such as Derek Walcott, Nissim Ezekiel or Vikram Seth demonstrate, interest in craft and form is not the sole province of native English-language writers. Traditional forms of poetry can be and have been naturalized by English-language writers from non-Anglo-European societies. In fact, the criticism that Parrish's "Anglo-European" base, seen in her choice of forms, topics, and images, marks her as non-national reflects a hegemonic ideology that promulgates a politicized canon of nationalist identities. If an Anglo-European orientation or influence excludes non-European writers from their national canons, where would we place writers such as Derek Walcott or Kamala Das? Malaysian and Singaporean Chinese-language writers whose works reflect a Chinese social world and concerns, as well as images and allusions drawn from Chinese literature, may then be considered non-national as well, an argument that has been used by some language policy makers (Hussein 1977). Such restrictive approaches to ensure the purity of the tribe have led to a legislation of strict cultural boundaries, as during periods of political repression in the People's Republic of China, resulting in the prohibition of the reading and teaching of "foreign" literatures and the dissemination of "foreign" media.[35]

Many of Parrish's metaphors — men's love as sailor and bird and woman as the abandoned; European civilization as static and decadent; Christian sentiment as Mariology and maternal — illuminate strong themes. Some of her best poems treat untimely death or fear of death. "Fear of Dying," specifically located in Singapore (22), manifests a sensitive dramatization on the well-worn themes of death and loss. However, her poems are most interesting when contextualized in a Malaysian/Singapore landscape. Read as "local poetry," where "local" characterizes themes and images related to particular places and concerns, poems such as "Ships at Singapore," "Low Tide, Johore," "The Scarlet Land," "Aftermath," and "Before a Storm" illustrate how 'locality' operates to secure feeling and sense. "Ships at Singapore" (10-11), for example, offers a naive vision of place. Twentieth-century realistic description of Singapore Harbor ("clanging dockyards. . . panting tugboats . . . iron ships, smoke ships . . . load rubber, tin") is contrasted with a romanticized past, figured as "the star-high ships." The lyrical form deliberately mythifies a material maritime history, providing a literary romance both relevant to a mercantile port like Singapore and necessary for a nation of economic immigrants whose legends and histories will inevitably have to be newly self-constructed. Moreover, its sentimental notions of Singapore's past and stereotypical maritime and harbor images offer an idealization of place, an imagined history that arguably helps transmute the technical, alien sense of "place" — an initial phase in a history of human settlement — to the emotionally-charged, communal sense of "home."

"Low Tide, Johore" shows a movement away from romanticization of the local to a strategic use of description to suggest strong emotion. Description is subordinated to the dominant impression of a time and place close to the eternal, although set within the temporal. Again, as in "Ships at Singapore" (and in the death poems), time is the underlying motif. Here description is economically focused on the impression of isolated suspension. The dialectic of stasis and movement, represented in the contrast between tropical inertia and life forces, is metonymically related to the ideal of eternal nature:

> The hour hangs motionless, before
> A rising sigh along the shore
> Heralds the returning sea. (12)

Playing on images of the promiscuous woman, "The Scarlet Land" is structured on the gendered constructions of the sea as a male lover and the country in its sensuous manifestations as the female anima. This feminized landscape contains "jarring subtleties . . . fragrant multiplicity." The female half embraces positive and negative associations; for example, the "orchid-bloom that clings/ Watching from sunless clefts in giant trees" are "sick and mottled" (13). Malayan flora and fauna, intoxicating to the senses, "enamored" "fawning," are also balanced against a jarring human edge: rice-blades are "sharp as boys' voices;" transient showers are "like children's anger." Echoing Auden's landscape poem, "Ode to Limestone," Parrish's ode offers a useful corrective to other Malaysian landscape poems, such as Wong Phui Nam's "How the Hills are Distant," that imagine the Malayan landscape as brutal, uninviting, and leached of sensuality. Parrish's still immature but sharply sensuous recognitions offer worthy, if different, resources for renewed connections to the Malaysian *genus loci* than Wong's poem, which is heavily influenced by Eliot's modernist waste land and Baudelaire's corrupt metropolitan visions.[36]

Love poems that explore the problems of union between Malayan (woman) and "foreign" or Western (male), the poems "Aftermath" and "Before A Storm" also offer description and a sense of locale. The female persona is identified with a tropical homeland; her "garden's covert" contains "pink frangipani." Even as the woman attempts to persuade her sailor/lover to "forsake your barren whore, the sea" for the "tropics" (29), her wrecked passion is figured in the tree overturned by the night storm. Rejecting the conventional trope of Ruth, the exiled woman, who follows her husband to a strange land, the speaker entreats her sailor to settle in her native land. The homeland represented here is no Europe but a romanticized tropical garden. Similarly, "Before a Storm" contrasts two localities: the man's "wind-beleaguered town" and the speaker's "ringed islands (which) burn to/ Saffron-sullen sky" (34). The contrast explores the complexities of relationships that cross geographical boundaries. A simple lyric of two quatrains, the poem alludes to a creative passion generated by love of place. The speaker cannot "print . . . passion down" in a geography not her own; only in her native habitat, one problematically different from the man's, can she write. "Before a Storm" suggests an identity that is constructed through relations defined by place, a profound identification of self with "homeland." Significantly also, the poem suggests Parrish's attachment to Malaysian/Singapore landscape and her resistance to leaving it.

Although Parrish is not a major figure in Malaysia/Singapore poetry, her 24 poems bear scrutiny because of their historical position in an evolving national literature, and for their insights, sensitivity of images and diction, and thematic interest. To omit her work is to deny the diversity of sources in Malaysian-Singapore English-language writing for ideological reasons that have not been consistently applied to other writers from the region.

Foreign-born Wong May

Wong May's status underlines the unstable nature of national identity discourse and its surreptitious reproduction of race discourse. Unlike Parrish's poems that generally have not been admitted as Malaysian/ Singapore writing, Wong May's poems appear in major anthologies of Singapore writing, including *The Flowering Tree, Seven Poets, The Second Tongue,* and the definitive canon under the ASEAN imprimatur, *Singapore Poetry.* Widely accepted as a Singaporean poet, Wong May, however, was born in Shanghai. She received a Chinese education in her early school years in Singapore, went on to do her B.A. in English Literature in the University of Singapore when she began publishing her poems with her contemporary Arthur Yap, worked briefly as an editor for Federal Publishing, then left for the University of Iowa around 1967. Except for brief visits back to Singapore, she has lived in the United States and in Germany ever since.[37] Wong May's years of residence in Singapore parallel those of a sojourner like the British writer Katherine Sim, who lived in Malaya for approximately twenty-two years, from 1938 to 1960.[38]

Despite her uncritical placement in the canon of Singapore writers, only a limited number of Wong May's poems has been accepted as Singaporean. In fact, most of her poetry remains undiscussed in the various studies on her work.[39] Only her early poems, containing features of local landscape and images reflecting local flora and fauna, are widely known to Singapore readers.

Wong May's uneven reception in Singapore has much to do with her break from British-based literary traditions and her later absorption with American and Continental experimental styles. Nevertheless, while her three collections show sharp dislocations of diction and imagery, these dislocations are more apparent than substantial. In *A Bad Girl's Book of Animals,* poems without recognizable local references have been neglected by Singapore anthologists; but an analysis of the development of her themes and style in the early poems and in the first collection demonstrates that a deeper integrity of philosophical concerns and a complex matrix of emotional experiences act as cohering agents that unify her Singapore-based writing with her later American-based production.

Her poems, written while she was an undergraduate in Singapore, contain images culled from Singapore flora and fauna or express autobiographical moments (see *Focus* 1963, 18, 31; 1964, 25-8). "The

Saw-dust," addressed to her older and only brother who died when a child, playing on the Christian notion of the dead as ashes and dust, imagines the brother as sawdust, and the sister as "the stairs/ The past is walking on me like a ghost" (31). The extended metaphor encompasses a childhood self ("The little girl. . . /who swept away/ The little crumbs of sawdust"), the theme of human mortality, and the speaker's love for her brother, concluding on a darkly necrophilic suggestion: "Ah, brother, you are dust now,/ I am the stairs —/ Will our dust be mingled? Soon?" (1963, 31). A similar love for the dead is expressed in "The rain is green," in which the speaker's fear that "you" will die is confirmed (1964: 27). The dead is felt as vitally present in her world: "I feel again your hair your arms your voice/ In the wind the grass the rain." Union with the dead is fearful, yet to be desired. Thus, even in Wong May's early poems, what is foregrounded is not the local landscape that national anthologists look for but internal states that thematize psychological and philosophical concerns.

The early poems also interrogate the subject of romantic love. The reiterated stance is that of loss of innocence, the movement from a child's illusions to an adult's complicated dissatisfactions. In "Only the Moon," the speaker traces her fancies, "When I was a child," to arrive at her present perception of reality. The new and full moon evolved from a cradle to sensuous delight, "a big cake," but now is "nothing but the moon" (1963 18). A longer and more sustained piece, "Once I thought" maintains a similar emotive and thematic structure, moving from a condition of innocence through the experience of sexuality to a vision of the sea as "soulless" and destructive. The poem ends in adult experience which is also incomprehension: "But I don't understand the sea" (1964 25-6).

The theme of a young woman moving into disillusionment enlarges from romantic loss to a metaphysical condition in a later poem, "Summer Guide" (1969, 67). The poem begins with a statement of radical distrust: "I distrust, mistrust you equally," in which the unexpected word, "equally," suggests that the speaker distrusts/ mistrusts herself as well. This interrogative relationship is located in an intensely physical world. While the mistrusted physical world is "accurate," the erotics of instinctual passion lie in a domain beyond ethical or rational influence: "blood-wise beyond/ all taste or distaste" (67). No longer concerned with simple adolescent disillusionment, Wong May's later poems assert a complex configuration of erotic and moral elements. Echoing the Lawrentian thesis of the primacy of the sexual and sub-conscious over the ethical and conscious, her poems in the first collection struggle to be "blood-wise."

Following her move to the United States in 1967, her poems also show an increasing willingness to forfeit the surface and local — elements that assume a mimetic function — to engage in an interrogation of reality, including a willfully indeterminate stylistics. The opening poem to the first collection, for example, moves in a series of statements that generate their own counter-statements:

> In his country they use water-
> hyacinths to feed pigs.
> Imagine
> the stuff pigs are made of!
> He lies in bed thinking this
> is but a zone of his life —
> As if life has zones. (3)

Even the modernist view of writing as stream-of-consciousness, a technique that the poem archly illustrates, is criticized:

> That is, if
> Consciousness is
> In streams.

The introductory poem signals the collection's postmodernist project — its consistently interrogative voice; its self-consciousness about the project of signifying ("Narration" 12; "Going Underground" 36); its deliberately illogical, absurd statements ("The Yellow Plague" 81); and its indeterminate constructions of imagery ("Macky Auditorium" 70; "Time" 45).

Underpinning the postmodern style is a world-view that supports and perhaps precedes it. This view assumes the absence of religious consolation ("no God/ walks the mauve hills," 83), and consequently falls back on an uncomfortable moral relativism ("Black on white/ or white on black?/ It certainly isn't any worse/ If you read the same lie" 24). In the absence of ethical signification, the poems suggest a psychologizing frame of which the speaker is also characteristically skeptical ("10 A.M." 33-4). Tying the philosophical gestalt together are narratives of emotional devastation ("Absence" 31; "The Whore" 73) that offer a nihilistic vision:

> Amazons cut off their
> breasts to bend the bow
> better, I am no stronger
> But more used-up — emptier. (37)

The collection ends with "A Lesson" in which the speaker asks for a direct apprehension of the senses without the intervention of signifying practices that carry moral judgements with them:

> Describe winter, I say
> without snow, or cold,
> or North. (83)

Although the human cannot escape signification, human experience is "given" — beyond our ability to rationalize — and, as the poem concludes, such experience is given "mostly as punishment." Wong May's early poems, written in Singapore, and those in *A Bad Girl's Book of Animals* that come from her American experience treat the lessons of growing up finally in a Blakean sense of "Nobodaddy," the punitive principle that rules the world of experience.

Her next two collections, reflecting her move to Europe, contain European-based themes and images. In these poems, the language has moved into an intranational arena with no recognizable base in a given national tradition, possessing instead multiple locations. Such geographical mobility permits a range of sensory and cultural choices and a wealth of global observations. But the same multiplicity may be seen as dislocating her work from its early regional context. The absence of local referent and setting helps to explain the neglect of Wong May's later work. Unable or unwilling to locate such poetry in a body of literature, the reader finds it difficult to name its significance.

The fate of Wong May's later books reminds us that while poems are the products of individuals, literary reputation is the result of converging social forces. A signifier or speech act has its fullest significance in social contexts; and intertextuality (of which poetic tradition is but one manifestation) and what I call the poetics of location are inextricably linked. No poem is read in isolation of other poems or of a sociocultural matrix. The difficulty posed by Wong May's later poetry comes from the difficulty (whether self-imposed, accidental or ideologically determined) of placing her work in a body of other similar works. To read Wong May's poetry as firstly located in Singapore, her original cultural home, and then to trace the changes and developments, or distortions and losses (depending on one's critical position) as manifested in the superimposition of American and European idioms on her early Chinese-British located stylistics would give her poems an originating sensibility.

The American-born white woman poet, Margaret Leong, presents a different problem of location. Identified with colonizing powers, white women writing in Malaysia/Singapore have also been identified as "expatriates" rather than as sojourners or immigrants. Leong came to Singapore in 1951, married a Malayan, and taught in the local schools. She was active in literary circles, published books of poetry and planned to write local fiction as well. Accepting a one-year lecturership at the University of Missouri, her home-state, she left Singapore in 1961.

The fact of "expatriation" raises the thorny question of what is meant by Malaysian/Singapore writing. The term "local" rests on an assumption of place. It asks that local writing be produced by a local writer. An expatriate, by definition, cannot be a Malaysian-Singapore writer because he or she is not of the place. Writers like D. J. Enright, Anthony Burgess, and Han Suyin are never claimed as national writers, although each lived in the region for a number of years and wrote fiction and poetry reflecting the local society. Because they were "expatriates," we assume their works lack the intimacy, identity, and closeness of observation we expect from local writers.

Barrington Kaye's poem "The Expatriate" is an amusing expression of the outsider position:

> In early manhood I am come,
> Having no arts but a second-rate brain,
> To strive within this swamp of stone
> To reconstruct my life again, . . .
> And so to Singapore I am come,
> Here in this foetid air to find
> Some comfort in the salary
> Commanded by a fourth-rate mind. (1)

In contrast, A. L. McLeod defined the literature of expatriation as "books written by men with a genuine love for the land, men who identified themselves almost wholly with it and regarded it as a home away from home: but none of them regarded it as home" (316). In the 1966 *Literature East and West* special issue on Malaysian literature, McLeod included two poems by Leong (374). Like McLeod, I place Leong's work as different in kind from the expatriate writing characterized by Kaye's poem. However, despite Leong's attempt to assimilate into the Malayan social world and to identify and speak for or as a Malayan, her adult and children's poems have received no critical attention in the thirty odd years since their publication. Leong explicitly denied an expatriate status in a 1960 interview with the *Singapore Free Press,* where, identified as "a Malayan poet," she "urged the formation of a poet's club as 'Malaya is sadly lacking in poets'" (7). The interview, however, reflects the problematic of her identity in an unselfconscious contradiction: "Though an American, Mrs. Leong is essentially a Malayan poet. . . . She is perhaps the only foreigner to have written poems which focussed almost wholly on Malayan themes which she describes as 'so very romantic'" (7). In this reportorial turn, Leong's American origin was distinguished from her Malayan poetic "essence," exhibited in her "Malayan themes," with "essence" and "themes" left undefined.

Later approaches to Malaysian/Singapore writing also demonstrate a similar contradiction and absence of definition. For example, the introduction to Singapore English-language poetry in the ASEAN anthology asserted that "the lack of accompanying cultural support in the way the [English] language was received posed questions of authenticity," and noted that certain problems were associated with "the search for an authentic idiom" (Lee Tzu Pheng 452-53). The more difficult aspect, according to this introduction, "concerns the role the poetry can be considered to have played — or would be expected to, in the poet's own view — in defining an authentic Singapore identity" (Lee Tzu Pheng 463). But the introduction did not define those questions of identity, or what an authentic local idiom was, or even what would be an authentic Singapore identity.

In fact, the concern with "authenticity," either identified with or distinguished from a national consciousness, thematized in the work of poets such as Lee Tzu Pheng, Arthur Yap, or Edwin Thumboo, is not a feature of Leong's poetry. Instead Leong shares the strenuous attempts of pioneer Malaysian/Singapore poets to ground their work in description and images drawn from local environment. The pressure to "name" or document local landscape was an urgent feature of early Malayan writing. Anne Brewster's excellent study points out that "an inventory of Malay and Chinese words in poems of the early fifties onwards reveals that most of them are in fact images drawn from the local natural and urban landscape" (10). These images, according to Brewster, form "a catalogue or taxonomy of the environment" (15). In 1953, for example, young writers were urged to add "local atmosphere" to adapt the English language "to suit the requirements of the region" (*Youth* 77, cited Brewster 16). Indeed, more than the male university writers Brewster examines, Leong provides a wide-ranging, unironic, and generous taxonomy of local landscapes, flora, fauna, images, legends, histories, folk-tales, customs, and sociocultural practices.

An earlier article on Leong in the *Straits Times* praises her use of the local: "She speaks of things that we all know about, her locales are always familiar ones, and the subjects she chooses are not strangers" (6). As seen in a representative list of her titles, the poems' themes and settings are recognizably multicultural Malayan: "Poem for Hari Raya," "The Wayang," "Ice Ball Man," "Rubber Tapping," "The Tin Mine," "Kinta Valley," and "Changi." Her adult poems include titles such as "Mist on Penang Hill," "Pasir Panjang," "Casuarina in Johore," and "Batu Caves." If one wants a taxonomy of place names and ready-made images of Malaysia/Singapore of the 1950s, such as Ee Tiang Hong had suggested compiling, Leong's poetry would make an excellent beginning.

In her children and adult poems, Leong was attempting what the Malayan male university writers had set out for themselves: "to express locality and a sense of self in the colonial language" (Brewster 10). Arguably, for Leong, English was not "the colonial language." Yet she also enlarged its resources by including Malay, Chinese, and Indian terms and names. Experiments to use the oral idioms of ordinary Malayans, including an admixture of ethnic syntactical structures and vocabulary known as *Engmalchin*, characterized the early 1950s writing, but they did not concern Leong. Her hewing to a neutral, internationally correct English, incorporating Malayan place names and Malay, Chinese, and Indian terms where necessary, setting her actions in a sharply particularized and sense-delighting landscape, separate her from the male university writers and prefigure some of the tendencies in later Malaysia/Singapore writing.

Leong's success in articulating a recognizable landscape for Malaysian-Singapore writing is undermined by a counter "orientalizing" discourse in the poetry. Although the physical and cultural scenes described were and are "native" to Malaysia/Singapore, they are often seen through the gaze of the occidental outsider seeking the romantic and exotic. The *kelongs* (fish-traps) and prawners with their *jalas* (pyramid-shaped nets), the *istanas* (palaces) and *hantus* (ghosts), are screened through a Western colonizing mentality as representations for the European visitor of the Orient; and these "Orientalist" representations offer a privileged position for the writer and for her Western readers (Edward Said 1).

In many of Leong's poems, romanticization of the Orient and acutely false notes remind the reader of her orientalist position. The lallang motif recurs frequently in her poems. Lallang, the local name for an ubiquitous, tough, weedy grass with cutting edges, appears as a visual detail (*RS* 8); as part of a tropical scene (*RS* 42), or foregrounded as a symbol of

Malaysian vegetation ("The Lallang," *AATT* 50). In "Lallang Along a Railway Track," it appears as a trope for transience. It is "Like an arsenal of emeralds" which is also a figure of "decay" (*RS* 46). But no native writer would romanticize lovers wading "in drifting lallang." Experience with its painful cutting edges immediately turns this image ludicrous.

Leong's exploitation of spirits, ghosts, and various religious rites also mark her as non-native. Local people were and many still are notoriously superstitious, fearful, and sensitive to the point of shunning other races' religious practices. Leong's use of imagery and subjects drawn from animistic belief, from Buddhism, Hinduism, and Islam, shows a curious, observant, omnivorous but shallow mind. Her poems are satisfied with recording surface color and scene but do not construct a deeper understanding of the emotional forces that make these scenes meaningful. Whether addressing "Kwei of the Trees" (*AATT* 110), "Lord Buddha's statue" (*RS* 23), "The Nonya Ghost" (*RS* 26), or "Pontianak" (*RS* 28), Leong's chief intention appears to be sensuous description. The over-dependence on description leads to a construction of local scene for the sake of color, rather than for an integration of scene and emotion toward self-expressive and/or sociocultural ends. While individual poems are garnished by gem-like images and lines, the achievement often misses engagement with the subject, and stops short of an evolving body of personal or sociocultural themes. "Thaipusam," for example, offers a vivid image of "the sky — a sari wound in blue yards . . . fastened to the temple with a giant pin" (*RS* 27); in "Song of the Fifth Guardian Spirit," "the west is splattered red/ With joss sticks of a dying day" (*RS* 35). Yet both poems remain vapid expressions lacking a grasp of the emotions and cultures that produced the spectacle recorded.

Some memorable poems rise above the Pre-Raphaelite attitudes that characterize her weakest work. Most successful are poems where description is least beset by a conventional poetic persona or where scene coincides with insight. "The Plane Crash" is simple description made emotionally effective through the sharp trope of weather for prayers (*RS* 66). "Chinese Funeral" avoids the hyperbolic, and remains close to actual observation, concluding on a convincing thought: "Along the horseshoe graves,/ west turning,/ funeral kites of incense rose/ . . . . While in the salt-consuming earth/ the dead were left alone" (*RS* 35). Leong's successful poems cover many Malayan localities — kampong (village), rural and sea scenes, urban landscapes, and multiplicities of a multiracial country. Description is integrated with or suggests deep thought, the whole evoking strong emotion. In "The Grave of Sir Francis Light — Penang" (*RS* 89), the imagery of "the heat that wraps colonial cities/ in winding sheets of sun" is subordinated to the pathos of "the paradox of burial/ in a foreign, distant/ and yet, somehow, native land." Poems treating themes of colonial contact (e.g. "To An Emperor's Envoy at Bukit China — Malacca"), eastern exile ("Sea Burial," *RS* 87), and geographical separation are the most realized. In "By the Great wall," the persona is a "foreigner and isolate" who remembers "home." Standing by the river bank, the exiled poet "wait[s] on a dark embankment/ For a ferry that never comes" (*RS* 66), suggesting an archetypal nightmare for exiles and isolates.

Leong's talent with diction and imagery, and her lavish attention to Malayan flora, fauna, and physical and cultural scenes are present in numerous poems on local subjects, e.g. "Kampong Sketches" (*RS* 27-29), "Changi temple" (*RS* 37), "Convent of Buddha — Ipoh" (*RS* 33), and "Festival of Lanterns" (*RS* 76). Her work has much to offer the evolving tradition of Malaysian/Singapore writing, as seen in how a Singapore poet like Arthur Yap has been influenced by her poem, "Polygamy — Three Views" (*RS* 73). The poem dramatizes the scene of polygamy in Chinese society in three passages, using the voices of three participants — the first wife, husband, and second wife. Yap follows Leong's use of this tripartite soliloquy to treat a similar plot in "a vicious circle" (52). Leong's position is more accepting and compassionate than the later-generation Yap's. The poem imagines the first wife, tired and childless, as reconciled to the prospect of the second wife: "Perhaps/ With a new wife here/ he shall not go abroad so much,/ And should she bear his child/ It shall be partly mine" (74). The elderly husband, aware that it is his money that has bought him a second wife, trusts that she will "learn to serve me/ And to do my will," while the second wife stoically accepts her fate and hopes for the best: "the master being old,/ Will be indulgent too" (75). In contrast to this benign construction, Yap's poem offers a critical view of polygamy as an institution in which women and men exploit each other economically. It would be misleading to apply the criterion of authenticity to either poem, for, as sociocultural constructs, they offer different reflections. Yet, it is instructive to note that Yap's poem, while strategically replicating Leong's narrative structure, subverts and hollows Leong's theme of social accommodation through a satirical drama of raw economic exchange.

Resistance to the "local" representation Leong's poems achieve — a graphic scene made to carry the perceiver's sentiment — ironically may arise as a consequence of a reader's "Europeanization." That is, a British education steeped the colonized imagination in images drawn from Anglo-European cultures. Thus, in the move towards self-representation, colonized writers often found their alienated representations in images derived from Eliot's *Waste Land,* as in Chandran Nair's poems. On the one hand, perceiving alienation as their theme, many pioneer

Malayan writers rejected vital images of the local world to represent their colonized selves. Choosing easily recognizable Malayan scenes and publishing locally, Leong, on the other hand, signalled her intention to write for a "native" audience. The term "native" was and remains ambiguous, difficult, politically under negotiation and ideologically controlled. As the work of a Caucasian whose assimilation into the immigrant Malayan population was cut short by her return to the United States, Leong's poetry presents an interesting case of cross-cultural cross-dressing. Hence, while many Malayan writers consciously or unconsciously imitated the forms, images, and values of Anglo-European cultures, Leong, identifying with the country of her marriage, adopted and imitated the beliefs and scenes of Malayan culture. As critics, we need to evaluate the shapes and expressions of such cross-cultural cross-dressing. If Leong's attempts at assimilating Asian images and cultural expressions in her poems are dismissed as "inauthentic," why do we accept as more authentic the early efforts of Wong Phui Nam who explicitly expressed the influence of T. S. Eliot and Rimbaud? Does cross-cultural cross-dressing work only one way, from an Asian base towards a Western metropolitan center? Or can the national canon be opened to sojourners and immigrants from the West who work toward assimilating into their Asian world? Simply put, is "nationalism" in Malaysia/Singapore wholly the province of indigenous and Asian-based immigrant populations? Or can one possess a white skin and also be a Malaysian or Singaporean writer? These questions are clearly beyond the province of criticism and literary studies.

Conclusion

The shaping phenomenon of displacement that characterizes the lives of the women in this study is, as Shulman points out in a similar context, "a theme as old as Eve; as familiar as the biblical story of Ruth following her mother-in-law, Naomi, into exile; as common as the practice in many cultures through the ages by which newly married women, many of them still children, must leave home and family to live far away among their husband's people" (19). In newly emerging nation states, women writers such as Aroozoo, Kathigasu, Janet Lim, Parrish, Wong May, and Margaret Leong lose visibility on account of their gender. Or as occasional poet or memoirist, they are assigned to the "inconsequentiality" of their choice of genre. Or their works have suffered erasure because they cannot be located within hegemonic cultural boundaries in which national identity is sublated with "Asian" or race identity.

When Wong May's first book, *A Bad Girl's Book of Animals,* appeared in 1969, it was praised by an American critic as "a genuine original . . . [reflecting] today's American world . . . and today's American speech." George Starbuck praised this "original" chiefly for its mastery of American idiom: "One incidental amazement is that an Oriental, learning English under British tutelage, should not merely master the American language, but should play the elaborate jokes on it which only a member of the family could get away with" (Blurb in *Reports*). Starbuck's "amazement" over Wong May's "American idiom" echoes the confused response that greeted Margaret Leong's poetry in Singapore in 1960. Both women were marginalized as "foreigners" who had successfully made another culture and idiom (Malayan for Leong, American for Wong) the subjects of their poems. The American Leong was read as Malayan, the Singapore-raised Wong as American. The works of these two women present a case of cross-cultural cross-dressing. While their language constructs have been read as "genuinely" rooted in, reflecting, and expressing their adopted cultures (Leong producing Malayan poetry, and Wong American poetry), their poems paradoxically remained identified with their original cultural bases (produced by the American poet, Leong and the Singaporean poet, Wong). Their poems can be said to represent productions that cross national cultural boundaries, so that a national-based interpretation is inadequate to explain the dialogical multinational multiculturalism in their texts.

Cross-cultural, multinational perspectival elements also pervade the apparently straightforward Anglophone "native" writers such as Edwin Thumboo and Arthur Yap. Both are generally praised as among Singapore's best poets writing today. Thumboo has claimed William Butler Yeats as a major influence (1983), while Yap admits to Larkin's influence on his poetry.[40] That the Anglo-cross-cultural intertextuality their poetry calls attention to has not created a problem in the reception of their poetry may be explained perhaps by the British colonial education base in Singapore. British poetic traditions have had a longer history of inculcation in Singapore than American literary traditions. American literature has not received as much attention in the O and A-level curriculum and in the university literature curricula, all administered until recently by British educational systems. Thumboo's introductions to the anthologies that appeared in the seventies and eighties, for example, alluded heavily to British poetic traditions, with a comparatively low reference to American literary sources (see Edwin Thumboo 1970, 1973, 1976, 1985). But such British-literature-bias is historically dated, as American and other comparative cultural influences assert more of a global presence, and as Singapore writers and critics receive more of their education and training outside of Britain.

The examples of women poets like Cecile Parrish and Wong May illustrate a cross-cultural dynamic of world literature in English, especially of writing from newly decolonized states. Exhibiting difference, upheaval, instability, and multiplicity, and resisting closure, dogma, and unitary state identity, this dynamic opposes nationalist ideologies that insist on monocultural, restrictive criteria. However, even an apparent multicultural ideology can become exclusionary, when serving the purposes of a restrictive nationalism. Brewster, for example, has argued that the multicultural ideology articulated as the official version of Singapore nationalism can be critiqued as reductive and formulaic, when constructed to serve an "hegemonic nationalism . . . to divert attention away from the inherent contradictions and conflicts of a pluralistic society" (1989a, 36-7). At the same time, however, such critiques by Western readers may be seen as attempts .to detract from the achievements of "authentic" native literatures, in support of Western metropolitan traditions.

To make women's writing visible, we have to make visible the forces that shape national canons of literary identity, and consequently that shape the omissions and gaps in these canons. The achievements of these writers, and their general absence from a national canon, indicate that a different notion of literary identity must be constructed to explain their work. Pioneer women's writing in English from or based in Malaysia/Singapore demonstrates a dynamic of Anglophone world literature that is cross-national or intranational in base, and that provides examples of cross-cultural production, across national lines. These works suggest that single nation-based interpretations are inadequate to explain transnational cultures that inhabit the hybrid "Third Space" in relation to Native and Other. They push us toward developmental, cross-cultural, multinational perspectival aesthetics that suggest that canons that exclude on restrictive national criteria, constructed by groups claiming hegemonic power and control, can and should become sites of contention for criticism.

1990

Notes

I thank the Asia Foundation for its support of my research carried out at the Centre for Advanced Studies, National University of Singapore; Professor Thumboo, Ms. Nambier, David Chng, Hedwig Anuar, Goh Eck Kheng, Shirley Hew, Jan Kemp, Koh Tai Ann, Leong Liew Geok, Rene Parrish, Irene Pates, and others for their assistance.

1. Literature from the Third World was, until very recently, visibly male-dominated, reflecting women's limited access to the discourse of nationalism that has taken central stage in this literature. Neil Lazarus's introduction to African Literature in *Longman Anthology of World Literature by Women 1875 - 1975* presents the case against women's literary production in Africa: "Literacy was used as a form of social control. Opportunities for formal education were rare, and when these presented themselves, they were conventionally awarded to male students. Since public life became increasingly dependent on a colonial education, women were more or less systematically excluded from this realm. The result was that when, in the first decades of this century, and above all in West and South Africa, nationalist leaders began to make a name for themselves by writing and speaking out against colonial abuses, the overwhelming majority of them were men. In these early years, which extended all the way to 1945, very few African women writing in English, French, or Portuguese managed to make themselves heard" (1062). See also Lloyd W. Brown, "Introduction" (1981). Similar questions about the absence of women in literary discourse were raised by Virginia Woolf, *A Room of One's Own,* Alice Walker, *In Our Mothers' Gardens,* and Lawrence Lipking, "Aristotle's Sister."

2. Lucy M. Friebert and Barbara A. White, for example, make a case for including writing disparaged as sentimental literature in the American canon (Preface, 1985). This study concentrates on non-canonical work — uncollected and occasional poems by Hedwig Aroozoo; two war memoirs, Sibyl Kathigasu's *No Dram of Mercy,* and Janet Lim's *Sold For Silver;* and three published poets, illustrating contrasting cases of ambiguous state identity, Cecile Parrish, Wong May, and Margaret Leong.

3. Nina Baym makes a convincing case for the dismissal of women's writing from the evolving canon of American literature by male interests and concerns in "Melodramas of Beset Manhood."

4. The discourse of nationalism has proceeded together with race and patriarchal discourses. See S. J. Smith for another view of this matrix (1990).

5. Chinweizu, et al. *Toward the Decolonization of African Literature,* is a classic postcolonial oppositional critique that reads African literature as "an autonomous entity separate and apart from all other literatures" (4). Its Afrocentric and separatist position, while an important strategic move in the process of decolonization, threatens to shape another hegemony that dictates acceptable and unacceptable styles based on ideological considerations that come close to tribalist argument: "an *extensional definition* in which *family resemblances* are pragmatically employed to decide which of any doubtful or borderline cases should be included with the indisputable canon of African literature" (308). [Italics the authors.]

6. Among other women poets the study could have included are Shirley Lim and Hilary Tham. Immigrating to the United States in the 1970s, Lim and Tham have continued to publish collections of poetry. Some passages in this study previously appeared in the essay, "Margaret Leong in Singapore: A Problematic of Location."

7. Hedwig Aroozoo was kind enough to share her uncollected poems and letters with me during the time of my research at the Centre for Advanced Studies in 1989. See also Hedwig Anuar, "Books in My Life," *Singapore Libraries* Vol. 15, 1985: 63-66.

8. Wang Gungwu is now Chancellor of Hong Kong University in which position he speaks as a scholar and representative of diasporic Chinese.
9. See Wendell Harris's essay, "Canonicity," for a comprehensive discussion of the various constructions of canons.
10. The push towards a Malay-based, Islamic monoculture as representative of the national culture in Malaysia is expressed by Ismail Hussein (1977). Fernando (1986) accepts this position uncritically: "When we speak of Malaysia's national literature, then, we speak of the main line of tradition which unquestionably is literature written in Bahasa Malaysia. This is the main line which has the weight and authority of history" (141).
11. European influence in this region began as early as 1511 with the capture of Malacca by Portuguese forces. The Dutch took over the colony in 1641. In 1824, the Anglo-Dutch Treaty made the Malay Peninsula, including Singapore, an exclusive British preserve. Britain enlarged its sphere of administration to include all the states in the Peninsula (Federation of Malaya), during which time large numbers of immigrant Chinese and Indians entered the region to work in the plantations, mines, and businesses. Led by nationalist Malays, Malaya received independence in 1957. Singapore, conjoined with Malaysia in 1962, became a separate state in 1965 (Bedlington 1978). British systems of administration, education, and entrepreneurship remain as models even today in Singapore. At the same time, paradoxically, the Singapore Government continues to express an anxiety over increasing Westernization, synonymous with 'Americanization'," as being "foreign" to an Asian population. The Prime Minister, Goh Chok Tong, for example, has declared "preserving the Asianness of Singapore society" to be "a major long-term goal of his government" *(The Straits Times* Weekly Overseas Edition 1990).
12. Information received from Hedwig Anuar in an interview in National University of Singapore, November 1989.
13. Bloom in *The Anxiety of Influence* quotes Malraux who sees the poet as "haunted by a voice with which the words must harmonize," and whose work therefore moves "from pastiche to style" (26).
14. T. S. Eliot's *The Waste Land* was a central literary reference for many writers of the generation of the fifties and early sixties from Asia, as it was for Anglo-American writers. See Bhagaban Jayasingh, E. V. Ramakrishnan, and Kathryn Van Spanckeren, *The Literary Half-Yearly,* 1988.
15. Homi Bhabha theorizes a "politics of the theoretical statement" that emerges in forms of hybridity and that emphasizes the "construction of discourse" as "the representation of the political" (12). According to Bhabha, political change comes in the "hybrid" moment, whose transformational value lies in the translation "of elements that are *neither the One . . . nor the Other . . . but something else besides* which contests the terms and territories of both" (13). Arguably, all the works (and their producers) discussed in this study manifest the instability of powerful cultural/political changes, inscribing culture's *hybridity,* as opposed to the canonical works that can be appropriated to serve state hegemony.
16. The idiomatic register of English evolving from the influences of Chinese and Malay linguistic presences is usually known as "Singlish," a regional patois that has received both academic attention and social acceptance. See John

Platt and Heidi Weber, 1980; Irene F. H. Wong, 1986, pp.97-110; John Platt and Kirpal Singh, 1984. See also Peter Lowenberg, 1986 and 1991.

17. For a discussion of the unease Malaysian and Singapore writers feel in their relationship to English-language use, see Thumboo (1976), Lee Tzu Pheng (1985), and Fernando (1986).

18. For an analysis of the history of the Communist insurgency in Malaysia and Singapore, see Lucien Pye.

19. Aside from Pye, much of the literature on the MPAJA that appeared during and after the course of the insurgency presented the MPAJA as less concerned with anti-Japanese activities and more focussed on political gains after the war, directly contradicting Kathigasu's first-hand testimony of the MPAJA's courage in anti-Japanese warfare. According to O'Ballance, "the MPAJA avoided Japanese troops and took practically no action against them at all. [The policy was] to collect arms, win local support or dominate the population by terror, and wait for the allies to win the war" (58-59). Miller portrays them as "overbearing, arrogant, insolent, and insulting" (51), whose terroristic brutalities led to a "hatred of the Chinese. . . . The Malay Governments felt the Chinese were nothing but saboteurs. . . . Even some senior British Civil Service officers, steeped in the pro-Malay tradition, developed a dislike of the Chinese. This feeling remains among some of them to this day" (57-58). Miller's portrait directly contradicts Kathigasu's sympathetic descriptions of Japanese brutality against the Chinese population and of Malay collusion with Japanese military rule.

20. After the Japanese surrender, the MPAJA was absorbed into the MCP (Malayan Communist Party) whose strike activities and later armed insurgency became conflated with the global struggle between the U.S. and the Soviet Union known as the Cold War. Thus, Anthony Short reports, "There is, however, a widespread belief that the order for an insurrection came from Moscow; that it was obeyed in Malaya; and that it formed part of an integral Soviet pattern of insurrection in South-east Asia" (152). Kathigasu's praise of the MPAJA, even if sincere, read in this context of global ideological struggle, is politically "incorrect" among the interpretations provided between the 50s and 70s, for it asserts an oppositional interpretation of MPAJA activities, one which locates them first as "nationalist" rather than as anti-nationalist tools of the then-feared Soviet Union.

21. The general stereotyping of Chinese immigrants as opportunistic sojourners by both Malay and British communities is discussed in Bedlington: "[The British] saw the Chinese as unscrupulous merchants whose word was less than their bond. . . . Malays generally share most of these stereotypes (adding some of their own) . . . as unreliable in interpersonal transactions, as exploiters of the Malay peasantry, as materialistic Sybarites, and significantly, as alien transients whose loyalty is directed outward toward a Communist China" (126).

22. Malaysia and Singapore, despite intertwined colonial histories and shared indigenous and immigrant populations, have evolved different national cultural policies. Malaysia, claiming the special status of the Malays as "sons of the soil," maintains a national language (Malay) and Malay-dominant national culture, while Singapore posits a multiracial, multicultural, and bilingual (English and the mother tongue, whether Chinese, Malay or Tamil) policy.

23. See Margery Wolf, "Women and Suicide in China," for an anthropological description of affects of oppressive patriarchal value-systems on Chinese women (111-142).

24. For a study of the patriarchal structure of traditional Chinese society and the participation of women in its asymmetrical constructions of gender roles and status, see Kay Johnson, *Women, the Family and Peasant Revolution.*

25. The injustices perpetrated by the *mui-tsai* system is also recorded by Ong Siang Song: "The case in which a Chinese woman was sentenced in February 1907 to four months imprisonment for inhuman treatment of a girl of 16, who had been bought for $230 by her husband, exemplifies the view still held by some Chinese people here as to the rights possessed by them over 'bought' maidservants . . . . Her life was no better than the slaves whose escape from the Sultan's harem was mentioned in the *Hikayat Abdullah*" (412-13).

26. More work needs to be done in the area of European missionary 'rescue' of women. An archival resource is the Wesleyan Methodist Missionary Society (London) Archive: *China: Women's Work Collection.* In the introduction to Mary Paik Lee's autobiography, *Quiet Odyssey,* Sucheng Chan discusses the "profound impact" (xxxviii) of Protestant missionaries on the "extremely excluded" (xxxvi) lives of Korean women; widows, for example, "accorded no rights whatsoever [found] a place in the new community of believers" (xxxviii).

27. Some male writers who have successfully negotiated crossing national boundaries to become accepted in another national canon include T. S. Eliot, who left the United States in his twenties, and Czeslaw Milosz, who left Lithuania and is now a Polish/American poet in Berkeley, California.

28. In the years before Malaya/Singapore received independence from Britain, most of the Anglophone literature about the region was written by visiting Westerners. See Somerset Maugham, *Ah King and Other Stories;* Maugham's *Malaysian Stories;* D. J. Enright, *Memoirs of a Mendicant Professor;* Anthony Burgess, *The Long Day Wanes: A Malayan Trilogy.* Han Suyin is an intersecting variant on the Western visitor or expatriate. Born of a Chinese father and Belgium mother, she practiced medicine in the region, later identified with the People's Republic of China in which she was raised, and most recently has been living in Switzerland. See Han Suyin, *And the Rain my Drink.*

29. The term was used by Paul C. P. Siu, a sociologist, in *The Chinese Laundryman: A Study in Social Isolation.*

30. See Etienne Balibar and Immanuel Wallerstein for a theoretical analysis of the simultaneous overlapping of race, gender, and nationality discourses.

31. This argument was offered by K. Singh in a rejoinder at a seminar on the subject, Singapore, November 1989. Parrish is represented in *The Second Tongue,* but omitted from other anthologies.

32. I am indebted to Mrs. Rene Parrish who provided me with invaluable information on her daughter's life in a series of interviews in Singapore, October/November 1989.

33. See *Who's Who in Malaysia,* 435.

34. Lee Tzu Pheng, "Introduction," *The Poetry of Singapore* 452-453, raises the issues of a writer's 'authenticity' as a national and cultural spokesperson,

if s/he writes in English, presented uncritically in the introduction as a "foreign" language.

35. While Anne Brewster critiques the discourse of nationalism in selected male-dominated poetry from Singapore, she does not interrogate their terms of references and reproduces them in her study, *Towards a Semiotic of Post-Colonial Discourse.*

36. See Fox Butterfield for accounts of state regulation of social contacts between the Chinese people and Westerners, "to prevent any bourgeois contagion from infecting China" (29).

37. In *How the Hills Are Distant,* poem Xlll is addressed to Rimbaud, whose symbolist manners are echoed in Wong's verse (13). The European orientation is even more noted in Wong's first collection, *Toccata on Ochre Sheaves,* in which Tan Han Hoe's introduction offers an apologia for the overt Eliotic "method."

38. Ironically, while Parrish was included in the 1965 *Who's Who in Malaysia,* Wong May is not included in *Who's Who in Singapore.* Gathering biographical information on Wong May was difficult. This information was taken from various interviews with her ex-university colleagues in October/November 1989.

39. Katharine Sim, a Welsh writer who lived with her British administrator husband in Malaya for over twenty years, published novels that take their subjects and materials from the region. Sim became proficient in the Malay language, and also wrote a study of the Malay poetic form, the pantun, *Flowers in the Sun.*

40. Compared to some other Singapore poets, little has been written on Wong May, despite her three published volumes and inclusion in major Singapore anthologies. The extant criticism bases interpretations of her work on identifiable local markers, found chiefly in her early work. Robert Yeo's qualifier, that her "early poetry have a definite niche in a developing canon of Singaporean poetry," for example, discounts her second and third volumes (1986 61).

Works Cited

Anderson, Patrick. *Snake Wine: A Singapore Episode.* London: Chatto & Windus, 1955.

Anonymous. "Margaret Leong — a woman with fascination." *Straits Times,* 31 May 1960, 6.

Anonymous. "Major long-term aim: To preserve Asianness." *Straits Times* Weekly Overseas Edition, Oct. 6 1990: 9.

Anuar, Hedwig. "Books in My Life." *Singapore Libraries* 15 (1985):63-66.

Aroozoo, Hedwig (nee Anuar). "Reflections on Doing Homework." *Convent of the Holy Infant Jesus Magazine,*1946; repub. in *CHIJ Victoria Street,* Singapore, 1983: 79.

————. "Rhyme in Time." *Litmus One (Selected University Verse, 1947-57).* Singapore: Raffles Society, 1958.

————. "The Ballad of David Marshall." *Suara Merdeka* May 1956: 24-25.

————. "Love-Match." *Suara Merdeka* June 1956: 26-27.

————. "Suez Canal Blues." *Suara Merdeka* July 1956: 23.

Balibar, Etienne and Immanuel Wallerstein. *Race, Nation, Class: Ambiguous Identities*. London: Verso, 1991.

Baym, Nina. "Melodramas of Beset Manhood: How Theories of American Fiction Exclude Women Writers." *American Quarterly* 33 (1981): 123-39.

Bedlington, Stanley S. *Malaysia and Singapore: The Building of New States*. Ithaca: Cornell University Press, 1978.

Bhabha, Homi. "The Commitment to Theory." *New Formations* 5 (1988): 4-23.

Bloom, Harold. *The Anxiety of Influence; A Theory of Poetry*. New York: Oxford University Press, 1973.

Brewster, Anne. "The Discourse of Nationalism and Multiculturalism in Singapore and Malaysia in the 50s and 60s." *SPAN* 24 (1987): 136-150.

—————. *Towards a Semiotic of Post-colonial Discourse: University Writing in Singapore and Malaysia 1949-1965*. Singapore: Heinemann for the Centre for Advanced Studies, 1988.

—————. *Post-colonial and Ethnic Minority Literatures in Singapore and Malaysia: A Cultural Analysis*, Ph.D. Dissertation. Flinders University, Australia, 1989.

Brown, Lloyd W. *Women Writers in Black Africa*. Connecticut: Greenwood Press, 1981.

Burgess, Anthony. *The Long Day Wanes: A Malayan Trilogy*. New York: Norton, 1964.

Butterfield, Fox. *China, Alive in the Bitter Sea*. New York: Times Books, 1982.

Chan, Heng Chee. "The Safer Art." *Focus* 1:1 (1961): 1.

China: Women's Work Collection: Zug, Switzerland: Interdocumentation Co., 1982 or 1983.

Chinweizu, Onwuchekwa, and Ihecgukwu Madubuike. *Toward the Decolonization of African Literature*. Washington, D.C.: Howard University Press, 1983.

Clammer, John. *Singapore: Ideology, Society, Culture*. Singapore: Chopman Pub. 1985.

Ee, Tiang Hong. "History as Myth in Malaysian Poetry in English." *The Writer's Sense of the Past*," edited by Kirpal Singh. Singapore: Singapore University Press, 1987.

Enright, D. J. *Memoirs of a Mendicant Professor*. London: Chatto & Windus, 1969.

Fernando, Lloyd. *Cultures in Conflict*. Singapore: Graham Brash, 1986.

Freibert, Lucy M. and Barbara A. White. *Hidden Hands: An Anthology of American Women Writers, 1790-1870*. New Brunswick, New Jersey: Rutgers University Press, 1985.

Hall, Edward. *The Hidden Dimension*. Garden City, New York: 1982.

Han, Suyin. *And the Rain my Drink*. London: Jonathan Cape, 1956.

Harris, Wendell V. "Canonicity." *PMLA*. (Jan. 1991): 110-21.

Hussein, Ismail. "Literary Organizations in Malaysia." *Conference of Asian Writer 1977*. Kuala Lumpur: Dewan Bahasa dan Pustaka, 1977.

Jayasingh, Bhagaban. "The Influence of T.S. Eliot on Contemporary Oriya Poetry." *The Literary Half-Yearly* (July 1988): 163-72.

Johnson, Kay. *Women, the Family and Peasant Revolution*. Chicago: University of Chicago Press, 1988.

Kathigasu, Sibyl. *No Dram of Mercy.* 1954. Singapore: Oxford University Press, 1983.

Koh, Tai Ann. "Biographical and Literary Writings and Plays in English by Women from Malaysia and Singapore: A Checklist." *Commentary* 7: 2 & 3 (Dec. 1987): 94-96.

Lau, Yok Ching. "Speaking as Women: The Poetry of Shirley Lim and Lee Tzu Pheng." *Commentary.* 7: 2 &3 (Dec. 1987): 102-17.

Lazarus, Neil. *Longman Anthology of World Literature by Women 1875 - 1975,* edited by Marian Arkin and Barbara Schollar. New York: Longman, 1989.

Lee, Chin Koon. *Mrs. Lee's Cookbook.* Singapore: Eurasian Press, 1974.

Lee, Geok Lan. Poems in *Bunga Emas,* edited by T. Wignesan, 1964.

Lee, Mary Paik. *Quiet Odyssey: A Pioneer Korean Woman in America.* Seattle: University of Washington Press, 1990.

Lee, Tzu Pheng. "Introduction." *The Poetry of Singapore.* Singapore: The ASEAN Committee on Culture and Information, 1985. 452-453.

Leong, Liew Geok. "Literature from History: Perspectives of the Pacific War in Malaya and Singapore." Paper presented in New Directions in Asian Studies Conference, Singapore, 1989.

Lim, Janet. *Sold For Silver.* London: Collins, 1958.

Lim, Shirley Geok-lin. *Crossing the Peninsula.* Kuala Lumpur: Heinemann, 1980.

————. "The English-language Writer in Singapore." *The Management of Success: The Moulding of Modern Singapore,* edited by Kernial Singh Sandhu and Paul Wheatley. Singapore: Institute of South East Asian Studies Press, 1989. 523-52.

————. "A Problematic of Identity: Margaret Leong in Singapore." *Perceiving Other Worlds,* edited by Edwin Thumboo. Singapore: Times Academic Press, 1991. 139-50.

Lipking, Lawrence. "Aristotle's Sister: A Poetic of Abandonment." *Critical Inquiry* 10:1 (1983): 61-81.

Litmus One (Selected University Verse, 1949-57). Singapore: Raffles Society, 1958.

Lowenberg, Peter. "Sociocultural context and second language acquisition: acculturation and creativity in Malaysian English. *World Englishes* 5: 1 (1986): 71-83.

————. "Variations in Malaysian English: The Pragmatics of languages in contact." *English Around the World: Sociolinguistics Perspectives,* edited by Jenny Cheshire. Cambridge: Cambridge University Press, 1991. 364-75.

Maugham, Somerset. *Ah King and Other Stories.* 1st pub. 1933. Singapore: Oxford University Press, 1986.

————. *Malaysian Stories.* Hong Kong: Heinemann, 1969.

Miller, Harry. *Menace in Malaya.* London: George G. Harrap, 1954.

Moran, J. W. G. *Spearhead in Malaya.* London: Peter Davies, 1959.

Nair, Chandran. "Writing in English — The Poetry to Date." *Commentary* 3:2 (July/August 1970): 29-34.

O'Ballance, Edgar. *Malaya: The Communist Insurgent War, 1948-60.* Hamden, Connecticut: Archon Books, 1966.

Ong, Siang Song. *One Hundred Years' History of the Chinese in Singapore.* Singapore: University of Malaya Press, 1967.

Parrish, Cecile. *Poems.* Singapore: Malaysia Printers Ltd, 1966.

Platt, John and Heidi Weber. *English in Singapore and Malaysia,* Kuala Lumpur: Oxford University Press, 1980.

Platt, John and Kirpal Singh. "The Use of Localized English in Singapore poetry." *English World Wide* V:l (1984): 43-54.

Pye, Lucien W. *Guerrilla Communism in Malaya.* Princeton: Princeton University Press, 1956.

Ramakrishnan, E. V. "Eliot in Malayalam Poetry." *The Literary Half-Yearly* (July 1988): 173-180.

Short, Anthony. "Communism and the Emergency." *Malaysia: A Survey,* edited by Wang Gungwu. New York: Praeger, 1964.149-60.

Shulman, Alix Kate. "Lost Women Writers ll: Far From Home," *PEN Newsletter* 71 (Spring 1990):18.

Singh, Kirpal. "An Approach to Singapore Writing in English." *ARIEL* 15:2 (1984): 5-24.

Siu, Paul C. P. *The Chinese Laundryman: A Study in Social Isolation.* New York: New York University Press, 1987.

Sim, Katharine. *Flowers in The Sun.* Eastern Universities Press, 1957, 1982.

Smith, S. J. "Social Geography — Patriarchy, Racism, Nationalism." *Progress in Human Geography.* 14:2 (June 1990): 261-71.

Straits Times. "First Milestone on the Road to Cultural Integration." 20 Jan. 1968.

Tham, Hilary. *No Gods Today.* Kuala Lumpur: the author, 1969.

Thumboo, Edwin, ed. "Introduction." *The Flowering Tree: Selected Writings from Singapore/Malaya.* Singapore: Educational Publications Bureau, 1970.

———, ed. "Introduction." *Seven Poets: Singapore and Malaysia.* Singapore: Singapore University Press, 1973.

———, ed. "Introduction." *The Second Tongue: An Anthology of Poetry from Malaysia and Singapore.* Singapore: Heinemann, 1976.

Thumboo, Edwin. "The Search for Style and Theme: A Personal Account." *Singapore Book World* 1983.

Van Spanckeren, Kathryn. "The Poetics of Urbanization: T. S. Eliot's *The Waste Land* and Mochtar Lubis' *Twilight in Djakarta.*" *The Literary Half-Yearly* July 1988: 203-19.

Walker, Alice. *In Our Mothers' Gardens: Womanist Prose.* San Diego: Harcourt and Brace Jovanovich, 1983.

Wang, Gungwu. *Pulse.* Singapore: Beda Lim, 1950.

———. "Trial and Error in Malayan Poetry." *Malayan Undergraduate.* Singapore, 1958a: 6-8.

———. (Anon.) "Some Suggestions for Malayan Verse Written in English." *New Cauldron.* Singapore: Raffles Society (1958b): 26-28.

Wee, Vivienne. "The Ups and Downs of Women's Status in Singapore: A Chronology of Some Landmark Events (1950-1987)." *Commentary* 7:2 & 3 (December 1987): 5-12.

Wignesan, T. ed. *Bunga Emas: An Anthology of Contemporary Malaysian Poetry (1930-1963).* Malaysia: Anthony Blond with Rayirath Pub., 1964.

Wolf, Margery. "Women and Suicide in China." *Women in Chinese Society,* edited by Margery Wolf and Roxane Witke. Stanford: Stanford University Press, 1975. 111-142.

Woolf, Virginia. *A Room of One's Own.* London: Hogarth Press, 1929.

Wong, Irene F. H. "The Search for a Localized Idiom in Malaysian English Literature." *ACLALS Bulletin* 7:6, Singapore,1986: 97-110.

Wong, Phui Nam. *Toccata on Ochre Sheaves*. Singapore: The Raffles Society, 1958.

——. *How The Hills Are Distant*. Kuala Lumpur: Tenggara, 1968.

Wong, May. Poems in *Focus* 2:2 (1963): 18, 31.

——. Poems in *Focus* 2:3 (1964): 25-28.

——. *The Bad Girl's Book of Animals*. New York: Harcourt, Brace & World, 1969.

——. *Reports*. New York: Harcourt, Brace, Jovanovich, 1972.

——. *Superstitions*. New York: Harcourt, Brace, Javonivich, 1980.

Yeo, Robert. "Poetry in English in Singapore and Malaysia," *Singapore Book World* 1 (1970a): 14-19.

——. "Poetry in English in the Seventies." *Singapore Writing*, edited by Chandran Nair. Singapore: Woodrose, 1977b.

——. "Wong May —*The Shroud*." *Critical Engagements: Singapore Poems in Focus*, edited by Kirpal Singh. Singapore: Heinemann Asia, 1986. 57-61.

Two new titles from PROF. SHIRLEY GEOK-LIN LIM:

Monsoon History (UK £6.99, USA $11.99)
Poems selected from "Modern Secrets" & "No Man's Grove" with the complete "Crossing the Peninsula" (winner of the 1980 Commonwealth Poetry Prize).

"The poet in exile, but a counter-exile that permits an embracing of all contradictions."

World Literatures Today

Writing S.E./ Asia in English: *Against the Grain* (UK £12.99, USA $24.99)
The ten chapters demonstrate that South East/ Asian Writing in English, Against the Grain of local speech, national languages and national canons, have much to tell us about place and region, and also about the nations that their imaginations press upon from the outside of linguistic borders.

Three from K.S. MANIAM:

The Return (UK £5.99, USA $11.95)
This novel of magical realism has become a Malaysian modern classic. Ravi attempts to come to terms with himself by sustaining the classical Hindu virtures of spiritual proportion, harmony and grace, and avoiding the decay of ethnic civilization through his pursuit of social mobility.

"THE RETURN bids fair to take a place among the top two or three of any published Malaysian/Singaporean fiction in English."

Ooi Boo Eng, Univ. of Malaya

In a Far Country (UK £5.99, USA $11.95)
This post-modernist novel is a potent cocktail of cultures, race and religions.

"The book seeks to free itself from the literary ghetto by addressing national issues and departing from realism to do so."

Dr. Paul Sharrad, Univ. of Wollongong, Australia

Sensuous Horizons, four stories & four plays (UK £6.99, USA $11.99)
The eight works explore the complex and varied lives of husbands, sons, wives, and lovers, all players in a game as old as time.

In The Name of Love by RAMLI IBRAHIM (UK £6.99, USA $11.99)

"This is daring theatre taking risks and living dangerously, reviving a spirit that at the time subverts and affirms the cultural concerns it displays, questioning and challenging, but never losing sight of that esential theatrical quality: entertainment. The plays mark a major contribution to South East Asia theatre, and one which will delight audiences everywhere."

Prof. John McRae, Univ. of Nottingham

Ways of Exile by WONG PHUI NAM (UK £5.99, USA $11.99)
This collection traces the development of the poet from student days to early maturity in lyrical litany, honouring the Malaysian soul as well as the geographical and spiritual ground of his country.

"Wong's poetic scenario is eschatological in that it discovers powerful destructive forces at work in the natural and social world."

Anne Brewster, *Towards a Semiotic of Postcolonial Discourse*

As I Please by SALLEH BEN JONED (UK £6.99, USA $11.99)

"Anybody who wants to understand cultural politics today should read this book. Anybody who wants to understand Malaysia today should read this book. And anybody who wants an insight into the confrontation of East and West, of Islam and the secular or Christian world, should read this book!"

Margaret Drabble

Skoob *PACIFICA* Anthology

No. 1: S.E. Asia Writes Back ! (UK £5.99, USA $11.99)

No. 2: The Pen is Mightier than the Sword (UK £6.99, USA $11.99)
The principle of Postmodern/Postcolonial writing is to deviate from the tradition and to develop a new direction of thought... The understanding of a writer involves anamnesis in the psychoanalytical context, the free association of ideas and imagery of the unconscious in situations past to discover the hidden meanings of his life.

"The **Skoob *PACIFICA*** series has provided a means for many writers to reach international readership... The Pacific Rim should not be seen just for its economic importance but also for the emergence of writings in English that call for recognition in the literary world."

British Council, Literature Matters

AS I PLEASE by **Salleh Ben Joned**

(UK £6.99, USA $11.99)

"Anybody who wants to understand cultural politics today should read this book. Anybody who wants to understand Malaysia today should read this book. And anybody who wants an insight into the confrontations of East and West, of Islam and the secular or Christian world, should read this book!" Margaret Drabble

Three from K.S. Maniam

SENSUOUS HORIZONS, four stories & four plays (UK £6.99, USA $11.99)

The eight works explores the complex and varied lives of husbands, sons, wives, and lovers, all players in a game as old as time.

THE RETURN (UK £5.99, USA $11.99)

This novel of magical realism has become a Malaysian modern classic. Ravi attempts to come to terms with himself by sustaining the classical Hindu virtues of spiritual proportion, harmony and grace, and avoiding the decay of ethnic civilization through his pursuit of social mobility. "THE RETURN bids fair to take a place among the top two or three of any published Malaysian/Singaporean fiction in English" Ooi Boo Eng, Univ. of Malaya

IN A FAR COUNTRY (UK £6.99, USA $11.99)

This post-modernist novel is a potent cocktail of cultures, race and religions. "The book seeks to free itself from the literary ghetto by addressing national issues and departing from realism to do so." Dr. Paul sharrad, Univ. of Wollongong, Australia

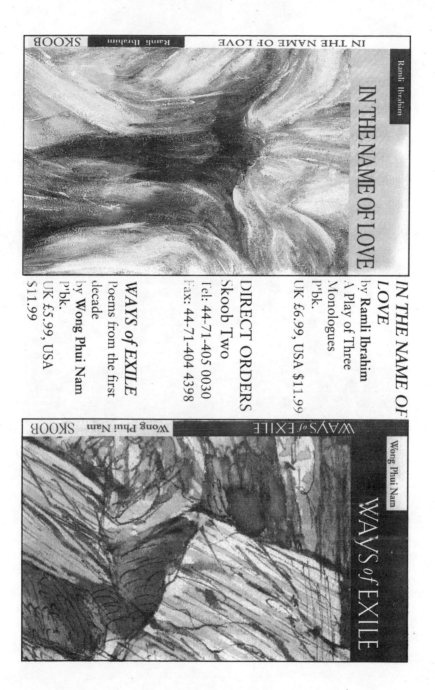

*IN THE NAME OF
LOVE*
by **Ramli Ibrahim**
A Play of Three
Monologues
P'bk.
UK £6.99, USA $11.99

DIRECT ORDERS
Skoob Two
Tel: 44-71-405 0030
Fax: 44-71-404 4398

WAYS of EXILE
Poems from the first
decade
by **Wong Phui Nam**
P'bk.
UK £5.99, USA
$11.99

SHANGRI-LA
HOTELS *and* RESORTS

SUPPORTING THE LITERATURES OF THE PACIFIC RIM

Beijing

Shanghai
Hangzhou
Taipei
Shenzhen   Hong Kong

Bangkok   Manila
Cebu

Penang   Kota Kinabalu

Kuala Lumpur
Singapore
Sentosa
Jakarta   Surabaya
Bali

MALAYSIA

Kota Kinabalu:
Tanjung Aru Resort

Kuala Lumpur:
Shangri-La

Penang:
Shangri-La
Golden Sands Resort
Rasa Sayang Resort
Palm Beach Resort

SINGAPORE

Shangri-La
Rasa Sentosa Resort

Shangri-La Hotels Marketing Sdn Bhd
7/F UBN Tower
Letter Box 5, 10 Jalan P. Ramlee
Kuala Lumpur 50250, Malaysia
Telex: 32421 KHKUL MA
Fax: (60-3) 230 6248
Reservations toll-free 800 1099